Learning Stencyl 3.x Game Development Beginner's Guide

A fast-paced, hands-on guide for developing a feature-complete video game on almost any desktop computer, without writing a single line of computer code

Innes Borkwood

PUBLISHING

BIRMINGHAM - MUMBAI

D1219191

Learning Stencyl 3.x Game Development Beginner's Guide

First published: May 2013

Production Reference: 1170513

Published by Packt Publishing Ltd.
Livery Place
35 Livery Street
Birmingham B3 2PB, UK.

ISBN 978-1-84969-596-1

www.packtpub.com

Cover Image by Vicki Wenderlich (www.vickiwenderlich.com) and Innes Borkwood (innes@borkwood.com)

Credits

Author

Innes Borkwood

Reviewers

Joe Dolivo

Jean-Marc "jihem" QUÉRÉ

James Vanderhyde

Acquisition Editor

Kartikey Pandey

Lead Technical Editor

Ankita Shashi

Technical Editors

Sharvari Baet

Sayali Mirajkar

Akshata Patil

Dheera Paul

Project Coordinator

Anugya Khurana

Proofreader

Lauren Tobon

Indexer

Rekha Nair

Graphics

Ronak Dhruv

Abhinash Sahu

Production Coordinator

Nitesh Thakur

Cover Work

Nitesh Thakur

Foreword

My journey began nearly 10 years ago creating a map editor for a Mario clone. I had just learned how to program, and like many, I wanted to make games with my newfound knowledge. Even before I learned how to program, I fostered an obsession over editing maps for games on TI graphing calculators, even going as far as drawing such maps out on graph paper as a way of sharing them with friends. Times have surely changed since then!

Over the years, I bounced from one project to another, each with increasingly ambitious scope. The Mario clone begat a general platformer engine, which in turn gave way to a completely general game engine. None of these experiments saw the light of day, but they set the stage for what eventually became Stencyl.

Stencyl was conceived during a time that, despite being a few years back, seems anachronistic. Facebook was closed to the public, YouTube was a novelty, and the iPhone had yet to be invented. Within the gaming world, creating a YouTube for games was considered the holy grail, and no fewer than a dozen companies sought this vision by democratizing game creation in various ways.

A few years later, Stencyl opened its doors to an eagerly awaiting public. Educators in particular loved the combination of a familiar brick-snapping interface with the incentives of building a real game. It was during this time that I met Innes and learned that he wanted to use Stencyl to teach programming and game design to young students. As we grew further acquainted with each other, he proposed this book.

Learning Stencyl 3.x Game Development: Beginner's Guide is a top to bottom treatise on how to build a game using Stencyl, from humble beginnings to the last 10% spent polishing and taking a game to market. Creating a game is portrayed not as a sprint, but as a journey upon which you'll build not just a working knowledge of Stencyl, but acquire a general toolbox of techniques and wisdom that will serve you well throughout your game-creating career.

When I applied to college, one of my essays detailed my early experiences with game programming. I was particularly fascinated by a magical spark of life I bestowed upon a lowly breakout clone when I got a ball to bounce off the paddle and break some blocks. It was a euphoric moment because I finally got my first game to work!

If you're new to the world of game creation, I offer you this one piece of advice: think big but start small. Complete some small projects to get the hang of things and see firsthand just how important that last 10 percent is. When you inevitably hit a brick wall, don't give up. Everybody starts somewhere, and when you get that first game working, you'll experience the same joy that I felt when I finally got my first game to work. Happy Stencyling!

Jonathan Chung
Creator of Stencyl

About the Author

Innes Borkwood is a freelance computer consultant and software trainer living in Perth, Western Australia.

Prior to moving to Perth in 2011, Innes was a full-time teacher at Chesterton Community Sports College in Staffordshire, England, where he taught Information & Communications Technology for four years.

In addition to consulting and teaching, Innes has also worked as a freelance journalist for national computer magazines in the UK.

Since the first personal computers arrived in the UK, Innes has been a dedicated technology enthusiast and electronics hobbyist, with an enthusiasm for participating in, and encouraging, life-long learning. He has a First Class Honours Degree in Business Studies with ICT, and continues to learn something new every day!

Innes is happily married to his very understanding wife, Ellen, with whom he has two wonderful children, David and Catherine.

Acknowledgement

Thanks to my wife, Ellen, and my children, David and Catherine, for being so accepting of my absence from family life during the many, many hours that I spent at my desk while writing this book.

I offer thanks and gratitude to the team at Packt Publishing, whose enthusiasm for this book has ensured that the process of creating it was an enjoyable, rewarding, and challenging experience; it has been a pleasure working with you. For the Technical Reviewers—thank you for your generous comments, helpful suggestions, and for your vigilance in detecting my errors.

For my daughter, Catherine; thank you for proof reading the early drafts, testing the accompanying code, and for providing such helpful, constructive criticism.

My final acknowledgements are reserved for Joe Dolivo and Jonathan Chung of Stencyl, LLC. Joe, thank you for responding to each of my many questions so promptly and comprehensively; I am indebted to you. Jon, thank you for creating Stencyl; it is a wonderful tool that has already enabled, and will continue to enable, many people to "find the fun!"

This book is dedicated to my dear wife, Ellen; thank you for your love, your support, and your encouragement. Here it is in print; I love you.

For David and Catherine—I love you too!

About the Reviewers

Joe Dolivo is a practicing electrical engineer (BSEE, UIUC-Illinois 2010) by day and Stencyl team member by night. Originally an inquisitive volunteer, he now handles numerous aspects of Stencyl's operations, including content development, site maintenance, social media, business partnerships, educational outreach, and support. Most recently, Joe's taken an interest in using innovative technologies such as Stencyl to improve STEM education in the US and abroad.

Jean-Marc "jihem" QUÉRÉ is a senior computer science engineer, and is also the author of numerous articles in the French specialized press and books (on WinDev). Self-taught, he provided software for more than 20 years in every domain: decision-making methods, artificial learning, robotics, and autonomous systems. Technology evangelist, he has chosen to support Stencyl (since the migration from Flash to haXe). He actively contributes to the community (extensions, translation, and support). Undoubtedly, you will meet him one day or another on the Stencyl forums. And you will be welcome!

Being part of something, implies to be welcomed by a community. Stencyl users are part of one of the best communities I have been in touch with as far as I can remember since the first steps of Internet (and Linux). You know that a person uses Stencyl because he (or she) has sparks in his (or her) eyes and a child-like spirit to create amazing games. I have found this in Innes. And if you go through this journey, you might have them too.

James Vanderhyde teaches computer science and math at Benedictine College in Atchison, Kansas. He has a PhD in computer science from Georgia Tech (2007). His research is in computer graphics and computer game development, especially for educational purposes. He has been writing computer games and other computer programs since the Commodore 128 days.

www.PacktPub.com

Support files, eBooks, discount offers and more

You might want to visit www.PacktPub.com for support files and downloads related to your book.

Did you know that Packt offers eBook versions of every book published, with PDF and ePub files available? You can upgrade to the eBook version at www.PacktPub.com and as a print book customer, you are entitled to a discount on the eBook copy. Get in touch with us at service@packtpub.com for more details.

At www.PacktPub.com, you can also read a collection of free technical articles, sign up for a range of free newsletters and receive exclusive discounts and offers on Packt books and eBooks.

http://PacktLib.PacktPub.com

Do you need instant solutions to your IT questions? PacktLib is Packt's online digital book library. Here, you can access, read and search across Packt's entire library of books.

Why Subscribe?

- ◆ Fully searchable across every book published by Packt
- ◆ Copy and paste, print and bookmark content
- ◆ On demand and accessible via web browser

Free Access for Packt account holders

If you have an account with Packt at www.PacktPub.com, you can use this to access PacktLib today and view nine entirely free books. Simply use your login credentials for immediate access.

Table of Contents

Preface

Creating video games has traditionally been a long and complicated process, requiring years of experience and a vast array of skills. However, with the introduction of comprehensive game-development toolkits such as Stencyl, the fun has returned to the art of game creation—anyone who has the desire to create his or her own video game can now do so with almost any desktop computer and a free software download from the Internet.

Stencyl eliminates many of the tedious and time consuming aspects of game development, but getting to grips with such a comprehensive software package can be somewhat daunting—there are so many great features that it's difficult to know where to start!

Learning Stencyl 3.x Game Development: Beginner's Guide will guide you through learning the essential skills that are required to create your own video games without knowing how to write computer code. We're going to start with a blank screen and, before we reach the end of the book, we'll have developed a complete game, ready for publishing. We won't stop with just the basics in place—we're going all the way, right through to including many of the important features that we would expect to find in a professional production!

Let's install Stencyl and create a video game.

What this book covers

Chapter 1, *Introduction*, explains what Stencyl is, how it works, and how we're going to learn the skills that we need to develop our own video games. We'll also install Stencyl and check that the installation is working as expected.

Chapter 2, *Let's Make a Game!*, guides us through the first steps of creating our game. We'll learn how to control our game's main character, design a game level with platforms, and create a scrolling display.

Chapter 3, Detecting Collisions, explores the management of different types of collisions within Stencyl. We'll add enemy characters and collectible items, and we'll fine tune the collision detection by modifying collision shapes.

Chapter 4, Creating Behaviors, explains how we can take full control of how our games work, by constructing our own custom gameplay routines. We'll learn how to use Stencyl's instruction blocks to introduce more advanced features into our game, such as random in-game events and decision making.

Chapter 5, Animation in Stencyl, introduces some of the different ways in which we can implement animation in our game. We'll discover how to bring our in-game characters to life with Stencyl's built-in animation and graphics editing tools.

Chapter 6, Managing and Displaying Information, focuses on managing information and sharing that information with players of our game. We'll be learning how to display text on screen, keep track of collected items, and also how to display a countdown timer bar.

Chapter 7, Polishing the Game, shows us how to add some essential elements to our game, such as an introductory screen, a game-over message, and a pause feature with a pop-up banner. We'll also be implementing an interesting visual effect and creating additional levels for our game.

Chapter 8, Implementing Sounds, concentrates on the skills that we need for implementing audio within our game. We'll learn many of the important techniques required for introducing sound effects and a soundtrack, to add that final professional touch to our games.

Chapter 9, Publishing and Making Money from Your Games, explains how we can publish our games on the Internet, and discusses some of the options available to us for selling or licensing our games. We'll also discover how to implement in-game advertising so we can earn some money each time our games are played.

Chapter 10, Targeting Mobile Platforms, discusses how we can test our games on mobile devices, and we'll also learn how to use the accelerometer and touchscreen features to control games.

Appendix, Planning, Resources, and Legal Issues, examines some of the important aspects of planning the development of a video game. We'll also consider the availability of third-party tools and resources and, finally, we'll review some of the legal aspects relating to the use of third-party assets within our video games.

What you need for this book

You will need to download Stencyl 3.x from `stencyl.com`.

Stencyl can be installed on Microsoft Windows XP (and later versions of Microsoft Windows), Mac OS X, and Linux (Ubuntu distributions recommended).

No prior knowledge of game development or computer programming is required.

Who this book is for

This book is for beginning game developers who have no prior knowledge of creating games or computer programming.

It's also an ideal resource for experienced game developers and designers who need to create rapid prototypes, or who want to speed up the game-development process.

Teachers and students, who think learning should be fun, will also benefit from this book!

Conventions

In this book, you will find several headings appearing frequently.

To give clear instructions of how to complete a procedure or task, we use:

Time for action – heading

1. Action 1
2. Action 2
3. Action 3

Instructions often need some extra explanation so that they make sense, so they are followed with:

What just happened?

This heading explains the working of tasks or instructions that you have just completed.

You will also find some other learning aids in the book, including:

Have a go hero – heading

These are practical challenges and give you ideas for experimenting with what you have learned.

You will also find a number of styles of text that distinguish between different kinds of information. Here are some examples of these styles and an explanation of their meaning.

Code words in text are shown as follows: "The game file named `5961_02_13.stencyl` represents how our game should look at this point in the book!"

New terms and **important words** are shown in bold. Words that you see on the screen, in menus or dialog boxes for example, appear in the text like this: "Before we can open up another game, we should close the **Adobe Flash Player** window in which the previously tested game is running, and we must close the current game in Stencyl by clicking on **File | Close Game** and follow any prompts that appear".

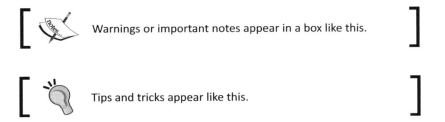

Warnings or important notes appear in a box like this.

Tips and tricks appear like this.

Reader feedback

Feedback from our readers is always welcome. Let us know what you think about this book—what you liked or may have disliked. Reader feedback is important for us to develop titles that you really get the most out of.

To send us general feedback, simply send an e-mail to `feedback@packtpub.com`, and mention the book title through the subject of your message.

If there is a topic that you have expertise in and you are interested in either writing or contributing to a book, see our author guide on `www.packtpub.com/authors`.

Customer support

Now that you are the proud owner of a Packt book, we have a number of things to help you to get the most from your purchase.

Downloading the example code

You can download the example code files for all Packt books you have purchased from your account at http://www.packtpub.com. If you purchased this book elsewhere, you can visit http://www.packtpub.com/support and register to have the files e-mailed directly to you.

Downloading the color images of this book

We also provide you a PDF file that has color images of the screenshots/diagrams used in this book. The color images will help you better understand the changes in the output. You can download this file from: http://www.packtpub.com/sites/default/files/downloads/5961OT_ColoredImages.pdf

Errata

Although we have taken every care to ensure the accuracy of our content, mistakes do happen. If you find a mistake in one of our books—maybe a mistake in the text or the code—we would be grateful if you would report this to us. By doing so, you can save other readers from frustration and help us improve subsequent versions of this book. If you find any errata, please report them by visiting http://www.packtpub.com/submit-errata, selecting your book, clicking on the **errata submission form** link, and entering the details of your errata. Once your errata are verified, your submission will be accepted and the errata will be uploaded to our website, or added to any list of existing errata, under the Errata section of that title.

Piracy

Piracy of copyright material on the Internet is an ongoing problem across all media. At Packt, we take the protection of our copyright and licenses very seriously. If you come across any illegal copies of our works, in any form, on the Internet, please provide us with the location address or website name immediately so that we can pursue a remedy.

Please contact us at copyright@packtpub.com with a link to the suspected pirated material.

We appreciate your help in protecting our authors, and our ability to bring you valuable content.

Questions

You can contact us at questions@packtpub.com if you are having a problem with any aspect of the book, and we will do our best to address it.

1
Introduction

Welcome to Stencyl — an exciting and fun game development tool used by many professional and amateur game developers around the world.

By the end of this book, we will know all the skills required to develop a product that exhibits all the features expected in a professionally-developed computer game.

However, before we start to create our game, we're going to learn about the Stencyl toolkit, install Stencyl, and test that everything is working as required, then experiment with some of the sample games that have been provided with the installation.

In this chapter we will learn the following:

- How Stencyl works
- How we'll learn to use Stencyl
- Why Stencyl is a great development tool
- Platforms that Stencyl runs on
- What makes Stencyl different
- Successful games created with Stencyl
- Using the free version of Stencyl
- Installing Stencyl and testing the setup

How Stencyl works

If you have purchased this book, then you may already have an idea of what Stencyl is and how it works.

However, if you are browsing online or standing in a bookstore flicking through the pages of this book, then you might want to know that Stencyl is a no-coding toolkit for creating 2D video games that will run on many different mobile and desktop devices.

Scenes, or levels, within a game are created using Stencyl's drag-and-drop **Scene Designer**. The screenshot below shows the Scene Designer being used to modify one of the levels in the game that we'll be creating:

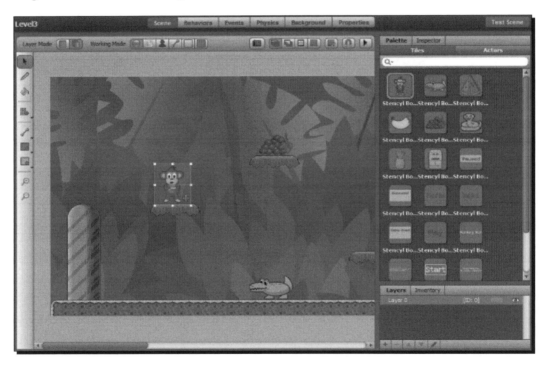

Downloading the color images of this book

We also provide you a PDF file that has color images of the screenshots/diagrams used in this book. The color images will help you better understand the changes in the output. You can download this file from: http://www.packtpub.com/sites/default/files/downloads/5961OT_ColoredImages.pdf

The instructions or logic for the gameplay can be created using Stencyl's **Gameplay Designer** — a clever system that utilizes building blocks which snap together to create a series of instructions that are used by the objects in our game. An example of some instructions being created in the Gameplay Designer is shown in the following screenshot:

How we'll learn to use Stencyl

All that is needed to follow the tutorials in this book are a desktop computer—Microsoft Windows, Mac OS X, or Linux will do just fine, along with the free version of Stencyl that can be downloaded from www.stencyl.com. The free version of Stencyl can be used to develop and publish Flash and HTML5 games, and it can also be used to develop and test games for desktop computers and mobile devices. If you want to publish games for platforms other than Flash and HTML5, then you'll need to pay for an annual subscription to Stencyl in order to access the additional publishing features.

A great way to learn to use a tool such as Stencyl is to complete a practical project, and over the course of this book, we will develop a game from a blank screen right through to completion, learning all the important features of Stencyl along the way.

The game will start in a very basic form and as we progress, we will use the tools within Stencyl to add features to our game until we have a final product that demonstrates many of the characteristics that a professional game should exhibit.

Later in this chapter, we'll install Stencyl and run some test games to ensure that everything is working properly. Then, in *Chapter 2, Let's Make a Game!*, we'll jump straight in and create a game with a character that we can control as it runs and jumps across a scrolling jungle scene and interacts with an interesting environment.

We're going to experience some amazing results very quickly, so the learning process is going to be fast paced and fun!

The following screenshot was captured while developing the game in *Chapter 2, Let's Make a Game!*, so it can be seen how quickly we will be progressing through the development of our game.

Why Stencyl is a great development tool

Stencyl is a ready-to-use, complete, game development studio that can be used by anyone from beginners to game development experts to create professional-quality games; there is no requirement to purchase or install additional software. The Stencyl game development process avoids the repetitive, complicated requirements of writing hundreds of lines of computer code, and gets you started with the creation of your games without being distracted by the intricate details that traditional computer programming languages require.

Rapid prototyping and development

If you have an idea for a game, Stencyl will enable you to rapidly create a working prototype, so that you can quickly progress to creating a completed game using the great features that come built into the Stencyl toolkit, including:

- Scene Designer
- Drag-and-drop Gameplay Designer
- Resource management (sounds and graphics)
- Animation editor
- Graphics editor
- Online resource sharing

We'll be learning how to use all these features to enable us to quickly build our video game.

No code development

Games can be created without writing a single line of computer code, by using Stencyl's drag-and-drop Gameplay Designer. Its clever system of building sequences of commands using specially designed instruction blocks means that we can only create instructions that make sense to the computer.

If you have ever tried writing computer games using a language such as Apple's Objective-C or Adobe's ActionScript, you probably know how frustrating it can be to ensure that every bracket, period, and special symbol appears in exactly the right place. That's a problem of the past with Stencyl!

Sharing resources with other Stencyl developers

One of the many great features of Stencyl is **StencylForge** — a ready-built repository of game resources that can be used for downloading graphics, audio, gameplay rules (known as **Behaviors** in Stencyl), and utilities. You can also upload your own resources to share with others.

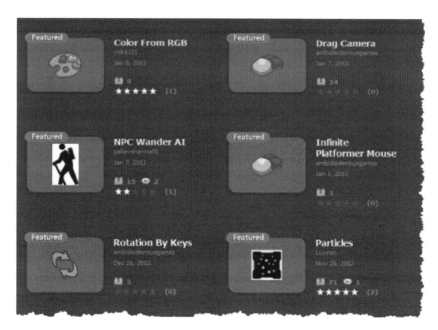

StencylForge is a remarkable asset to the Stencyl community, and it's one of the exciting features of Stencyl that we'll be learning to use while we develop our game.

In addition to being able to share resources using StencylForge, there is a great community of helpful Stencyl users for both beginner and experienced users at `community.stencyl.com`.

Platforms that Stencyl runs on

The Stencyl game development toolkit can be installed on the following desktop computer platforms:

◆ Microsoft Windows (XP, Windows Vista, Windows 7, and Windows 8)

◆ Mac OS X

◆ Linux

The installation process for each of the above platforms is detailed later in this chapter.

Stencyl target platforms

When we talk about target platforms, we mean the devices that our game can run on.

Games created with Stencyl can be played on most common platforms including web browsers, Microsoft Windows, Mac OS X and iOS devices (for example, iPhone and iPad), Android, and Linux. The main issues that we need to think about, when it comes to the target platform, are the screen size of the game and how our game will be controlled (that is, keyboard, mouse, or touch). Stencyl does all the hard work for you!

Currently, at the time of publication, Stencyl can target the following platforms:

◆ Apple mobile devices running iOS Version 4.1 and above, including:

❑ iPod touch

❑ iPad

❑ iPhone

◆ Google Android devices running Android Version 2.2 and above, including:

❑ Phones

❑ Tablets

◆ HTML5 web browsers:

❑ Many web browsers and devices that support the HTML5 web standard

◆ Microsoft Windows desktop PCs and laptops:

❑ Windows XP and above

◆ Mac desktop operating systems:

❑ Mac OS X

◆ Linux desktops:

❑ Ubuntu distributions recommended

Targeting specific devices

If you need to target a specific device, it is important to ensure that it is supported. So, check the Stencyl website for the most up-to-date information, as details may have changed since publication.

Publishing desktop games

When creating games for desktop platforms, it's important to understand that you can only publish games for the platform on which you are running Stencyl. For example, if you are running Stencyl on a Windows PC, you can only create desktop games for other Windows PCs, and if you are running Stencyl on Mac OS X, then you can only create desktop games for other Mac OS X computers.

Publishing to iOS devices

Amazingly, if you want to publish to Apple's iOS devices using Stencyl, you don't need to own an Apple computer, which has been, until now, an expensive barrier to entry for would-be iOS game developers! The Stencyl *Mobile* and *Studio* annual subscriptions include access to the StencylBuilder service that enables Windows and Linux users to publish their Stencyl games to the Apple App Store as long as they are current members of the Apple iOS Developer Program.

Publishing to Android

Publishing to Android is a very straightforward process with Stencyl running on any supported desktop platform, and testing on an Android device does not require a developer license.

What makes Stencyl different

There are many game development tools available, but Stencyl has some stand-out features that make it very different from its competitors.

Stencyl runs on almost any desktop computer

Stencyl can be installed on nearly all popular desktop computers, and Stencyl files can be freely exported and imported between the different desktop platforms, which is very useful when working with friends or colleagues who use different platforms for game development.

Stencyl creates native code

Whichever platform we want to publish our game onto, Stencyl does all the hard work for us! It creates the game code specifically for that device, and it will not have to run the game in a wrapper that can slow our games down.

Although that might sound fairly technical, it just means that our games will run at the fastest possible speeds without us having to learn a new programming language for each target platform. Stencyl takes care of all the hard work when it comes to publishing to different target devices; we can just concentrate on creating our games!

You don't need to be a coder

Probably the greatest differentiator between Stencyl and other game development tools is the way in which the gameplay instructions are built. With many game development tools, you must hand-code the instructions in a specific programming language, which can be very tedious and time-consuming. Or, with some other development tools, you are required to point and click on the instructions that you want to select in order to build rules that the objects in your game will follow, which can be very restricting when it comes to complex gameplay.

The developers of Stencyl have created a system that offers an impressive set of options when compared to other currently available game development methods. There are four different options available to game developers when using Stencyl, so we can do the following:

◆ Use Stencyl's built-in gameplay routines (called **behaviors** in Stencyl)

◆ Download existing behaviors from StencylForge

◆ Create our own behaviors using an intuitive drag-and-drop system

◆ Hand-code our own gameplay instructions using a traditional programming language called Haxe

The magic of Stencyl is that we can mix and match any combination of the above development methods!

For example, if we want to create a basic game with common gameplay features, it's very easy to use Stencyl's built-in behaviors, and it's quite possible to develop a complete game in this manner.

At the time of publication, there were more than fifty built-in behaviors, a small sample of which is shown in the following screenshot:

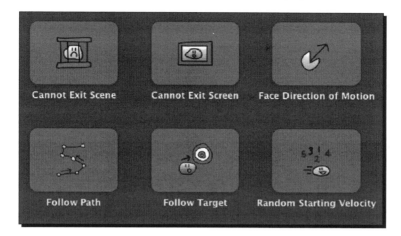

Once we understand how the prebuilt behaviors work, we can either customize existing ones or we can create our own from scratch using the drag-and-drop behavior editor.

The following screenshot shows an example of a custom-built behavior, and even if you have never seen Stencyl before, you might be able to understand some of the instructions.

Finally, more advanced developers may choose to hand-code their own special game routines using the Haxe programming language (pronounced Hex, according to the main developer). This is certainly not a requirement for creating games, and many Stencyl users have never even tried this kind of development! Most Stencyl developers use a combination of prebuilt behaviors, customized behaviors, and also behaviors that they have created themselves, and these are the methods that we are going to be using throughout this book.

When our game is finished, we just need to decide which platforms we want to target, and Stencyl will do the rest with a few clicks of the mouse!

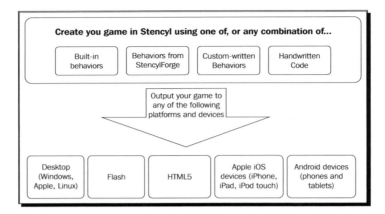

Using the free version of Stencyl

The free version of Stencyl has very few limitations compared to the subscription versions and in practice, you can use all the important game development features and make any kind of game with the free version that you can make with the subscription versions.

The main limitations of the free version of Stencyl are:

◆ Only Flash and HTML5 games can be published

◆ A Stencyl splash screen is displayed for a few moments when a published game loads

◆ Custom preloaders can't be implemented (these are the loading screen and progress bar that you see when your game first loads)

◆ Some monetization features are limited

The great thing about the free version of Stencyl is that we can develop our games to completion, publish them for Flash or HTML5, and even sell them if we wish.

If, after publishing for Flash or HTML5, we find that a game is very popular, we can then pay for the appropriate Stencyl subscription and sell the game in the Apple App Store, or for Android devices in the Google Play store. We can learn how to use Stencyl and develop games for free to see if people like them, before paying for an annual subscription!

If you are a member of the Apple iOS Developer program, games can be created and tested for the Apple iOS devices with the free version of Stencyl, but they can't be published to the Apple App Store. In *Chapter 10*, *Targeting Mobile Platforms*, we'll look in more detail at the options available, and the requirements for publishing to mobile devices running iOS and Android.

Using the free version of Stencyl with this book

In order to follow the game development tutorials in this book, only the free version of Stencyl is required. Subscriptions to Stencyl are only necessary for publishing to mobile devices and desktop applications.

The following matrix shows the major differences between the free and subscription versions of Stencyl:

	Free	Indie	Mobile	Studio
Platform Support				
Flash Publishing	Yes (w/ watermark)	Yes	Yes (w/ watermark)	Yes
HTML5 publishing	Yes (w/ watermark)	Yes	Yes (w/ watermark)	Yes
Chrome Store publishing	Yes (w/ watermark)	Yes	Yes (w/ watermark)	Yes
Windows 8 Store publishing	Yes (w/ watermark)	Yes	Yes (w/ watermark)	Yes
Native desktop publishing	Yes (w/ watermark)	Yes	Yes (w/ watermark)	Yes
iOS publishing	No	No	No	Yes
Android publishing	No	No	No	Yes

Please note that the previous matrix provides only a summary of differences between the available versions of Stencyl. It is vital to check the Stencyl website (`www.stencyl.com`) for the latest features prior to making a purchasing decision, as the feature list may have been updated since publication.

Successful games created with Stencyl

Many successful games for Flash and mobile devices have been created with Stencyl. In some cases, they have been created by experienced developers who have switched to Stencyl to speed up the development process, and in other cases, the games have been developed by newcomers to game development, who had previously been unable to create their own games due to the complexity of traditional programming languages, or who had simply not attempted to create a game previously.

Following are three examples of successful games that were created using Stencyl:

◆ **Making Monkeys**: Making Monkeys is an original, fun, platform game created by Greg Sergeant of `greg-anims.com`. The idea of the game is that very weird-looking monkeys can use a special weapon to duplicate themselves and solve various puzzles. Making Monkeys was sponsored by Armor Games and has gained over 1 million game plays.

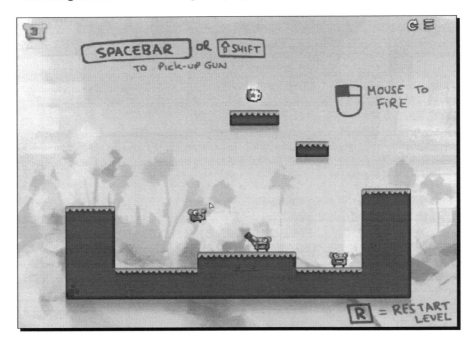

Greg has stated that it only took him a few days to create the prototype of the game and that Stencyl enabled him to try out new gameplay elements very quickly.

- **Kreayshawn Goes to Japan**: The first game that Beth Maher (www.bethmaher.com) created was called Kreayshawn: The game. The game, shown in the following screenshot, was created by her with Stencyl during a workshop project that was designed to encourage women to become involved in the indie game industry.

The development of this fan game led to Beth working with Columbia Records (part of the Sony group of companies) to produce Kreayshawn Goes to Japan, for Kreayshawn's fan website (arcade.kreayshawn.com). The game is a bright, imaginative platform game featuring Kreayshawn as the main character.

- **Impossible Pixel**: Impossible Pixel and the Fate of Destiny, created by 99 Up Games, is a challenging platform game with 93 levels, available on iPad and iPhone. This game takes advantage of the touchscreen features provided by iOS; the buttons for controlling the player can be seen in the lower-left and lower-right corners of the following screenshot:

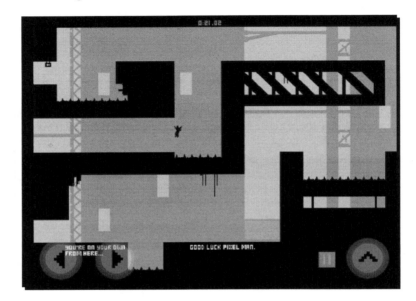

At the time of writing, Impossible Pixel, according to the developer's figures, had been downloaded from the Apple App Store approximately 700,000 times and had reached the position of the most popular free download on the App Store in nine countries. It was also the second most popular free download in thirty other countries, including the US App Store.

Impossible Pixel includes many professional features including Game Center achievements, high score leaderboards, atmospheric retro soundtrack, and many interesting challenges throughout the game.

The Stencyl Showcase

The listed games are a very small sample of the successful games that have been published using Stencyl. The Stencyl website contains areas dedicated to showcasing games, and it's certainly worth visiting Stencyl Showcase for inspiration, and to see some examples of impressive games that have been created with Stencyl.

- `www.stencyl.com/stencyl/showcase/`
- `www.stencyl.com/stencyl/successes/`

Installing Stencyl and testing the setup

We've had a look at what Stencyl can do and how we are going to learn to use it. So, let's jump right into the next vital step and install Stencyl. The following section of the book is split into four parts. The first three parts will explain how to install and run Stencyl on each of Microsoft Windows, Mac OS X, and Linux, and the fourth part will step through creating an account and quickly testing Stencyl to make sure that everything is working.

Once we have Stencyl up and running, we'll head off into *Chapter 2, Let's make a game!*, where we'll quickly progress with the development of our first game.

Installing Stencyl

Let's look at how to install Stencyl on each of the three desktop platforms that it supports: Microsoft Windows, Mac OS X, and Linux.

Microsoft Windows

Stencyl will currently install on the versions of Windows listed as follows:

◆ Windows XP

◆ Windows Vista

◆ Windows 7

◆ Windows 8

The download and installation methods are the same for each version of Windows, but the following screenshots have been captured in Windows 7.

Time for action – downloading and installing Stencyl on Windows

In this session, we're going to download and install Stencyl on Windows:

1. Visit www.stencyl.com.

2. Click on the **Download Now** button on the home page.

3. Depending on which web browser you are using and how you have configured it, the latest Stencyl installation file will start to download automatically, or you may have to confirm that you accept the download and specify the download location.

4. When the installation file has downloaded, find it in Windows Explorer and double-click it to start the installation process. You can see the dialog box shown in the following screenshot:

5. Click on **Next** to accept the default installation folder.

6. Click on **Install** to set the installation process running. Usually, the installation process will take less than a minute to complete, but the time may vary depending on the specification of your computer.

7. When the installation has completed, click on **Next** again to display the final dialog box shown in the following screenshot:

8. I recommend clicking on the **Run Stencyl** option to remove the checkmark so Stencyl does not run automatically.

9. Click on **Finish** to complete the installation of Stencyl.

Because of the system access that Stencyl requires, you may need to run Stencyl as the Administrator on a Windows PC when updating or the first time after purchasing a subscription. This can easily be achieved by right-clicking on the Stencyl application icon and selecting **Run as administrator**.

What just happened?

We have just downloaded the latest version of Stencyl for Windows, and the installation is now complete. If you want to delete the installation file that you downloaded, then that's fine; it's not needed any more.

When running Stencyl for the first time, we are asked to sign in. The signing in process is the same for all platforms and is detailed under the heading, *Creating a Stencyl account*, (after the Linux installation procedure in this chapter).

Mac OS X

Stencyl will currently install on all versions of Mac OS X, but it should be noted that Java 6 must be installed in order for Stencyl to work.

At the time of writing, Java 6 was a mandatory requirement for correct operation of Stencyl; Java 7 is not compatible.

The download and installation methods are the same for each version of Mac OS X, but the following screenshots have been captured in Mac OS X 10.7.4.

Time for action – downloading and installing Stencyl for Mac OS X

In this session, we're going to download and install Stencyl for Mac OS X.

1. Visit `www.stencyl.com`.

2. Click on the **Download Now** button on the home page.

3. Depending on which web browser you are using and how you have configured it, the latest Stencyl installation file will start to download automatically, or you may have to confirm that you accept the download and specify the download location.

4. When the installation file has downloaded, double-click on the `stencyl.dmg` file to automatically mount it and start the installation process.

5. When the application's files are ready to install, the following window will be displayed:

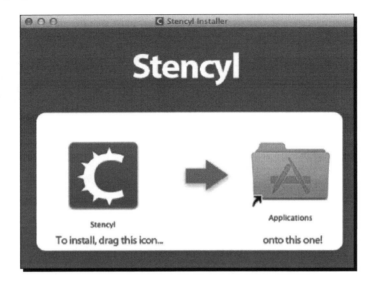

6. To complete the installation, click-and-hold on the **Stencyl** icon and drag it on top of the **Applications** icon. The Stencyl files will be copied into the `Applications` folder, and Stencyl is then ready to run!

What just happened?

We have just downloaded the latest version of Stencyl for Mac OS X, and the installation is now complete.

The `stencyl.dmg` file can now be unmounted and deleted; it's not needed anymore.

 When running Stencyl for the first time, we are asked to sign in. The signing in process is the same for all platforms and is detailed under the heading, *Creating a Stencyl account*, (after the Linux installation procedure in this chapter).

Linux

Stencyl should install on most recent versions of Linux, but Ubuntu distributions are recommended. For the following screenshots, Stencyl was installed and tested on Ubuntu Version 10.10.

Time for action – downloading and installing Stencyl for Linux

In this session, we're going to download and install Stencyl on Linux.

1. Visit www.stencyl.com.

2. Click on the **Download Now** button on the home page.

3. Depending on which web browser you are using and how you have configured it, the latest Stencyl installation file will start to download automatically, or you may have to confirm that you accept the download and specify the download location.

4. When the download has completed, right-click on the downloaded tar.gz file and select the **Open With Archive Manager** option as shown in the following screenshot:

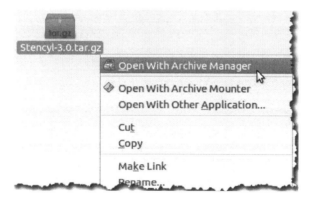

5. Open the folder where the files were extracted.

6. Stencyl is now ready to run!

What just happened?

We have just downloaded the latest version of Stencyl for Linux, and the installation is now complete.

The Linux version of Stencyl doesn't really need installing – we just needed to extract the files to create the `Stencyl` folder so that the application files are accessible.

If you want to delete the original download file, that's fine; it isn't needed anymore.

Creating a Stencyl account

Now that we have installed Stencyl, the next step is to run a quick test to ensure that everything is working, so we can then dive into the next chapter and create our first game.

Time for action – creating an account and signing in

Although it is not a requirement to sign in to create games with Stencyl, we won't be able to publish any games, access StencylForge, or contribute to the Stencyl online forums without an account.

In order to follow the tutorials in this book, we'll need access to StencylForge, and we'll also need to be able to publish our games, so I highly recommend creating a Stencyl account and signing in.

1. Run Stencyl and the following screen will be displayed:

2. If you do not see the sign-in screen, ensure that you have Stencyl running, and select **File | Sign In** on the main menu at the upper-left corner of the **Stencyl** screen.

 If you have already signed up for an account on the Stencyl forums, you do not need to create a separate account in order to log into Stencyl. The Stencyl application login and the Stencyl forum login use the same credentials; so, you can sign in to Stencyl without any further action!

3. Click on **Create an Account** and enter your username, password, and e-mail address in the right-hand side of the dialog box shown as follows. Note that Stencyl usernames and passwords are restricted to alphanumeric characters (letters and numbers only).

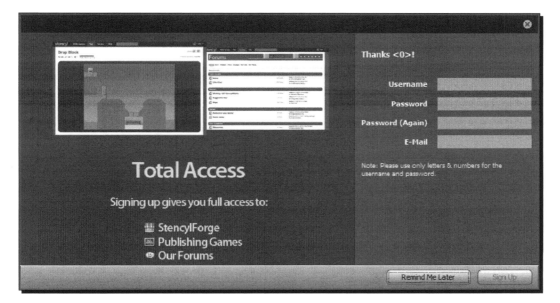

 Choose your username carefully as it will be your permanent Stencyl login name and username on the Stencyl online forums!

4. When you are confident that you have entered the correct details, click on the **Sign Up** button, and after a few seconds a confirmation message will be displayed as shown in the following screenshot:

5. Click on **OK** to confirm, and we are ready to start using Stencyl!

What just happened?

We have created an account so that we can access the important features of Stencyl. The same account credentials can be used to log in to the Stencyl forums at `community.stencyl.com`.

You do not need to sign in and out of the Stencyl application each time you use it, because your login details are remembered unless you specifically choose to sign out using the **File | Sign Out** option in the Stencyl menu.

Have a go hero

Why not visit the Stencyl community forums and say hello?

Fire up your web browser and visit `community.stencyl.com`, sign in to the forums using the account details that you have just created, and have a browse.

You could go to the **Chit Chat** forum, find the topic entitled **Introduce Yourself!**, and well, introduce yourself!

Testing the Stencyl installation

Now that we have installed Stencyl, it would be a good idea to carry out a test so that we know that everything is working as it should be.

Time For action – testing Stencyl

We're going to load up Stencyl, open one of the sample games that has been provided, and run the game to make sure that Stencyl is working properly.

 From this point onwards, all the tutorials will be the same whether Stencyl is running on Microsoft Windows, Mac OS X, or Linux, although the screenshots have mainly been taken using the Microsoft Windows version. On the rare occasion that there is a difference between the versions, it will be explained clearly in the tutorial.

1. If Stencyl is not already running on your computer, load it up and make sure that you have signed in with the account username and password that you created earlier, so you will see a screen that looks something like the following screenshot:

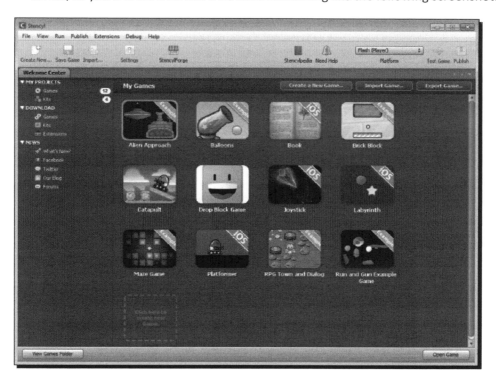

Don't worry if the list of games isn't identical on your screen, because the sample games packaged with Stencyl may be changed as software updates are released.

2. Double-click on the game icon for **Alien Approach** to open the game.

3. When the game has loaded, ensure that the target-platform drop-down option is set to **Flash (Player)**, and click on the blue arrow labeled **Test Game**, both of which can be found at the upper-right corner of the screen, as shown in the following screenshot:

4. Wait for Stencyl to create the game and display it in the **Adobe Flash Player** window as shown in the following screenshot (this may take up to 30 seconds, perhaps more on a very old computer).

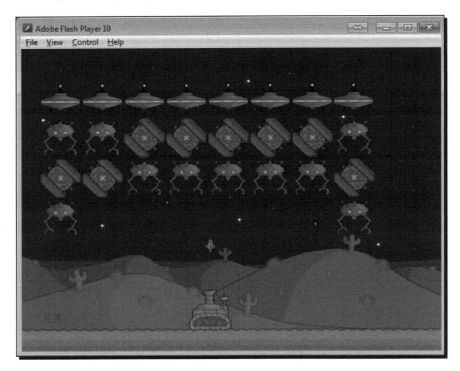

5. Play the game using the arrow keys to move left and right, and the spacebar to fire your weapons.

6. When you have finished playing the game, close the **Adobe Flash Player** window.

What just happened?

We just loaded a game into Stencyl and compiled it for the first time! Compilation is the process of converting the Stencyl game-code into a format that will run on our target platform. The default target platform is Flash, so when the compilation process has finished, the game will be displayed in an **Adobe Flash Player** window.

It's important to be aware that the sample games are not completed projects – they are just examples that have been provided so that we can see the kind of games that can be created. We can also use the samples to understand how the games have been put together, which is a great way to learn!

Have a go hero

We've loaded and compiled one sample game and have had a play, so why not try some of the other sample games that have been provided?

Before we can open up another game, we should close the **Adobe Flash Player** window in which the previously tested game is running, and we must close the current game in Stencyl by clicking on **File | Close Game** and follow any prompts that appear.

Now, experiment with the other sample games, so that you become comfortable with the process of loading, testing, and closing games in Stencyl.

Summary

We've reached the end of this chapter!

We have examined what Stencyl is for and who will find it useful. We have also looked at why Stencyl is different from other game development tools, and we've discovered that Stencyl can run on virtually all desktop computers, and can create games for many different target platforms, including the latest Apple iOS and Android devices.

Finally, we stepped through the procedures for installing Stencyl on Microsoft Windows, Mac OS X, and Linux PCs, and then rounded off with a quick test, using a sample game to ensure that Stencyl was working properly.

We've learned a lot in this chapter, but now that our Stencyl installation is complete and has been tested, it's time to roll up our sleeves and start using Stencyl! In *Chapter 2, Let's Make a Game!* We'll very quickly build up the basics of our game, so that we will have a character that we can control as it explores the environment we are going to create for it.

2
Let's Make a Game!

In Chapter 1, Introduction, I promised that we'd have the basics of a working game in place by the end of this chapter, and I plan to keep my promise!

Throughout this book, we are going to create a platform game, based in the jungle, in which the player will control a cheeky monkey that will have the ability to run and jump around the scene. As our monkey character runs, the screen will scroll horizontally to display more of the jungle and, along the way, there will be various obstacles, some items to collect, and some enemies to avoid.

Although some of the preceding features will be added to our game later in the development process, when we have learned more features of Stencyl, in this chapter, we will put in place many of the basic mechanics of the game.

The skills we will be learning in this chapter are:

- ◆ Creating a new game
- ◆ Creating a blank scene
- ◆ Downloading resources from StencylForge
- ◆ Understanding the Stencyl Dashboard
- ◆ Adding an actor into a scene
- ◆ Downloading and using tiles for scenery
- ◆ Using behaviors to interact with our game
- ◆ Improving the scene mechanics
- ◆ Making the screen scroll

By the end of this chapter, our game should resemble the following screenshot:

Using the downloaded game files

When starting a practical activity in the book, we can either continue in Stencyl, using our progress from the previous tutorial or, if we are coming back to the book after a break, we can load the last version of the game that we saved at the end of the previous session.

If we want to start afresh at the beginning of a practical activity, we can import the appropriate downloaded game file into Stencyl, so we know that we are starting at the right point in the game development process!

 The game files accompanying each chapter can be found in the *Support* section of this book's web page at www.packtpub.com.

Before each practical activity, there will be a note advising which Stencyl game file should be imported prior to starting the exercise, but it's not necessary to use the import files if we are following the tutorials consecutively.

It's very easy to import a Stencyl game file—just load up Stencyl and, on the main menu, go to **File | Import Game...**, then double-click the relevant file.

Let's get started!

Grab your keyboard and mouse, load up Stencyl, and let's start developing our game!

Creating a new game

We'll start by setting up Stencyl with a new, blank game to work with.

Time for action – creating a new game

We are starting with a blank game, so there's no need to import a game file!

1. Load up Stencyl on your computer.

2. Click on the **Click here to create New Game** cutout box, which appears after all the existing games on the **My Games** screen.

3. Click on **Blank Game** at the bottom of the left-hand side panel of the **Create a New Game...** dialog box.

4. Click on the **Next** button.

5. Type the name of our game `Monkey Run` into the **Name** text box under the **Basic Info** heading.

6. Click on the **Create** button.

7. Wait a few seconds while the blank game is created.

8. On the main menu, click on **File | Save**, or click the **Save Game** icon on the toolbar.

What just happened?

We have created and saved a blank game, but there are no game characters, no scenes, and no gameplay instructions!

It's a basic task, but we've taken our first step into game development with Stencyl.

Creating a blank scene

Every game needs a "world" in which to play, and this is where we will start to build our game. We already know that our game is going to be based in the jungle. So, let's take the next step and create a world for our monkey to play in.

The **Dashboard** should currently be displayed on the screen and, if we look at the left-hand side panel, under the heading **RESOURCES**, we can see a list of the types of resources that can be used in our game. The fourth item in the list is **Scenes**, and it should be highlighted, which is helpful, because the next step we are going to take is to create a scene for our game.

Time for action – creating a blank scene

The game file to import and load for this session is `5961_02_01.stencyl`.

1. Click on the message, **This game contains no Scenes. Click here to create one**, that appears in the middle of the right-hand side panel.

2. Give the scene a name. I prefer keeping scene names to one word if possible, so let's call it **Jungle**.

3. In the **Background Color** section of the dialog box, click on the long, thin, white rectangle so the color-selector pops up, and change the color to **Sea Green**—hovering the mouse over a color will pop up a tooltip with the name of the color.

4. Click on the **Create** button.

What just happened?

We have just created a **scene**!

In Stencyl, a scene is most easily described as being a "level" in a game. Our game will have just one level during the initial development stages, and it's now being displayed in the Scene Editor.

If we have a look at the upper-left side of our Stencyl screen (under the toolbar), we can see that we have two tabs—one is the **Dashboard** tab, and the other is our new **Jungle** tab that represents the scene we have just created. Just in case you're wondering, an asterisk next to the name on a tab means that the work in that tab has not been saved yet—we'll save our jungle scene at the start of the next step!

Downloading resources from StencylForge

We don't have any objects in our game yet, so we can't do anything interesting with our scene. Our next step is to insert a controllable character into our game and, as mentioned at the start of this chapter, our main character is going to be a monkey—so let's find that monkey!

Time for action – downloading an actor

The game file to import and load for this session is `5961_02_02.stencyl`.

We're going to add a character into our game, right now, by downloading it from Stencyl's online resource, which is called **StencylForge**.

1. On the Stencyl menu, click on **File | Save Game** (or click the **Save Game** toolbar icon).

2. Click on the **StencylForge** icon on the Stencyl toolbar.

3. Click on **Actor Types** in the **Resources** section of the left-hand side panel.

4. In the search box at the upper-right corner of the screen, type `Stencyl Book Monkey`.

5. Press *Enter* on the keyboard and wait for the search results to appear.

6. Double-click on the **Stencyl Book Monkey** thumbnail that appears in the right-hand side panel and wait for the monkey actor's information to be displayed—this may take a few seconds.

7. Read the information under the **Description** heading.

8. Click on the green **Download** button at the upper-right corner of the screen and wait for the actor to be downloaded into our game—the download may take a few seconds to start.

9. When the actor has downloaded, the monkey animations will appear in the **Animation Editor**.

10. Save the game.

Downloading the example code

You can download the example code files for all Packt books you have purchased from your account at http://www.packtpub.com . If you purchased this book elsewhere, you can visit http://www.packtpub.com/support and register to have the files e-mailed directly to you.

What just happened?

After saving the game, we downloaded an animated monkey from StencylForge. In Stencyl, the controllable characters in our game are called **actors**, and we are now looking at the **Animations** editor which shows the available animations for the monkey.

As we can see, there are eight different animations for our monkey, which provides plenty of scope for the movement of our monkey actor within the game.

We can see that the **Waiting** animation in the left-hand side panel has a star icon attached to it, which means it is the default animation for the actor. When we later place the actor into the jungle scene, the **Waiting** animation will be displayed by default.

> The actor graphics for our jungle game have all been created by the talented Vicki Wenderlich—www.vickiwenderlich.com—who has generously made the images available under the Creative Commons Attribution license. This means that anyone can use these graphics in their games—even commercial ones—as long as Vicki Wenderlich is clearly given credit for her work. We'll be having a closer look at legal matters relating to licensing and copyright in *Appendix 11, Planning, Resources, and Legal Issues*.

Have a go hero – searching StencylForge for interesting actors

In the previous *Time for Action* steps, we learned how to search StencylForge for actors. It's a good idea to become familiar with the resources that are available to us for use in our games, so have a go at browsing through the various actor resources that are available for download from StencylForge.

Open up the **StencylForge** tab, and have a good rummage around to see what interesting actors you can find! Although it is quite easy to delete unwanted actors from a game, if you want to download some more actors, to have a look at their animations, I would recommend creating a blank game to experiment with.

Understanding the Stencyl Dashboard

The Dashboard in Stencyl is the control center—it's where we will find all the resources in our game, whether they are scenes, actors, or any of the other resources that we'll be working with throughout the game development process.

It's a good idea to become familiar with Dashboard, so click on the **Dashboard** tab and note that the **Actor Types** heading and the **Scenes** heading both have a digit **1** next to them. This is telling us that there is currently one actor and one scene in our game, so it's a useful way to know, at a glance, what resources we have in a game that we are developing.

Adding an actor into a scene

We have a jungle scene, and we have downloaded our monkey actor, so let's do the right thing and put the monkey in the jungle using Stencyl's **Scene Designer**!

Time for action – adding an actor to the jungle scene

The game file to import and load for this session is `5961_02_03.stencyl`.

We need to ensure that the Animation Editor is displaying the monkey animation so, click on the **Actor Types** heading in the **Dashboard**, then double-click the **Stencyl Book Monkey** thumbnail in the main panel.

1. Click on the green **Add to Scene** button at the upper-right corner of the screen.
2. Click on the green **Jungle** scene that is shown in the **Choose a Scene** dialog box.
3. Click on the **OK** button to display the scene.
4. Move the mouse cursor (which shows the monkey) into the center of the green jungle scene.
5. Click on the mouse once to place the monkey into the scene.
6. Press *Escape* on the keyboard.
7. Click **File** | **Save** Game to save the game (or click the **Save Game** icon on the toolbar).

What just happened?

We have placed the monkey actor into the jungle scene, which was as easy as selecting the scene and then clicking on the mouse where we wanted the actor to appear. We only have one scene in our game, so it wasn't a difficult choice to make!

We are currently looking at the **Scene Designer**, which shows the design of the scene, and, to the right of the scene view, we can see the **Actors** in the **Palette** tab.

Currently, we can only see one actor in the palette—the monkey—because this is the only actor in our game. As we add more actors, they will be added to the **Actors** palette, and then we can click on any actor and add it to the scene as required.

If we wanted to place several copies of the actor into the scene, then we could have done so by moving the mouse and clicking on it each time we wanted to add a copy of the actor. It's not strictly necessary, but pressing *Escape* cleared the monkey actor from the mouse cursor so we didn't accidentally place more than one copy of the actor into the scene.

If we accidentally add more than one monkey to the jungle scene, it is easy to remove the unwanted actors—ensuring that the *Escape* key has been pressed, click on the unwanted actor and press the *Delete* key to remove it.

Testing the game

So far, we have a scene with a single actor placed on it, so now would be a good time to test the game to make sure that we know what we have achieved in the development process!

Time for action – testing the game

The game file to import and load for this session is `5961_02_04.stencyl`.

Fortunately, Stencyl makes it very easy—and quick—to test our games:

1. Click the **Test Game** icon on the right-hand side of the toolbar.
2. Watch the progress messages that appear while the game is prepared.

3. The Flash Player window opens so that we can see our game.

4. Press the arrow keys on the keyboard. Don't worry—nothing should happen!

5. Close the Flash Player window.

What just happened?

We tested our game, but it wasn't very exciting to see, was it?

However, when we clicked on the **Test Game** icon, Stencyl saved the game file, put together all the information that we have provided and compiled it into a Flash game that was displayed in the Flash Player window.

When we pressed the arrow keys on the keyboard, absolutely nothing happened because we haven't provided Stencyl with any information about how the monkey actor will be controlled by the player!

The other problem we have is that we have no scenery in our scene. If we don't make the scene interesting, it's not going to be a very interesting game, so let's make that our next task.

Downloading and using tiles for scenery

Currently, our monkey is floating in midair, which doesn't present the player of our game with a very interesting scene! We need to build some scenery, made from tiles, so that our monkey can run and jump on something.

Once again, we're going to visit StencylForge and search for some resources that we can use in our game, so let's get on and do that:

Time for action – downloading tiles from StencylForge

The game file to import and load for this session is `5961_02_04.stencyl`.

1. If the **StencylForge** tab is still available at the top of the screen, then click on it. If the StencylForge tab is not visible, click on the **StencylForge** icon on the toolbar to open it up again.

2. In the left-hand side panel, under the **MEDIA** heading, click on **Tilesets**.

3. In the search box, found at the upper-right corner of the screen, type `Stencyl Book Tileset`, and press *Enter*.

4. Double-click on the thumbnail image for the **Stencyl Book Tileset** and read the information under the **Description** heading.

5. Click on the **Download** button at the upper-right of the screen.

6. Wait a moment for the tileset to download.

What just happened?

In the same way that we downloaded the monkey actor from StencylForge, we have just downloaded a **tileset**—a collection of predesigned tiles that will help us build our jungle scene.

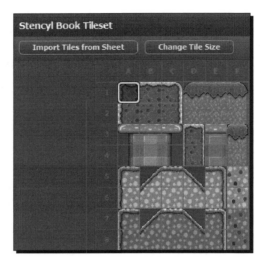

 The tileset that we are using in our game is based on a design by a Stencyl user called Ceric. The tileset was generously released by Ceric as a **public domain** resource, which means that we can use the graphics for absolutely any purpose we desire, without any licensing requirements or copyright-related issues.

We're currently looking at the Tileset Editor, which enables us to modify the tileset's graphics along with various other aspects of tile management, but we don't need to make any changes right now—for our purposes, the tiles are just fine as they are.

Now that we have downloaded the tiles, they are available for us to use in our game.

Have a go hero – searching StencylForge for tilesets

Search StencylForge and see which other tilesets are available—but don't download any of them into our game! If you would like to experiment with downloading some tilesets, it would be a good idea to create a blank game to practice with.

Adding tiles into the scene

Adding tiles into the scene is usually a fun process—it's when we really start to see how the game will look—and we can experiment to our heart's desire until we get the layout just right.

Time for action – adding tiles into the scene

The game file to import and load for this session is `5961_02_05.stencyl`.

We're currently looking at the Tileset Editor, but we're not going to be using it in this chapter, so we can close the tab and ensure that we are viewing the Scene Designer.

1. Close the **Stencyl Book Tileset** tab by clicking on the small **x** icon in the tab.

2. Close the **StencylForge** tab.

3. Click on the **Jungle** tab to display the green jungle scene. If the **Jungle** tab isn't visible, click on the **Dashboard** tab, click on **Scenes** in the left panel, and then double-click on the **Jungle** scene thumbnail image in the right-hand side panel.

4. In the **Palette** panel, on the right of the screen, click on the **Tiles** palette button, to display the tileset as follows:

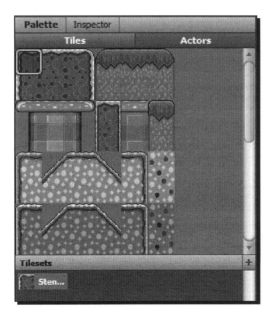

5. The tile in the upper-left corner of the tileset is already selected, so move the mouse cursor to the lower-left corner of the green jungle scene and click the mouse once to place the tile.

6. In the **Tiles** palette, click on the second tile present in the top row of the tileset to select it.

7. Place the newly-selected tile by clicking on the green jungle scene, immediately to the right of the first tile, so the lower-left corner of the jungle scene looks like the following screenshot:

What just happened?

We've started to design the layout of the jungle scene, but, so far, we have only placed two tiles.

Designing a scene using tiles is a straightforward process—we just click in the **Tilesets** palette to select a tile, and then we click on the scene to place the tile.

Our next step is to complete the basic layout for the jungle scene but, before we do that, we're going learn to make use of the design tools that are available to us.

Working with tiles

If we had to click once on the scene *every* time we wanted to place one tile, the fun of designing a scene would soon turn into frustration! Let's have a look at some tips that will help us to speed up our placement of tiles in the Scene Designer.

Deleting tiles from a scene

To delete a tile from a scene, we first need to ensure that we do not have a tile attached to the mouse cursor, and this is done by pressing the *Escape* key on the keyboard. We can then click on any tile and press *Delete* on the keyboard to remove it.

Replacing existing tiles in a scene

If we want to replace an existing tile, we don't need to delete it first—we can simply place a new tile over the top of it.

Moving tiles in a scene

We can move a single tile by clicking on the tile in the scene and then dragging it to a new location or, once we have clicked on a tile, we can use the arrow keys to position it. Again, we need to press *Escape* first, to ensure that we do not have a tile selected in the tile palette.

Selecting multiple tiles

We can select multiple tiles by clicking-and-dragging a selection box around the tiles that we want to select. The trick is to ensure that we start the click-and-drag on an unused part of the scene—or start the click-and-drag outside the edge of the scene—as shown in the following screenshot:

When we draw the selection box and let go of the mouse button, the selected tiles will be highlighted as a group, so they can be dragged or deleted together, which is much quicker than moving or deleting one tile at a time!

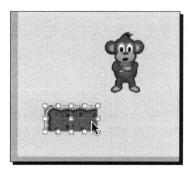

Placing multiple copies of tiles

If we really want to speed things up, we can place multiple copies of the same tile on the scene, by "painting" the tiles into place, rather than clicking once to position each individual tile. To paint a tile onto a scene, we select the required tile from the **Tiles** palette and then click-and-drag the mouse to cover the areas where we want the tile to appear.

We can also select multiple tiles from the **Tiles** palette by clicking-and-dragging on the tiles that we want from the palette. We can then single-click to add that block into the scene or, we can "paint" the block onto the scene by clicking and dragging, just as we can do with a single block.

Have a go hero – experimenting with tiles in the scene

The game file to import and load for this session is `5961_02_06.stencyl`.

Using the skills that we have discussed earlier, we can now go ahead and experiment with placing tiles in the scene. Go wild—after all, we're in a jungle, but don't spend too much time making the perfect scene—this is just an experiment, and our next task will be to delete our experimental tiles!

Try experimenting with the following techniques in our jungle scene:

- Placing a tile over the top of an existing tile
- Adding a single tile
- Painting a single tile onto the scene
- Deleting single and multiple tiles
- Moving single and multiple tiles
- Painting blocks of multiple tiles into the scene

The more we experiment with the tools, the more familiar we will become with them, and the easier it will become to design our scenes in the future!

It really doesn't matter what our scene looks like after experimenting with the tile-placement techniques—we're going to tidy it up shortly!

Finalizing the initial design

We've had fun experimenting with tiles in the Scene Designer, but we need a scene layout that we can work with for the rest of the tutorial, so the next task is to clear up the scene.

Have a go hero – tidying up the scene

The game file to import and load for this session is `5961_02_06.stencyl`.

We have now discovered all the tools that we need to place tiles into a scene, so let's delete our experimental tiles and set up our scene for the rest of the tutorial.

We need to do the following:

- Delete the experimental tiles that we have just placed in the scene.
- Ensure that the jungle scene looks like the following screenshot.
- Save the game!

We're going to keep the layout very basic to start with, as it will allow us to build up our game without becoming distracted by too many tiles—later on, we'll be adding to the scene to make it more challenging for the player.

Reviewing our progress

We've already made a lot of progress and have discovered many of Stencyl's game-design features, so let's review what we have achieved so far—we have:

- Created a blank game
- Created a game scene
- Downloaded an actor from StencylForge
- Added an actor to a scene
- Downloaded a tileset from StencylForge
- Added tiles to a scene
- Modified the layout of tiles within a scene

We now have a basic scene layout for our game, but there is currently a vital element of the game that we still need to add.

Using behaviors to interact with our game

We can't really call our current creation a *game*, because there isn't any interaction! Players need to be able to react to what is happening in our game, or it won't be much fun so, in this part of the book, we are going to implement the following gameplay elements:

- Controlling the monkey with the keyboard
- Scrolling the scene as the monkey runs

Working with behaviors

Behaviors are the instructions, or rules, for our game. Currently, we have a scene and an actor, but we haven't implemented any rules relating to how our game will work.

Think of behaviors as the answers to questions that are asked when certain events occur in our game, such as the ones listed here:

- What happens when the player presses keys on the keyboard?
- What should happen when my actor reaches the edge of the screen?
- What happens when my player actor bumps into an enemy actor?

The behaviors in our game can listen out for these mentioned **events**, and can then apply the rules that we have specified. Understanding events is a very important aspect of game development—hundreds of events will occur within our game every second, and it is up to us, as developers, to decide how we will respond to those events.

The good news is that Stencyl, as we might now expect, will manage all the hard work for us. All we need to know is that events will occur, and that our behaviors will manage how our game reacts to those events.

Adding behaviors

We are now going to start adding some behaviors into our game so that it will start coming to life! First of all, let's get that monkey moving.

Time for action – attaching a behavior to an actor

The game file to import and load for this session is `5961_02_06.stencyl`.

 We will be working with the monkey actor, so ensure that it is currently on display in the **Animation Editor**.

Stencyl comes packaged with many useful behaviors—and we first need to tell Stencyl to attach the required behaviors to the relevant objects within our game. In this case, we need to attach a behavior to the monkey actor, so that we can control it with the keyboard.

1. Click on the **Stencyl Book Monkey** tab to display the monkey in the Animation Editor.

2. Click on the **Behaviors** button in the row of buttons at the upper-center of the screen.

3. Click on the message **Click here to choose a Behavior to attach to this Actor Type** that appears in the main panel.

4. In the left-hand side panel of the **Choose a Behavior** dialog box, click on the **Controls** option that appears under the **FROM YOUR LIBRARY** heading.

5. Scroll down the list of behaviors that appears, until you can see the thumbnail image for the **Jump and Run Movement**, then double-click on it.

What just happened?

We needed to find a behavior that would allow us to control the monkey with the keyboard, so we first selected the tab for the monkey actor, and then we chose the **Jump and Run Movement** behavior, so it is now attached to the monkey actor.

The instructions in the newly-attached behavior will now apply to the monkey actor but, before we test our game, we need to provide the behavior with some information, so that it knows exactly what to do.

Configuring behaviors with Attributes

Some behaviors must be provided with information so that they can do their job but, at the moment, the **Jump and Run Movement** behavior doesn't have all the information that it needs.

The configuration information that we supply to a behavior are called **attributes**, and an attribute could be almost any type of data such as a number, text, a type of actor, or even a list of items.

As we can see, if we scroll down the configuration information for the **Jump and Run Movement** behavior that we have onscreen, there are quite a lot of attributes needed to configure this behavior!

Fortunately, the **Jump and Run Movement** behavior only needs us to provide the following attributes to get started:

- ◆ The keys that will control the actor.
- ◆ The animations that will be used when then actor moves.

Our next task is to specify these attributes so that we can move the monkey with the keyboard and see the correct animations as the monkey moves around the scene.

Time for action – configuring the behavior

The game file to import and load for this session is `5961_02_07.stencyl`.

Ensure that we can see the attributes for the *Run and Jump Movement* behavior by opening the monkey actor and clicking on the **Behaviors** button at the upper-center of the screen.

Let's get the keyboard and animation information into the behavior:

1. Click on the drop-down arrow next to the heading **Left Control** and select the item labeled **left**.

2. Click on the drop-down arrow next to the heading **Right Control** and select the item labeled **right**.

3. Click on the drop-down arrow next to the heading **Jump Control** and select the item labeled **up**.

4. Scroll down the configuration screen so that the section with the red warning triangle icons can be seen.

5. Click on the **Choose Animation...** button next to the first icon, which is labeled **Idle Left Animation**.

6. In the **Choose Animation** dialog box that appears, click on the thumbnail for the monkey's **Idle Left** animation.

7. Click on **OK** to confirm your choice.

8. Click on the **Choose Animation...** button next to the second icon, which is labeled **Idle Right Animation**.

9. In the **Choose Animation...** dialog box that appears, click on the monkey thumbnail image labeled **Idle Right**.

10. Click on **OK** to confirm your choice.

What just happened?

We have selected the keys that we are going to use to control the monkey—arrow left, arrow right, and arrow up—and we have specified which animations are going to be displayed when the monkey actor is idle facing left or idle facing right.

However, we haven't quite finished configuring the *Jump and Run Movement* behavior yet—we need to specify the last few animations, and that's our next task.

Have a go hero – configuring the remaining animations

We have already configured the first two animations, so go ahead and configure the final four:

◆ Run left

◆ Run right

◆ Jump left

◆ Jump right

Just click on the **Choose Animation…** buttons and select the appropriate animation from the dialog box.

If we make a mistake when choosing the animations, it doesn't matter! We can simply click on the **Choose Animation…** button again, and select the appropriate animation.

Save the game!

Always save the game after changes have been made!

Testing the game

Now that we have attached a behavior to the monkey, and we've configured the behavior to respond to the required key presses and display the appropriate animations, it's time to test our progress so far.

When developing a game, it is advisable to test often—perhaps even after every significant change that is made to the game. This allows us to see when things have gone wrong, and to be able to easily step backwards through any changes and fix anything that we might have done wrong. Of course, testing also enables us to see what has gone *right*, so we can enjoy the progress that we are making in the development process!

It doesn't cost anything to test a Flash game in Stencyl, and it's a very quick process, which usually takes a few seconds, so why not test as often as we can?

 This is a *deliberate mistake* alert! It can be very frustrating to follow the steps in a tutorial, only to find that we do not experience the results that we are expecting.

Be aware that when we test the game this time, it's not going to work quite how we expect it to. However, don't worry—it will only take a few moments to fix the problem, and it's a good opportunity to learn that sometimes things go wrong when developing a game, so we can have the experience of putting them right!

Time for action – testing the game to find a problem!

The game file to import and load for this session is `5961_02_08.stencyl`.

Let's test the game so we can see what's going to go wrong!

1. Save the game.
2. Click the **Test Game** icon on the toolbar.

3. Wait for the game to compile and display in the Flash Player Window.

4. Press the left and right arrow keys to move the monkey and press the up arrow key to try to make the monkey jump.

Clearly things aren't working as we would expect!

What just happened?

We've experienced our first **bug**—however, it's not a fault with Stencyl—we just haven't set the game up quite right!

Although the left and right arrow keys are making the monkey move in the correct direction, the monkey is floating in midair, the animations for running left and right aren't working, and the jump button isn't doing its job.

It's almost impossible to develop a useful computer application—including a game, without introducing a mistake, or bug, during the development process, so when this happens, we need to find the problem and fix it!

Improving the scene mechanics

To fix our bug, we need to make a single change to the game. Currently, there is no gravity to make the monkey fall to the ground, so we need to make an adjustment to a setting in the Jungle scene.

Time for action – adding gravity to the Jungle scene

The game file to import and load for this session is `5961_02_08.stencyl`.

Gravity in a game enables actors to fall or float, depending on the configuration that we specify, and we need the gravity in our game to allow the monkey actor to fall—just as it would in a real jungle—so let's make that change to the Jungle scene:

If the **Jungle** tab isn't visible at the top of the screen, we'll need to open up the Jungle scene first.

1. Click on the **Dashboard** tab.

2. Click on **Scenes** under the **RESOURCES** heading in the left-hand side panel.

3. Double-click on the thumbnail image for the **Jungle** scene.

Now that we can see the **Jungle** scene, we can change the required setting:

1. Click on the **Physics** button in the row of buttons in the upper-center of the screen, as shown in the following screenshot:

2. Change the contents of the text box next to the label **Gravity (Vertical)** so that it contains the number 85 as shown in the following screenshot:

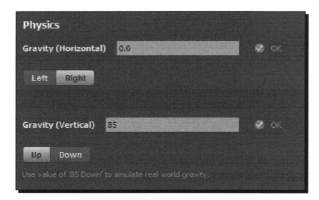

3. Click on the **Test Game** icon on the toolbar to save and test the game.
4. Wait for the game to compile and display in the Flash Player window.
5. Use the left, right, and up arrow keys to control the monkey.
6. Try to move the monkey off the left or right edge of the scene.

What just happened?

We added gravity to our game, so now the monkey actor's behavior can do its job properly!

The Jump and Run Movement behavior needs the scene to have a gravity setting before it will work properly, because the running and jumping actions rely on the monkey being on the "ground"—which is represented by the tiles in our game.

If we have a closer look at the **Physics** settings on the screen, we can see that gravity can be set vertically and horizontally, which can provide some very interesting gameplay in the appropriate places!

We set the vertical gravity value to 85, because this number most closely represents the effects of real gravity on our actor, but do remember that we are only using a game physics engine—not a scientific simulation of real life!

Keeping an actor in a scene

While testing the game, it may have become apparent that there is another problem—when the monkey actor completely leaves the scene, by running off the sides, it disappears and never returns!

If that problem didn't occur during the last test, then test the game again right now, and make the monkey run off the side of the scene so that it disappears.

Time for action – attaching another behavior to the actor

The game file to import and load for this session is `5961_02_09.stencyl`.

We can easily prevent actors from leaving a scene by attaching another behavior, so our next task is to do just that!

1. Ensure that the **Stencyl Book Monkey** tab is active.

2. If the **Stencyl Book Monkey** tab isn't currently open, go to the **Dashboard**, click on **Actor Types** under the **RESOURCES** heading, and double-click on the thumbnail image for the monkey.

3. Click on the **Behaviors** button at the upper-center of the screen.

4. Click on the **+ Add Behavior** button at the very lower-left corner of the screen.

5. In the left-hand side panel of the **Choose a Behavior** dialog box, click on the **Motion** option that appears under the **FROM YOUR LIBRARY** heading.

6. Find the **Cannot Exit Scene** behavior in the main panel, and double-click it. Be careful not to select the similarly named **Cannot Exit Screen** behavior—it doesn't do exactly what we need!

7. Read the information on the behavior screen that is now being displayed:

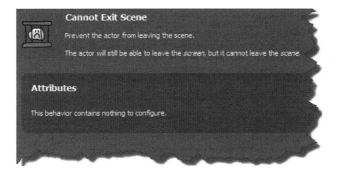

8. Click the **Test Game** icon to see if the monkey can still leave at the edges of the scene, then close the Flash Player window.

What just happened?

We've attached a second behavior to the monkey actor, and this additional behavior is designed to prevent the actor from leaving the scene. Hopefully, we could see that the behavior did its job when we tested the game!

Unlike the **Jump and Run Movement** behavior, which had some information that needed to be configured, the **Cannot Exit Scene** behavior does not have any attributes that can be changed, so we were able to jump straight into testing the game, as soon as the behavior had been attached to the actor.

Increasing the width of the gameplay area

Currently, our monkey only has a very small area in which to play, as he is restricted to moving within the confines of our game window which is quite small—640 pixels wide and 480 pixels high. This is a common screen size for Flash games, which is why it is the default size for Stencyl games.

It might be possible to create an interesting jungle scene in such a small space but, we can make the game more interesting for our players, if we make the gameplay area much wider, so let's change the settings for the Jungle scene to make it three times as wide.

Time for action – increasing the width of the scene

The game file to import and load for this session is `5961_02_10.stencyl`.

We're going to change the width of the scene, so we need to display the jungle scene's properties:

1. On the **Dashboard**, click on the **Scenes** heading.

2. Double-click the thumbnail image for the **Jungle** scene.

3. Ensure that the **Scene** button is selected in the row of buttons at the upper-center of the screen.

4. Click on the **Properties** button in the same row of buttons.

5. In the **Edit Scene Properties** dialog box, under the **Size** heading, change the **Width** from 20 to 60.

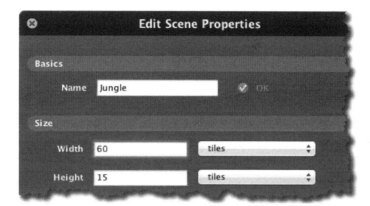

6. Click on **OK**.

7. Test the game by making the monkey run past the rightmost edge of the scene, and then close the Flash Player window—expect a problem to occur when the monkey leaves the edge of the screen!

What just happened?

We've increased the width of the scene from its original 20 tiles to 60 tiles—three times its original width. We can see that, as soon as we confirmed the changes to the width of the scene, it immediately increased in size—it's now so wide that we need to use the horizontal scroll bar at the bottom of the Scene Designer in order to see the whole scene!

However, we have a problem because, when the monkey ran off the edge of the screen, he disappeared, never to be seen again.

Another problem that may not immediately be apparent, is that there aren't enough tiles for the monkey to run along—when he ran past the edge of the screen, the poor monkey fell off a cliff!

Our next task is to fix both of these problems, starting with the tiles:

Have a go hero – adding more tiles to the scene

The game file to import and load for this session is `5961_02_11.stencyl`.

We already know how to add tiles, and we're already looking at the Scene Designer, so go ahead and add enough tiles to reach the far, right-hand side edge of the scene, as shown in the following zoomed-out screenshot:

When designing scenes that are too wide to fit on our screen, we can either scroll along the scene using the horizontal scroll bar, or we can zoom in and out of the scene using the zoom utility buttons in the toolbar at the left-hand side of the Scene Designer. Clicking on the zoom tools and then clicking on the scene, enables us to zoom in and out as required.

When we have added the extra tiles, we can test the game again and, this time, instead of running off a cliff when we hold the right arrow key down, the monkey will run off the side of the scene and disappear but, if we hold the left arrow key long enough, he will run back into the scene so we can see him again.

That just leaves us to solve the problem of the disappearing monkey—we'd like to see him, wherever he is, on our wide scene!

Making the screen scroll

Rather than losing our monkey off the side of the screen, we're going to ensure that the screen scrolls automatically as he runs.

Once again, behaviors come to our rescue—in just a few clicks, we will have a scrolling scene for our monkey to enjoy.

Scrolling through a scene in Stencyl is easily managed by using the **Camera Follow** behavior, and we attach the behavior to the actor that we want to follow—in our game, that's the monkey.

Time for action – attaching the Camera Follow behavior

The game file to import and load for this session is `5961_02_11.stencyl`.

1. Go to the **Dashboard** tab and click on the **Actor Types** heading.

2. Double click on the **Stencyl Book Monkey**.

3. Click on the **Behaviors** button in the row of buttons at the upper-center of the screen.

4. Click on the **+ Add Behavior** button at the lower-left corner of the screen.

5. In the **Choose a Behavior** dialog box, click on the **Game** option in the left-hand side panel, under the heading **FROM YOUR LIBRARY**.

6. Locate the **Camera Follow** behavior and double-click on it.

7. Do *not* change the scroll speed attribute in the behavior configuration screen!

8. Test the game and try to make the monkey run off the right edge of the screen—run around and see how far the monkey can go!

What just happened?

Attaching the **Camera Follow** behavior to an actor forces the scene to scroll whenever the actor tries to pass the center of the current screen view. Once our actor reaches either the leftmost or rightmost edge of the scene, it will stop scrolling, which allows our actor to move to the edge of the scene.

It would be a good exercise to test our game again, just to be sure that we are familiar with the way in which the Camera Follow behavior allows the actor to move around the wide jungle scene.

Adding some interesting scenery

Although we now have the basic game mechanics in place, we don't yet have a very interesting design for our platform game—our monkey can only run to left and right, but there are no obstacles!

Our next task is to add some detail to the scene, starting with additional tiles to make the scene more fun for our players:

Have a go hero – adding some interesting tiles to the scene

The game file to import and load for this session is `5961_02_12.stencyl`.

We already know how to add tiles to a scene but, before starting, we just need to make sure that:

- ◆ We are viewing the **Jungle** scene in the Scene Designer
- ◆ We have clicked on the **Tiles** button in the palette, in the panel on the right-hand side of the screen, so we can see the tileset

Go ahead and add some tiles from the tileset—it really doesn't matter too much, what the scene looks like, as long as the monkey can run around and jump without too many obstructions. There's an example of the left-hand side part of the scene in the following screenshot:

Don't forget to scroll along scene in the Scene Designer, and add platforms and obstructions along the whole length of the scene. Remember that, to view the whole width of the scene, we can use the zoom tools on the left-hand side of the Scene Designer.

 Do include the green pillars at the leftmost and rightmost edges of the scene, as shown in the following screenshot, which shows the whole scene, as these pillars are used in a later session.

Fine-tuning the level design

When creating a platform game we'll often find that it is too hard, too easy, or just too frustrating!

The skill of the game designer is to ensure that the players of our game will find it fun—there's no point making it ridiculously difficult, because the player will give up and move on to another game very quickly. Equally, we need to make sure that the game is not too easy to complete, otherwise the game will be finished very quickly.

While designing the layout of the game, it is important to test our progress very frequently. Make sure that it is possible for the monkey to navigate the whole length of the scene, and try to introduce some interesting challenges along the way.

The following screenshot shows an example of a level design which is not too difficult, but which has some interesting challenges. For example, if the player decides to make the monkey take the easiest route, and run along the floor of the jungle, then it will soon hit the walls of an old ruined temple, and have to run back to jump up the platforms to get over the ruins!

If this was a time-based platform game, with a countdown and bonus points for finishing the level quickly, then this is the type of challenge that can encourage a player to play the same level over and over until they can complete it in the shortest time, and gain maximum bonus points!

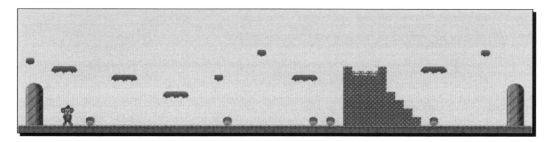

Finding game testers

The life of a game developer can be an isolated one! It's very easy to become lost in the development of a game without taking time out to look at it from someone else's point of view.

For this reason, it's a good idea to find someone else to test our game designs for us—it could be a friend, colleague, or a family member, but it is important to watch and listen to others while they test the game and, most importantly, make notes about what they say, so that we can improve the design of the game and make it more fun!

Summary

Wow! We've learned a lot in this chapter.

We created a blank game and added a jungle scene. We then downloaded a monkey actor from StencylForge and added a behavior to control it with the keyboard.

The next step was to use StencylForge again, to find an appropriate tileset to create some interesting content for our Jungle scene.

To ensure that the actor couldn't fall off the edge of the scene, we attached the **Cannot Exit Scene** behavior, and then we attached the **Camera Follow** behavior to the monkey, so it could run and jump along the whole length of the scene, while the scenery automatically scrolled to keep up with it.

In the final part of the chapter we made the platform game design more interesting and considered some challenges that might make our game more fun to play.

We've made quite amazing progress in just one chapter—we have all the basic mechanics in place for our platform game. However, there are two vital elements missing—we need some enemies to avoid, and we also need a challenge for our monkey to complete, so let's head off into *Chapter 3, Detecting Collisions*, and really make our game come to life!

The game file named `5961_02_13.stencyl` represents how our game should look at this point in the book.

3
Detecting Collisions

In this chapter, we will continue to develop the game that we started to create in Chapter 2, Let's make a game. Although we have many of the basic game mechanics in place, we do not yet have a very interesting game that will engage our players, so we're going to introduce an additional element of interactivity to make the game more challenging.

In its current form, the game allows our monkey to navigate the jungle scene without any difficulty, and that isn't going to be much fun for players of our game — we need a more interesting environment!

To make the game more challenging, we're going to add some dangerous enemies for the monkey to avoid, and we're also going to create a challenge for the player to complete — the monkey will have to collect some items as it makes its journey through the jungle.

In order to be able to collect these items, we need our monkey to detect collisions with other objects, so our game can respond accordingly. In this chapter, we're going to learn the important aspects of implementing collision detection within Stencyl.

By the end of this chapter, we will have a good understanding of the following topics:

- ◆ Working with collision detection in Stencyl
- ◆ Modifying an actor's collision shapes
- ◆ Configuring collision shapes for tiles
- ◆ Adding enemies and collectibles
- ◆ Working with collision groups
- ◆ Using collision sensors
- ◆ Implementing terrain collision shapes

The target for this chapter is to progress with our development of the game so that it looks something like the following screenshot:

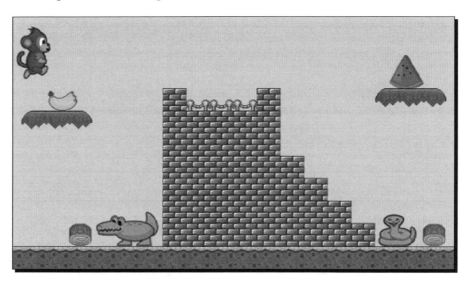

As we can see, our monkey now has fruits to collect and dangerous animals to avoid!

Working with collision detection in Stencyl

If our monkey has to collect items and avoid enemies, we will need to detect collisions between the monkey and the various actors that will represent the enemies and collectible items. In other words, our game needs to know when these objects have bumped into each other!

Stencyl, as we may now expect, makes the job of working with collisions much easier than it would be if we had to hand code our game using a traditional programming language. We can easily specify which parts of our tiles and actors will cause a collision event, and we can also easily configure behaviors to carry out certain actions for us when collision events occur.

In fact Stencyl is already automatically managing collisions within our game! Let's have a look behind the scenes, using a very useful feature that has been built into Stencyl to help us manage the collision detection:

Time for action – enabling the Debug Drawing feature

The game file to import and load for this session is `5961_03_01.stencyl`.

Stencyl makes it incredibly easy to see how collision detection is configured within our game; all we have to do is use the `Enable Debug Drawing` feature.

1. On the main menu in Stencyl, select **Run | Enable Debug Drawing**.
2. Test the game.
3. Navigate the monkey around the scene and take note of where the colored lines appear around the monkey and the tiles.
4. Close the **Adobe Flash Player** window.

What just happened?

We've enabled the option that displays the debug drawing feature in Stencyl. When we tested the game with debug drawing enabled, we could see that colored lines are drawn around the monkey actor and the tiles.

These lines, which are normally invisible to players of our game, are used by Stencyl to determine when collisions have occurred, that is, when the lines of any two objects intersect (or touch) each other. If we examine some of the colored lines more closely, we can see that they completely enclose each object; for example, the monkey and the floating leafy platforms are each enclosed by their own rectangles.

When adjoining tiles form a larger, more complex shape, Stencyl will automatically create a single, large collision object. As we can see in the following screenshot, the ground, the walls of the temple ruins, and the logs are all considered by Stencyl to be a single solid object, even though we know that we created the jungle environment using small rectangular tiles.

The combining of tiles in this manner is an optimization process automatically carried out by Stencyl; we don't need to do any extra work in order for this to happen!

 Optimization is the process of making computer code do its job more efficiently, which, in practical terms, means that our games will run more smoothly, even when there is a lot of onscreen action and background calculation.

Debug drawing is extremely useful when designing a game, because it enables us to visualize the way in which Stencyl processes collisions, and this can help us see problems that we may otherwise have overlooked; we can debug collision detection within our game!

The colored lines around the objects represent the collision shapes for those objects, but we didn't need to define the collision shapes, because they had already been configured in the actor and the tiles that we downloaded from StencylForge.

We can also see, in the previous screenshot, that most of the tiles are enclosed within collision shapes, but some are not. For example, the rope barrier on top of the temple ruins does not have a collision shape defined, which is why the monkey doesn't bump into the rope during gameplay. This feature allows us to use tiles that are purely for decorative purposes. There is no technical reason for them to be in our game; they just look nice.

Modifying an actor's collision shapes

Now that we know what collision shapes are, we can learn about modifying these shapes to meet our exact requirements.

Although the initial testing of our game demonstrated that the monkey can successfully traverse the jungle environment by running on the ground and jumping on the various obstacles that we created with tiles, there are some improvements to be made!

Note how the collision box around the leafy platform is larger than it needs to be; it projects far lower from the bottom of the platform than is necessary. This is likely to be annoying for players of our game, if the monkey jumps up when it is beneath the platform, it will bump the top of its head before it actually hits the platform. Even worse, the collision box around the monkey is also too large, which may lead to even greater frustration for our players.

To examine this problem more closely, test the game again, and make the monkey jump up when it is standing immediately beneath a platform. Although it's not a major issue while we're designing the game, players of our game will quickly give up if the same problem occurs when the monkey is standing close to an enemy actor – a collision will occur before a player can see the actors touching, and they will consider it to be unfair. This is a guaranteed way to annoy players, and they'll quickly start looking for a more fun game elsewhere!

We can see how this problem occurs in the following screenshot; a collision is detected whenever the collision shapes of the monkey and the platform intersect, but there is still quite a big gap between the image of the monkey and the platform.

The good news is that Stencyl equips us with the tools to make the required adjustments. We can use the **Animation Editor** to alter an actor's existing collision shapes and to add new ones. We can even add multiple collision shapes to an actor, so that we can form more complex shapes that closely represent the shape of our actor.

 When discussing collision detection, we can also refer to an actor's **collision bounds**; this simply denotes a single collision shape or multiple collision shapes that are used to specify the collision-detection areas for an actor.

Let's have a look at how we can improve the collision detection for the monkey.

Time for Action – modifying the monkey's collision shapes

The game file to import and load for this session is `5961_03_01.stencyl`.

We're going to fine-tune the collision shapes for the monkey, so ensure that the monkey actor is visible in the Animation Editor:

1. Go to the **Dashboard** tab, click on **Actor Types**, then double-click on the monkey actor's thumbnail.

    Now that we can see the monkey animations, we can go ahead and modify the collision bounds.

2. Click on the **Collision** button in the row of buttons at the upper-center of the screen.

3. Look at the center of the screen, where the collision shape for one of the monkey animations is displayed.

4. Click on the **Idle Left** thumbnail in the **Animations** (left) panel to display the collision bounds for the **Idle Left** animation.

5. Click somewhere just inside the border of the orange rectangular collision shape, so that the box is selected and press the *Delete* key on the keyboard to remove the collision shape.

6. Locate the collision shapes tools at the top of the screen.

7. Click on **Add Circle** to display the **Add Circle** dialog box.

8. Click on **OK**.

9. Click inside the orange border of the new collision circle to ensure that it is selected.

10. Use the arrow keys on the keyboard to position the circle over the monkey's head. It should have an **X position (Left)** of 18 units and a **Y position (Top)** of 10 units as displayed in the **Current Shape** panel at the upper-right of the screen.

The position of the collision circle and the configuration of the **Current Shape** panel are shown in the following screenshot.

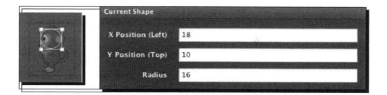

What just happened?

Firstly, we displayed the collision configuration screen for the monkey's **Idle Left** animation, and then we deleted the existing rectangular collision shape.

The next step was to add a new collision shape. In this case, we chose a circle because it more accurately represents the shape of the collision that we want to detect. We then moved the collision circle so that it was positioned over the monkey's head.

It's not desperately important for the collision circle to exactly cover the monkey's head. In fact, it's often better if the collision shapes for actors are very slightly smaller than the image of the actor, because it will appear to be fairer to the player, than if the collision shape is too large.

It's the game designer's decision to make sure that the collision bounds for each actor are appropriate for the game, and often an appropriate configuration can only be determined by playtesting the game. This is why it's important to find impartial testers to play our games and provide feedback, as discussed in the *Chapter 2* section entitled, *Finding game testers*.

At this point, we can clearly see that we have a problem; the collision circle that we have added will not detect when the monkey's body and feet collide with other objects! We can resolve this problem by adding more collision shapes; we aren't restricted to only one shape for each animation.

Adding multiple collision shapes

We're going to add two more collision shapes to ensure that the collision detection for the **Idle Left** animation is accurate, and our goal is for the collision shapes, for the **Idle Left** animation, to look like the following screenshot:

Time for action – adding more collision shapes to the monkey

The game file to import and load for this session is `5961_03_02.stencyl`.

We will use the following information to position the additional collision shapes correctly in step 3:

	X Position (Left)	Y Position (Top)	Radius
Circle 1 (head)	18	10	16
Circle 2 (body)	21	35	16
Circle 3 (feet)	24	65	8

1. Ensure that the monkey's **Idle Left** animation is visible in the center panel of Collision Editor.

2. Click on the **Add Circle** tool at the top of the center panel.

3. Referring to the previous diagram, enter the **X Position (Left)**, **Y Position (Top)**, and **Radius** information for the body's collision circle (Circle 2) into the **Add Circle** dialog box, and click on **OK** to confirm.

4. Repeat steps 2 and 3 to create a collision circle for the monkey's feet.

5. Save the game.

What just happened?

We've added two more collision shapes to the monkey actor to ensure that it can more appropriately interact with tiles and other actors in our game.

We can see that the collision bounds for the **Idle Left** animation now consists of three circles. Circular collision shapes were chosen for the monkey actor because they enable it to more easily slide off the edge of platforms and other obstacles. However, it's a good idea, when developing a game, to experiment with different collision shapes in order to achieve the best results for collision detection.

We can test the game now, if desired, but be aware that we have only made changes to the **Idle Left** animation. We still have to modify the collisions for the remaining animations for the monkey actor.

Planning the collision shapes

Before spending too much time refining the collision shapes for each of an actor's animations, it's a good idea to plan in advance and carefully consider the requirements for each animation. Also, consider the following tips, which could save some time!

- Don't spend too long agonizing over each collision shape; to start with, only reasonable accuracy is required. We can always revisit the collision bounds at a later stage in development if the existing configuration doesn't work as required.

- Consider the requirements for each animation. For example, in our game, the monkey's *dead* animation does not require any collision detection. So, no collision shapes are required!

- Once a collision shape has been created, the arrow keys on the keyboard can be used to adjust the position of the shape; this can be much faster than retyping the coordinates in the Animation Editor's **Current Shape** panel.

- When several animations are similar, configure one of them, and then jot down the collision shape settings, so they can be copied for the other similar animations. It will then just take a few moments to enter these settings and adjust them slightly, if required.

- We don't have to use circles for the collision shapes; rectangular collision shapes, and even polygonal shapes should be used if appropriate for the shape of the actor!

- Take into account what a player might consider to be fair or unfair when playing the game. Don't make collision shapes too large or too small.

- Remember to save the game regularly!

Have a go hero

The game file to import and load for this session is `5961_03_03.stencyl`.

We've configured the collision bounds for the monkey's **Idle Left** animation, but all the other monkey animations (**Idle Right**, **Jump Left**, and so on) need their collision bounds updated.

Update the collision bounds for each of the monkey's animations, taking note of the planning tips provided previously.

Testing the updated collision bounds

When all the monkey animations' collision bounds have been created and adjusted, we can save and test the game again. Be sure to thoroughly test to ensure that the collision shapes for the monkey are suitable for the environment; for example, if the monkey jumps into a small gap, can it jump out again, or will it become trapped?

We may need to move some objects, such as the log tiles, within the scene to ensure that the monkey can move around the scene freely. These are the types of problems that need to be resolved before a game can be released to the public, so don't be afraid to make changes to the collision bounds or to adjust the layout of the scene to account for any gameplay difficulties that are discovered during the testing process.

There should now be a great improvement in the collision-detection accuracy when the monkey collides with other objects and with most of the tiles, but we still need to do some work on the collision shapes of the leafy platforms.

Configuring collision shapes for tiles

When we need to fine-tune the collision bounds for tiles; the process is slightly different than it is for actors, so let's learn how we can improve the collision detection for the leafy platform.

Time for action – modifying the collision bounds of a tile

The game file to import and load for this session is `5961_03_04.stencyl`.

As we've seen, the collision box is too large for the leafy platforms; it only needs to surround the top two-thirds of the tile, so let's create a new tile collision shape that meets that requirement.

We're going to be modifying tile collisions, so we need to display the Tileset Editor:

1. Go to the **Dashboard** tab, click on **Tilesets**, then double-click on the thumbnail for our tileset in the main panel.

2. Click on any tile in the tileset in the left-hand panel; the collision-shapes panel will be displayed at the top of the right-hand panel.

3. In the upper-right panel, click on the gray **+** button and then select **Create Box...** in the pop-up menu.

4. In the **Create a Box...** dialog box, enter the **Name, X Position, Y Position**, and the **Width** and **Height** information as shown in the following screenshot:

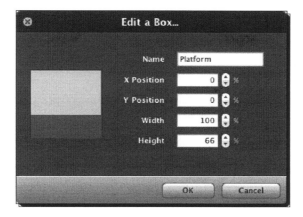

5. Click on **OK**.

6. In the left panel, click-and-drag the mouse on the first leafy platform tile (position A9 in the grid) across to the fourth leafy platform tile (position D9), and then release the mouse. The four tiles are selected as shown in the following screenshot:

7. In the right-hand panel, click on the newly created **Platform** collision shape. It may be necessary to scroll down to the bottom of the right-hand panel in order to see the new collision shape.

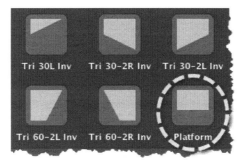

8. Select the **Jungle scene** tab (or open it, if it is not already open) and save the game.

What just happened?

Using the Tileset Editor, we created a new tile collision shape called `Platform`. We then selected the four tiles that we wanted to modify, and clicked on the icon for the new collision shape, so that it was applied to all the platform tiles that we selected.

Because we changed the collision shape for existing tiles in a scene, we had to open the scene and save it to ensure that the changes to the collision shapes were applied to the relevant tiles in the scene.

 Note that the new collision shape we created in the Tileset Editor is also available to the *whole* tileset, so any other tiles can use it without us having to define it again.

We could have specified the collision shape for each tile one at a time, but selecting the four tiles was much quicker, and if an appropriate collision shape had already existed in the upper-right panel, we could have just clicked on the existing collision shape to apply it to the selected tiles.

Have a go hero

The game file to import and load for this session is `5961_03_05.stencyl`.

Now that we've updated the collision shapes for both the monkey actor and the platform tiles, the collision detection in our game should be much improved.

Test the game, ensuring that the **Enable Debug Drawing** option is selected in the **Run** menu, and have a look at the accuracy of the collision between the monkey and the platforms that we have just modified.

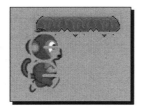

We can see that the collision is now very accurate; there isn't a large gap between the monkey's head and the platform. In fact, there is no gap at all. The monkey's hair slightly overlaps the overhanging leaves on the platform, and this interaction between the actor and the platform will be much more acceptable to players of our game.

Perhaps a little more fine-tuning of the collision bounds might be required before the game is completed, but that is the time to ensure that some serious playtesting is carried out, and feedback from our testers should be reviewed, with adjustments to the game being made as required.

Adding enemies and collectibles

Now that we have refined the collision detection for the monkey and the tiles, it's time to add some enemies for our monkey to avoid, and we also need to find some interesting items for the monkey to collect. Adding these objects into our game will introduce the first level of challenge for our players.

We've already learned how to import actors from StencylForge, and that's where we'll find the new actors we're going to place into the jungle scene.

Downloading the enemies and collectibles

The game file to import and load for this session is `5961_03_05.stencyl`.

We already know how to search for and download actors from StencylForge, so let's download the actors with the following names:

- ◆   `Stencyl Book Croc`
- ◆   `Stencyl Book Snake`
- ◆   `Stencyl Book Melon`
- ◆   `Stencyl Book Bananas`
- ◆   `Stencyl Book Pineapple`
- ◆   `Stencyl Book Grapes`

If we now go to the **Dashboard** tab and click on **Actor Types**, we should see the following display in the main panel:

Now that we have added all the actors, we need to save the game!

Placing the new actors into the jungle scene

The game file to import and load for this session is `5961_03_06.stencyl`.

Now that we've downloaded the actors from StencylForge, it's time to place them into the jungle scene. As a designer, it's our job to place the enemies and collectibles into locations that will provide a challenge for players of our game, but as with the design of the collision bounds for the actors, we must not make the game too frustrating nor should we make it too easy.

We have already added actors to the scene by clicking on the **Add to Scene** button when viewing the actor in the Animation Editor. However, there is a more efficient way to add multiple actors into a scene without having to display each actor's animations first.

If we display the scene, we can see two buttons at the top of the right-hand panel: one is for displaying the available tiles and the other is for displaying the available actors. If the available actors are not already on display, click on the **Actors** button. We can now add actors to the scene in exactly the same way that we added tiles: click on an actor, then add it to the scene by clicking on the required location. It's great to know that all the skills we learned when adding tiles work equally as well for actors!

Here's another useful tip before we start adding more actors to the scene; holding the *Shift* key on the keyboard while positioning actors on a scene snaps the actor into place on an invisible grid. This can be very useful for placing actors at regular evenly spaced positions within a scene. Also have a look at the tools available within the Scene Designer, at the upper-right of the main panel. Hovering the mouse pointer over each tool will provide a tip. We're most interested in the three grid tools at this point!

- ◆ Add each of the new actors (fruits and enemies) to the jungle scene.
- ◆ Save the game.

> If we test the game right now, we'll see that there is a problem with the collision testing, and we may also experience some strange effects, such as some of the fruit or enemies moving unexpectedly.
>
> Don't worry, it's just the Stencyl's physics engine behaving as it should; we're going to fix these problems!

We can now test the game. Although all the enemy actors and the collectible fruits are clearly visible, when the monkey collides with them, nothing happens; he runs straight past them without even the slightest bump!

This might lead us to believe that there is a problem with the collision bounds of the newly added actors. However, if we have a look at the collision bounds for these actors, we can see that they are all in place. The collision shapes of two of the new actors are shown as follows.

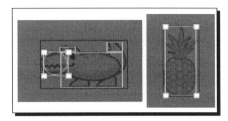

Clearly, something is wrong with the collision detection! We have one final task to complete to ensure that Stencyl can detect collisions correctly.

Working with collision groups

Behind the scenes, collision detection is quite a complex process, but Stencyl gives us great control over which collisions will be detected between different actors and tiles. This control is achieved by allowing us to place actors into groups, and then providing us with the ability to specify which groups will collide with each other.

For example, we may want our monkey actor to collide with enemy actors and also with the collectible fruit actors, but we might not want the enemy actors to collide with the fruit actors.

Let's have a look at how the collision groups are currently configured.

Time for action – examining the collision group settings

The game file to import and load for this session is `5961_03_07.stencyl`.

We need to open up the **Collision Groups** window in the Stencyl **Settings** dialog box:

1. Click the **Settings** icon on the main Stencyl toolbar.

2. Look down the list of icons that are shown in the left panel of the **Game Settings** dialog box and click on **Groups**.

3. In the **Collision Groups** window that is now being displayed, click on **Tiles** under the **GROUPS** heading at the top of the right-hand panel.

What just happened?

We have displayed the current collision settings for the **Tiles** group as shown in the following screenshot:

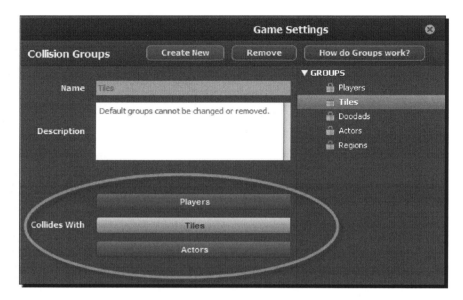

The **Collides With** section in the previous screenshot, which has been highlighted with an oval shape, shows which other collision groups have been configured to collide with the **Tiles** collision group. Currently, both the **Players** and the **Actors** collision groups are configured to collide with the **Tiles** group (remember, the **Tiles** group is the one we selected in the right-hand panel). Note that the **Players** button and the **Actors** button are shaded darker than the **Tiles** button, which shows us that they are currently selected.

This means that any actor that is placed in the **Players** group or the **Actors** group will react to a collision with a tile. Note that, if we configure a group such as **Tiles** to collide with **Players**, then the **Players** group will automatically be updated to reflect this change!

Viewing the actors' collision groups

We now know that tiles are configured to react to collisions with any actor which is in either the **Players** or **Actors** group, so let's see which groups **Players** and **Actors** are configured to detect collisions with.

Time for action – examining the Players and Actors groups

The game file to import and load for this session is `5961_03_07.stencyl`.

1. Click on **Players** in the right-hand panel (under the **GROUPS** heading).

2. Examine the buttons at the bottom of the main panel in the **Collides With** section; make a note of which group or groups are selected.

3. Click on **Actors** in the right-hand panel (under the **GROUPS** heading).

4. Examine the buttons at the bottom of the main panel in the **Collides With** section; make a note of which groups are selected.

5. Click on the **OK** button to hide the **Game Setting** dialog box.

What just happened?

We examined the collision settings for the **Players** group and the **Actors** group, and we should have noted that any actor in the **Players** group can detect collisions with tiles only. We should also have noted that actors in the **Actors** group can detect collisions with both **Tiles** and other actors in the **Actors** group.

It's useful to know that actors do not have to detect collisions with other actors in the same group.

The ability to configure collisions between actors in different groups gives us an amazing amount of flexibility in our game, when we need to manage collisions between actors and tiles.

Let's put this new found knowledge into practice!

 The collision groups entitled **Doodads** and **Regions** have special features that we will not be using. However, it's useful to note that actors in the **Doodads** group will never cause collision events to occur, and that **Regions** is a special type of group that enables us to specify arbitrary areas of a scene that can cause collision events.

Creating a new collision group

We know from our previous game test, that the monkey completely ignored the enemy actors that it ran past. If we need to remind ourselves what happened, we can test the game again; the monkey is able to run straight through the enemy actors without a collision occurring!

Time for action – creating a collision group for enemy actors

The game file to import and load for this session is `5961_03_07.stencyl`.

We're now going to configure the collision detection, so that the monkey will collide with the enemy Croc.

1. Display the **Stencyl Book Croc** actor in the Animation Editor (click on the **Dashboard** tab, then **Actor Types** and double-click on the **Stencyl Book Croc** thumbnail).

2. Click on the **Properties** button in the row of buttons at the upper-center of the screen.

3. Click the **Edit Groups** button in the **Choose Group** section to display the **Collisions Groups** window in the **Game Settings** dialog box.

4. Click on the **Create New** button at the top of the dialog box.

5. In the **Create a New Group...** dialog box that appears, type `Enemies` into the **Name** textbox and click on the **Create** button.

6. Look at the bottom of the list in the right panel, and we can now see that the new group has been added to the list.

7. In the main panel, click on the **Players** button and the **Tiles** button.

8. Click on **OK** to return to the Stencyl Book Croc **Properties** window.

9. In the **Choose Group** section, click on the **Group** drop-down list and select **Enemies**.

10. Test the game; make the monkey collide with the Croc!

What just happened?

We have created a new collision group called `Enemies`, which will contain actors that collide with the players and tiles, and we have added the Croc actor to this new collision group.

Creating a new collision group requires us to view the **Collision Group** window in the **Game Settings** dialog box, and then either select the group that we want to work with, or create a new group. We can then click on the buttons for the other group names to specify which other collision groups our currently selected group will collide with.

Have a go hero

The game file to import and load for this session is `5961_03_08.stencyl`.

We have already created an **Enemies** collision group and added the Croc actor to this group, so we know how to add the Snake actor to the **Enemies** group by changing its collision group in the actor's **Properties** window.

◆ Add the Snake actor to the **Enemies** group.

◆ Don't forget to test the game to ensure that the monkey collides with the snake!

Configuring collisions for the fruit actors

The game file to import and load for this session is `5961_03_09.stencyl`.

The enemy actors are now configured so that they are part of the **Enemy** collision group, but we haven't set up a collision group for the collectible fruit.

We have already learned the skills required for creating collision groups and for adding actors into a collision group, so our next task is to put those skills into practice and configure the collision group for the fruit.

In order to ensure that our game can detect collisions between the monkey and the fruit, we must complete the following steps:

1. Create a `Collectibles` collision group.

2. Configure the **Collectibles** group so that it detects collisions with **Tiles** and **Players**.

3. Add each fruit actor to the **Collectibles** collision group.

Remember, to create a new group, we can either click on the **Settings** icon on the toolbar, and then click on the **Groups** option in the left panel, or we can display one of the fruit actors in the Animation Editor, and click on the **Properties** button for that actor, which will enable us to see the **Edit Groups...** button.

The buttons determining the collisions for the **Collectibles** group should be configured as shown in the following screenshot:

When the **Collectibles** collision group has been created, remember to view the **Properties** window for each of the pieces of fruit, and change the collision group to **Collectibles**.

It's vital to test the game at this stage to check that all the collisions are working as expected. Make sure that the monkey collides with all four types of fruit to ensure that the collision group is configured correctly.

 If, when the game is tested, we find that the collisions with the fruit actors aren't working as expected, review the *Time for action – creating a collision group for enemy actors section*, which contains the steps for creating a new group, specifying which groups collide, and adding an actor to the newly created group.

Using collision sensors

In most platform games, when the player's character passes a collectible item, it doesn't normally bump into it and stop. The player will run straight through the item, collecting points as it passes, and the collectible item will disappear so that it can't be collected more than once.

We know from the previous game test that when our monkey collides with a piece of collectible fruit, it crashes into it and stops, or lands on top of the fruit if the monkey is jumping. We need the collision to be detected so that our game can reward the player with a bonus, but we don't want to stop the flow of the game by having to stop and start the monkey each time a piece of fruit is collected.

When we want a collision to be detected, but not cause a physical reaction in the game, we need to specify that the colliding actor is a **sensor**.

Time for action – configuring the fruit as a sensor

The game file to import and load for this session is `5961_03_10.stencyl`.

We'll start by setting up the banana actor as a sensor:

1. Display the banana actor in the Animation Editor (click on the **Dashboard** tab, then **Actor Types**, and double-click on the **Stencyl Book Banana** thumbnail).

2. Ensure that the **Collision** button is selected in the row of buttons at the upper-center of the screen.

3. Click on the left collision circle on the banana so that it is selected.

4. In the right panel, under the heading **Physical Properties**, click on the **Is a Sensor?** option so that a checkmark is shown as follows:

5. Click on the right collision circle on the banana so that it is selected.

6. Click on the **Is a Sensor?** option so that a checkmark is shown.

7. Click on the **Physics** button in the row of buttons at the upper-center of the screen.

8. Change the **Affected by Gravity?** setting to **No**.

9. Test the game; make the monkey collide with the banana (it will run through it)!

What just happened?

We have changed the banana actor into a sensor; our game will still detect collisions between the banana and the monkey and cause a collision event, but the collision will not cause a physical reaction in the game. It's important to note that, because the banana has two collision shapes (two circles), we had to configure both of those shapes as sensors.

Because the banana is now a sensor, we also needed to change a physics setting so that it will no longer be affected by the scene's gravity. If we do not tell sensors to ignore gravity, they will fall straight through the tiles!

Don't these changes put us right back where we started? Before we created the **Collectible** collision group, the monkey ran straight through the banana actor, and that's what's happening now!

Although it looks like we have taken a step backwards, behind the scenes Stencyl is still detecting the collision, but instead of making the monkey bump into the banana actor, it is just sensing when the collision occurs and creating a collision event. This means that we can use or create behaviors that depend upon a collision being sensed between the monkey and the banana actors, and that's exactly what we need in our game!

Have a go hero

The game file to import and load for this session is `5961_03_11.stencyl`.

We have only configured the banana to be a sensor, but we also have grapes, a melon, and a pineapple, which should also be configured in the same way, so go ahead and configure each of the fruit actors as sensors. Remember to change each actor's **Affected by Gravity?** setting to **No** so the actors don't fall through the tiles.

When this task has been completed, our monkey should be able to run through each piece of fruit without bumping into it!

Implementing terrain collision shapes

We've already learned about setting up collisions for tilesets and actors, but there is a third type of collision that we can use in the design of our games.

Terrain collision areas enable us to set up arbitrary areas within our scene that actors can collide with. This feature can be helpful if there are large areas of tiles that do not have collisions defined, but it is also very useful when a scene has not been designed using tiles; for example, a background may consist of a single artistic image onto which collision areas can be placed using the terrain feature.

Let's implement a practical example, so we can see how it works.

Currently, our monkey can run all the way to the edges of the scene, and when it gets there, it just bumps against nothing but the imaginary edge of the scene. Rather than modify the tiles' collision shapes in the Tileset Editor, we're going to draw custom terrain shapes over the green pillars that we placed at the extreme ends of the scene, to prevent the monkey from running through them.

Time for action – adding a terrain collision area to the scene

The game file to import and load for this session is `5961_03_12.stencyl`.

We're going to be working in the Scene Designer.

1. Go to the **Dashboard** tab, click on **Scenes**, and double-click on the thumbnail for the jungle scene.

2. Ensure that we can see the leftmost part of the scene (scroll all the way to the left).

3. Click on the **Add Terrain** tool in the vertical toolbar which can be found at the left edge of the Scene Designer (highlighted by the dotted oval in the following screenshot):

4. Referring to the following screenshot, click-and-drag a rectangle over the green pillar at the left of the scene, as shown:

5. Right-click on the same **Add Terrain** tool on the **Scene Designer** toolbar and select **Add Terrain (Circle)** from the pop-up menu.

6. Click-and-drag a circle over the curved section of the green pillar, as shown:

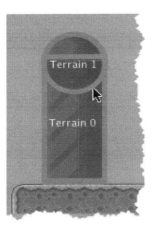

7. If necessary, it is easy to adjust the position of the new terrain shape by clicking on the shape and using the arrow keys. If the shapes need redrawing, they can be deleted by clicking on them and pressing the *Delete* key on the keyboard.

8. On the **Working Mode** section of the horizontal toolbar at the top of the Scene Designer, click on the **Work with Tiles and Actors** (globe) icon.

9. Test the game and try to make the monkey run past the pillar at the left of the scene.

What just happened?

We have created two custom terrain collision shapes within our scene: one rectangle and one circle. The shapes were positioned to overlay scenery that did not have its own collision bounds, but we could have placed our custom terrain shapes absolutely anywhere within the scene, if required.

When testing the game, we can see that the monkey can no longer run past the green pillar at the left side of the scene; it just bumps into the pillar as though it were another actor or a collection of tiles with the appropriate collision bounds.

Have a go hero

The game file to import and load for this session is `5961_03_13.stencyl`.

There is a second pillar at the rightmost edge of the scene, and this should also have custom terrain objects drawn over it so that the monkey cannot run past the pillar, to the edge of the screen.

◆ Use the skills that we have just learned to draw custom terrain shapes over the pillar at the rightmost edge of the scene.

Remember to test the game regularly during the design process to ensure that the monkey can traverse the scene as planned.

What else can we improve?

When testing the latest changes, if we had controlled the monkey so that it jumped onto the various platforms and then onto the pillar, we would have found that we could make the monkey land on top of the pillar! Is that something that we want the monkey to do? If not, we'll need to make the pillars taller by moving and adding tiles in the Scene Designer. If we modify the tiles that are used to construct the pillar, then we'll also need to redraw the custom terrain shapes to cover the modified pillars.

Again, it's up to us as game designers to determine a scene layout that works, is fun and challenging (but not too challenging) for players to explore, and which does not exhibit any strange behavior, such as being able to make actors jump onto edge-of-scene markers (for example, our pillars).

Summary

The development of our game and our game development skills are progressing at a great pace!

In this chapter, we have learned about three different types of **collision bounds** that can be implemented within Stencyl games:

◆ Actor collision shapes

◆ Tile collision shapes

◆ Custom terrain shapes

We've also seen how we can create very accurate collision shapes in our game, and we have learned about setting up **collision groups**, so that collisions are only detected when necessary, thereby improving the performance of our game.

Another useful feature that we have examined is the ability to configure an actor's collision shapes as sensors, so that although a physical collision does not take place, our game-code will still be able to react when a collision with a sensor occurs.

Although collisions are now being detected in our game, we still have some work to do! We need to make the game more interesting by providing some feedback to the player when these collisions occur. What should happen when the monkey bumps into an enemy actor? What should happen when the monkey bumps into the collectible fruit actors?

We'll find out the answers to these questions in *Chapter 4, Creating Behaviors*.

4
Creating Behaviors

In Chapter 3, Detecting Collisions, we configured collision shapes for the actors and tiles so that collisions are detected when required, and our game now allows the player to traverse the scene with some basic, predictable interactivity. However, although the monkey is now colliding with other actors, there are currently no responses to these collisions, other than a bump when some of the actors collide.

We need to take control of the game, so in this chapter, we're going to learn how to create instructions that will carry out specific actions when collisions and other events occur within our game.

In this chapter we will be:

◆   Creating custom behaviors

◆   Understanding the instruction block palette

◆   Creating a timed event

◆   Examining screen size and scene size

◆   Introducing randomness into our game

◆   Implementing our first special effect

◆   Understanding active actors

◆   Creating a countdown timer

◆   Implementing decision making in our game

◆   Repositioning an actor during gameplay

◆   Triggering custom events in our behaviors

Creating custom behaviors

When an event such as a collision occurs during gameplay, we would like to be able to decide exactly what happens, rather than being limited to using the built-in behaviors that have been provided for us. We're going to create our own custom behaviors that;

- Respond to collisions and other events
- Use a random number to make gameplay less predictable
- Utilize a timer to carry out actions at regular or delayed intervals
- Implement custom events that can be triggered by other behaviors

Creating our first custom behavior

As we discovered in the *Using behaviors to interact with our game* section in *Chapter 2, Let's Make a Game!*, behaviors are the instructions and rules that our game will use. We've already used some behaviors that have been built for us and are provided with Stencyl:

- Camera Follow
- Cannot Exit Scene
- Jump and Run Movement

We found the previously mentioned behaviors in the built-in behavior library, and we attached them to the monkey actor so that it would follow the specified instructions. Up until now, we haven't concerned ourselves with how these behaviors work. We've just accepted that they do the required job, but now it's time to learn about what is going on in the background, and to create a custom behavior of our own.

Currently, when our monkey runs past a piece of fruit, nothing happens, not even a bump, because in *Chapter 2, Let's Make a Game!*, we configured all the fruit actors to be **sensors**.

However, we would like something to happen. In this case, we want the fruit to disappear so it can't be collected twice.

Time for action – creating a behavior

The game file that needs to be imported and loaded for this session is
`5961_04_01.stencyl`.

We are going to use Stencyl's **kill...** instruction block to remove the collected fruit from the game, remembering that each fruit actor is a member of the `Collectibles` group. Execute the following steps in order to create a behavior:

1. On the **Dashboard**, under the **LOGIC** heading, click on **Actor Behaviors**.

2. Click on the green **Create New** button situated at the top of the right-hand panel.

3. In the **Create New...** dialog box, enter the words `Collect Fruit` into the **Name** textbox and click on the **Create** button.

4. The behavior editor will be displayed.

5. Click on the **+ Add Event** button at the top of the left-hand panel.

6. In the pop-up menu that appears, move the mouse over **Collisions**.

7. In the next pop-up menu, in the **Any actor collides with...** section, click on **Member of Group**.

8. Double-click on the **Actor – Group** event label towards the top of the left-hand panel (immediately under the **+ Add Event** button).

9. Change the text to **Collides with Collectibles** and press *Enter* on the keyboard.

10. In the orange **when Actor hits a ...** block, displayed in the center panel, click on the **Actor Group** selector and click on **Choose Group** in the pop-up menu, as shown in the following screenshot:

11. In the **Choose an Actor Group** dialog box, select **Collectibles** and click on **OK**.

12. Save the game. It's not ready for testing yet!

What just happened?

We have created a new actor behavior called `Collect Fruit`, which has a single empty event called **Collides with Collectibles**, but we haven't provided any instructions yet.

The event was initially called **Actor – Group** and although that is quite descriptive (we're responding to a collision between an actor and a group), we might have several **Actor – Group** collision events, for example, we will also need to check for collisions with actors in the **Enemies** group. To make it easier to identify what each event does, it's a good practice to give each event a descriptive name and, in this case, **Collides with Collectibles** is an appropriate name, because it describes the event that we're listening for.

Note that this name is not used by Stencyl for referencing the event. It is simply a human-readable label, with the purpose of helping the developer to easily identify the events that we have created.

Stencyl behaviors can listen out for many different types of events, but we have chosen to listen for a very specific event, which is triggered when the actor collides with any actor in the specified group. When we clicked on the **Actor Group** option in the orange block, and specified the Collectibles group, we were telling the behavior to listen out for a collision event between this actor and any actor that is a member of the Collectibles group.

The orange **when** block in our new Collect Fruit behavior will listen out for a collision between **Self** and the Collectibles group, but which actor is the **Self** instruction referring to? The answer to this question demonstrates the beauty of Stencyl behaviors, because **Self** is whichever actor we attach the behavior to and we can attach it to any type of actor that we want. In other words, behaviors are reusable, they are not limited to being attached to a single type of actor. They can be attached to as many different actor types as we wish.

 The reusability of behaviors within Stencyl can be compared to **Object Oriented Programming (OOP)** methodologies in traditional programming languages.

Currently, the behavior is not attached to an actor and we have not specified what action we want to take place when the collision event occurs, so let's do that now.

Time for action – adding an action and attaching to it an actor

The game file that needs to be imported and loaded for this session is 5961_04_02.stencyl.

Ensure that the Behavior editor is currently displaying the orange **when** block for the **Collides with Collectibles** event in the Collect Fruit behavior, as shown in the following screenshot:

When following the given steps, carefully refer to the screenshots, as they will assist you in correctly placing the blocks.

1. Click on the **Actor** button above the instruction block palette at the top of the right-hand panel, to ensure that it is selected, as shown in the following screenshot:

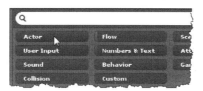

2. Click on the **Properties** category button in the row of buttons that is displayed immediately below the top buttons in the instruction block palette, as shown in the following screenshot:

3. Locate the blue **kill Self** block in the **Alive / Dead** subcategory of the right-hand panel.

4. Click and drag the blue **kill Self** block, and drop it into the blank area of the orange **when Self hits a...** block in the center panel as shown in the following screenshot. When the white snap-line appears, let go of the mouse button. This will allow the block to snap into place:

5. Locate the blue **of group** block at the top-right of the orange **Self hits a ... of Collectibles** block, and drag it onto the word **Self**, which is inside the blue **kill Self** block that we just added, as shown in the following screenshot:

6. Click on the green **Attach to Actor Type** button at the top-right of the block palette as per the following screenshot:

7. In the **Choose an Actor Type** dialog box, double-click on the **Stencyl Book Monkey** icon, the behavior list for the monkey will be displayed.

8. Click on the `Collect Fruit` tab to return to the completed event, which should now look like the following screenshot:

9. Test the game. Make the monkey collide with a piece of fruit.

What just happened?

When the monkey collides with a piece of fruit, the fruit disappears!

We had already created the `Fruit Collected` behavior, and had specified that it must listen out for a collision event between `Self` (the monkey) and any member of the `Collectibles` group. However, we had not specified which action should take place when the collision occurred, so we added the `kill Self` instruction block to the `when Self hits a... of Collectibles` event, and configured it to remove the actor that we just collided with. The blue `of group` block is a label that provides a reference to the other actor involved in the collision, that is the actor we want to kill.

Finally, we attached the behavior to the monkey actor. Now, in our game, when the behavior runs, any references to `Self` in the behavior blocks will be considered to mean this monkey actor, and any references to `of group` will refer to the member of the `Collectibles` group that the monkey collided with.

 A very common mistake is to forget the final step, attaching the behavior to the appropriate actor! If a behavior appears not to run at all, this is the first mistake to check for.

Sometimes when developing or reviewing the design of a behavior, it can be helpful to express it in English, rather than in technical terms. If we were to write our new event in English, it could be stated as follows:

When this actor hits a member of Collectibles, kill the Collectibles actor that we just collided with.

In the previous sentence, the phrase before the comma is the event that is being listened to in the orange `when self hits a ... of Collectibles:` block. The phrase after the comma is the action that is to be carried out when the event is triggered, that is the instruction in the blue `kill Self` block.

Almost all behaviors in Stencyl are designed with this basic principle—what am I listening for, and what should I do when it happens? Behaviors can be far more complicated than this, but this is the essence of most behaviors.

The actor's behavior screen

When we attached the `Collect Fruit` behavior to the monkey actor, the actor's behavior screen was displayed. However, we switched back to the `Collides with Collectibles` event, so that we could compare it with the screenshot. Let's return to the monkey's behavior screen by opening the monkey actor from the **Dashboard** option, and by clicking on the **Behaviors** button at the top of the right-hand panel.

The actor's behavior page provides some information that is useful for us to know. If we look at the left-hand panel, we can see a list of behaviors that are currently attached to this actor:

- Jump and Run Movement
- Cannot Exit Scene
- Camera Follow
- Collect Fruit

Also, at the top of the right-hand panel, there is a red **Deactivate Behavior** button, which can be used to disable the currently selected behavior. This feature can be useful for debugging because we can disable behaviors during the process of tracking down a problem. It's also useful to know that behaviors can be deactivated and reactivated within instruction blocks. This is a more advanced feature but it's a feature that's worth remembering for future use.

Adding an additional event to a behavior

We have created an event that makes fruit disappear when the monkey collects it, and we now need to add a new event that will kill the monkey when it collides with an enemy actor.

It is quite possible to create a brand new behavior that will do this job, but we're going to add an additional event to the behavior that we have just created. This means that the behavior will have two events to listen out for, namely:

- A collision between the monkey and a member of the `Collectibles` group
- A collision between the monkey and a member of the `Enemies` group

Originally, we created the behavior to do one job, and we gave it a sensible name `Collect Fruit`. However, as we're going to add a second event that is not related to fruit collection, this name won't make sense any more, so we need to give the behavior a more relevant name.

Time for action – adding an event and renaming the behavior

The game file that needs to be imported and loaded for this session is `5961_04_03.stencyl`.

If we're following on immediately from the previous instructions, we should be looking at the monkey actor's behavior page. However, we need to return to the behavior editor so, click on the `Collect Fruit` tab or, if the tab is not visible, go to the **Dashboard**, click on **Actor Behaviors** (under **LOGIC** in the left-hand panel) and double-click on the **Collect Fruit** behavior, which is currently represented by an image of a hammer.

We can now see the orange **when ...** block that we created earlier. Now perform the following steps:

1. Click on the **+ Add Event** button at the top of the left-hand panel.
2. In the pop-up menu, move the mouse over the **Collisions** option, and select **Member of Group**.
3. Double-click the new **Actor – Group** item in the left panel.
4. Change the text to `Collides with Enemies` and press *Enter* on the keyboard.
5. On the orange **when Self hits a...** block, change the **Actor Group** option to **Enemies** by clicking on it, selecting **Choose Group** and double-clicking **Enemies** in the **Choose an Actor Group** dialog box.
6. In the right-hand panel, ensure that the **Actor** button is selected at the top of the panel, click on **Properties** from the row of silver buttons in the right-panel, and drag the blue **kill Self** block into the orange **when Self hits a...** block.

7. In the row of buttons shown at the upper-center of the screen, click on the **Properties** button, as shown in the following screenshot:

8. In the **Edit Properties** dialog box, change the name from `Collect Fruit` to `Manage Player Collisions`.

9. In the **Description** box, type `Manages all collisions for the player's character`.

 Note that we could also change the icon for this behavior from the default hammer to any image of our choice, although we're going to leave it as it is.

10. Click on the **Apply Changes** button.

11. Test the game. First, make the monkey run into a piece of fruit, then make it bump into one of the enemy characters.

What just happened?

We have added a new event to the behavior that we created earlier, and we renamed the behavior.

The procedure for creating the `Collides with Enemies` event is very similar to the one we followed when creating the `Collides with Collectibles` event. We specified what type of event we wanted to create. In this case it is another group collision. Then, we specified which group we wanted to detect the collisions with, by changing the `Actor Group` to `Enemies` in the orange `when Self hits a...` block.

The next step was to tell the event what to do when a collision occurs with the `Enemies` group—we need to kill the actor—so we dragged the `kill Self` block into the orange `when Self hits a...` block.

We might ask ourselves the question, "Which actor is going to be killed?" To find the answer, we first need to know that the `kill Self` block is going to kill `Self`. Remembering that this behavior is attached to the monkey actor, we can determine that `Self` refers to the monkey. So, the monkey will be killed when the collision occurs.

This is an important difference when compared to the `Collides with Collectibles` event because, in that event, it is the actor `of group`—the member of the `kill Self` group—that was killed.

The final step was to give the behavior a more relevant name, it doesn't just manage collisions with the fruit anymore. It manages all of the monkey's collisions so the name `Manage Player Collisions` seems more appropriate, and will help us to more easily identify the behavior if we need to make changes in the future.

When we test the game, we will find that both events are doing their jobs—when our monkey touches a piece of fruit, the fruit disappears but, when the monkey runs into one of the enemy actors, the monkey is killed.

Understanding the instruction block palette

When we are creating or editing behaviors, we have access to the block palette, the rightmost panel from which we have been selecting the instruction blocks.

The palette has been arranged so that it is easy to locate the blocks that we require, and it is organized as shown in the following screenshot:

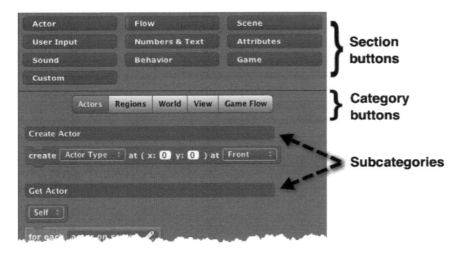

We have already used the section buttons to select blocks from the **Actor** and **Scene** sections, but it is worth noting that each section has different category buttons. For example, in the previous screenshot, we can see that the currently selected **Scene** section has five categories namely **Actors**, **Regions**, **World**, **View** and **Game Flow**. Underneath the category buttons, the blocks are separated into subcategories so, for example, the **Actors** category, in the **Scene** section, has the subcategories **Create Actor** and **Get Actor**.

If we click on the **Actor** section button, we will have a different selection of categories from which we can choose—**Position**, **Motion**, **Properties**, **Draw**, **Tweening**, and **Effects**. If we then click on the **Position** category button, we can see that the subcategories are **Position** and **Direction**.

As we learn more about Stencyl behaviors, we will become familiar with the sections, categories and subcategories, but one of the keys to mastering Stencyl is to understand which all instruction blocks are available to us, and where to find them.

 To learn more about how individual instruction blocks work, right-click on the block in the palette, and select **View Help**. This will open up the relevant help page on the `stencyl.com` website.

Considering future refinements

We've created a new behavior for the monkey, and it correctly manages the monkey's collisions, but we still have some work to do in order to refine the actions that take place when the collisions occur.

For example, rather than fruit disappearing instantly when it is collected, it might be more visually appealing if a special effect occurred. Perhaps the fruit could fade away gently or, for a more dramatic effect, it might explode, with the pieces fading away.

When the monkey collides with an enemy actor, the monkey vanishes without warning, which isn't very elegant, so we'll need to make some decisions about how that process is handled.

However, rather than holding ourselves back with the technicalities of special effects, we're going to carry on building the important mechanics of the game, and we'll consider options for some of the refinements and implement them later in the development process.

A review of the gameplay

We are making fantastic progress with our game; we're only one quarter of the way through this chapter, and we have implemented several features and learned several new skills.

However, in its current state, the gameplay is not going to be very exciting for players of Monkey Run. The game will be exactly the same every time it is played and, as a designer, our job is to create a game that people will want to come back to play time and time again.

There is an important element missing from our game, and that is the element of chance, our game needs some randomness!

Random gameplay is very difficult to get just right. If a game has too many random elements, it will be too difficult to play, our players will give up very quickly and move on to more interesting games. For this reason, even when we, as designers are happy with the gameplay, it is vital that we find the opportunity to allow independent, unbiased game testers to provide us with feedback, so we can fine-tune the game and make it enjoyable to play.

Introducing a new challenge

We're going to introduce a new actor into our game—a mysterious Aztec statue that will fall from the sky at random locations and block the monkey's path. Our first task is to find the statue on StencylForge, download it and configure it for our game.

Because we are going to be building a more complex behavior in this section of the book, rather than jumping in and trying to create the whole behavior in one session, we'll break down the process so we can be sure that each step is working correctly.

As we create the behavior step-by-step, we'll notice that some things aren't working quite as they should. Don't worry we'll fix the problems as we work our way through the development process.

Building behaviors step-by-step is a good practice, jumping in and trying to create a complex behavior without regular testing can be a recipe for disaster. So, it's a good idea to get into the habit of working through the development process methodically, rather than rushing ahead and introducing difficult to fix bugs.

Have a go hero – downloading and configuring the statue

The game file that needs to be imported and loaded for this session is `5961_04_04.stencyl`.

The skills required to complete the following tasks were covered in *Chapter 3, Detecting Collisions*, so if required, refer to the relevant sections and review the detailed steps to complete the tasks listed.

The tasks we need to achieve here are:

◆ Downloading the actor called **Stencyl Book Statue** from StencylForge

◆ Creating a new collision group called `Droppers`

◆ Configuring the new `Droppers` group to collide with `Players`, `Tiles`, `Enemies`, and `Droppers`

◆ Adding the statue to the `Droppers` collision group—this is a vital step, so don't forget to complete it

◆ Saving the game, so we're ready for the next section, *Time for action – creating a behavior to drop the statues*

We now have a statue actor that is a member of a new group called `Droppers`, and we have configured it to collide with actors that are members of the specified groups.

Creating a timed event

We've already decided that we are going to drop the Aztec statues into the jungle at random locations but, first we need to decide how often our game is going to drop them. So the first step is to automatically create the actor inside the jungle scene every few seconds.

Time for action – creating a behavior to drop the statues

The game file that needs to be imported and loaded for this session is `5961_04_05.stencyl`.

We're going to start by creating a behavior to drop the statues into a single location in the scene, and then we'll refine the behavior as we progress. Execute the following steps in order to create a behavior to drop the statue:

1. On the **Dashboard**, under the **LOGIC** heading, click on **Scene Behaviors**.

2. Click on the message **This game contains no Logic. Click here to create one.** in the main panel.

3. In the **Name** textbox, type `Drop Actors Randomly` and click on the **Create** button to display the behavior editor.

4. At the top of the left-hand panel, click on **+ Add Event**.

5. In the pop-up menu, move the mouse over **Time**, then click **Every N seconds** (*not* **After N seconds**).

6. Double-click on the **Every N secs** item in the left-hand panel, and change the name of the event to `Drop statues`.

7. In the orange **do every … seconds** block, enter the digit `3` into the white textbox.

8. Click on the **Scene** button at the top of the instruction block palette, as shown in the following screenshot:

Scene

9. Drag the red **create Actor Type …** block into the orange **do every 3 seconds** block.

10. On the new red **create Actor Type at …** block, click on the **Actor Type** option and select **Choose Actor Type** from the drop-down menu.

11. In the **Choose an Actor Type** dialog box, double-click on the icon for the **Stencyl Book Statue**. The red block will change to **create Stencyl Book Statue at …**.

12. In the red **create Stencyl Book Statue at …** block, enter the number 320 into the white textbox to the right of **x:.**

13. Enter the number 10 into the white textbox to the right of **y:,** as shown in the following screenshot:

14. Click on the green **Attach to Scene** button above the instruction block palette.

15. Double-click the icon for the **Jungle** scene.

16. Test the game.

What just happened?

We've created a new scene behavior that drops the statue actor into the jungle scene every 3 seconds. Rather than being attached to an actor, this behavior is attached to the scene, because the scene is going to create the statues for us.

We needed to tell the `create Actor Type at …` block which actor to create, and where to create it, so we selected the statue actor type in the **Choose Actor Type** dialog box. The numbers that we entered in the **x:** and **y:** textboxes represent the location on the screen where the statue will be created. Although we have some work to do to position the statue correctly, the numbers we provided are adequate for testing if the behavior is carrying out its main task correctly.

 Note that we don't need to manually add the statue actor to the jungle scene using the Scene Designer, as we have done with the monkey, fruit, and enemy actors, the `create Stencyl Book Statue at …` block will do all the work for us.

When we test the game, we can see that a new statue actor appears at the top-center of the screen every three seconds. However, we can quickly determine that things are not quite right. If we move the monkey, we can see that the statue is always dropping into the scene at exactly the same position, which is probably not what we're hoping for, because it won't present much of a challenge for players of our game when the monkey progresses to the other end of the scene.

Identifying and resolving problems

We've already identified one unexpected issue—the statues always fall in the same location—but it's now time to give the game a really good testing and make a note about what happens when, for example, many statues are allowed to fall into the scene. Try it.

There may be other problems to be found, but it's important to understand that these bugs aren't necessarily faults with Stencyl, they may be system limitations (that is, known features) or they could be caused by the way that we have designed the game—for example, the player's character may become stuck at a certain point in a scene if we haven't carefully considered the placing of tiles.

Sometimes these effects are desirable in a game but, if they are not, we will need to change our game so that it works differently, so it's a good idea to note any problems as early as possible (always keep a notepad and pencil at hand). It's all part of the learning process.

We'll fine-tune the behavior that drops the statues as we progress through this chapter but, before we can do that, we need to understand a little more about the relationship between screen and scene sizes.

Examining screen size and scene size

In our newly created behavior, we specified the **x** position as `320` and the **y** position as `10`. It's a good idea to examine what these numbers mean so that we have a good understanding of why the statue actor is appearing exactly where it does.

The coordinates on a computer screen are measured from the upper left-hand corner of the screen, which has an x position of zero and a y position of zero. As we move from the left of the screen to the right, the x coordinate increases in value. As we move from the top of the screen to the bottom, the y coordinate increases in value, as shown in the following figure, in which the dotted lines represent the edges of our screen:

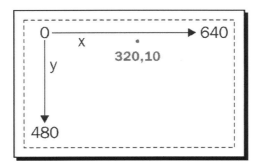

When we initially created our game, at the beginning of *Chapter 2, Let's Make a Game!* we accepted the default screen width of 640 pixels and screen height of 480 pixels. The screen size determines the area of the game that we can see on the computer screen at any one time. We can see this configuration by clicking on the **Settings** icon on the Stencyl toolbar, and clicking on **Setting**, and then on **Display** in the **Game Settings** dialog box.

 A pixel is the smallest controllable point on a computer display. In Stencyl, although it is easy to do, it is fairly unusual to draw on the screen at pixel level. We usually create actors and tiles, or draw shapes that are constructed for us, without having to worry about individual pixels.

The point on the previous figure, labeled 320, 10 represents the x and y coordinates at which our statue is being created, that's 320 pixels horizontally from the left of the screen, and 10 pixels vertically from the top of the screen.

Later on in *Chapter 2, Let's Make a Game!*, when we made the jungle scene scrollable, we changed the scene width from 20 tiles to 60 tiles. In our game, each tile is 32 pixels wide, which means that we changed the width of the scene from 640 pixels wide (20 tiles x 32 pixels) right up to 1,920 pixels wide (60 tiles x 32 pixels). We can see this information about the scene width by looking at the properties dialog box for the Jungle scene. Open the Jungle scene and click on the **Properties** button at the top of the screen.

The following screenshot shows how our screen size (the area that is displayed) relates to the scene size (the whole area in which our game is played).

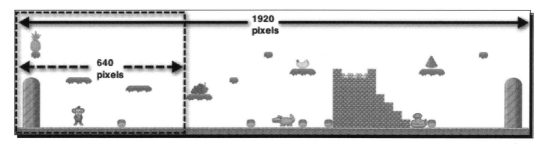

In the previous screenshot, the dotted rectangle, which is 640 pixels wide, represents the size of the screen, that is, the area of the game that we can see at any one time while the game is being played, and this is also known as the **viewport**. The solid line, which is 1,920 pixels wide, represents the width of our scene. As the monkey runs towards the right-hand side of the screen, we can imagine that the dotted black rectangle will slide along the scene in order to prevent the monkey disappearing off the side. It's the camera that we set up back in *Chapter 2, Let's Make a Game!*, that manages this process for us.

The reason that the statues always fall at the same location, is that we have specified a fixed x coordinate of 320 pixels (that's the horizontal location) for the statue. This means that, as our monkey runs towards the right edge of the screen, the statues will always fall at 320 pixels from the left-hand edge of the scene.

We need the statues to be dropped in the center of the screen (or viewport), so let's resolve that issue.

Time for action – adjusting the drop-location of the statue

The game file that needs to be imported and loaded for this session is
`5961_04_06.stencyl`.

Ensure that the `Drop Actors Randomly` behavior is displayed onscreen. Execute the following steps:

1. Click on the drop-down arrow to right of the **x** textbox (it currently contains the number `320`).

2. Move the mouse cursor over **Math** in the drop-down menu.

3. In the **Arithmetic** section of the pop-up menu, click on the **0 + 0** block.

 Note that the zeroes in the new green instruction block do not appear in our event blocks, they have been replaced by empty textboxes.

4. In the left-hand blank textbox of the new **of camera + ...** block, click on the drop-down arrow.

5. Select **Scene** from the drop-down menu.

6. In the **Basics** section of the pop-up menu, click on the red **x of camera** block.

7. In the right-hand blank textbox of the **of camera + ...** block, enter the number `320`, as shown in the following screenshot:

8. Test the game. Make the monkey run to the right of the scene.

What just happened?

Instead of the statues dropping at a location that is always 320 pixels from the left-hand edge of the scene, they will now always drop at a location 320 pixels from the left-hand edge of the screen.

To achieve this result, we used the `x of camera` block and a little bit of basic math (addition). The position `x of camera` is always the left-hand edge of the screen, which is zero pixels from the left of the screen. The screen width is 640 pixels, so if we add half the screen width (half of 640 = 320) to the camera's x position (0 pixels), we will always be specifying an x position of 320 pixels from the left of the screen. No matter where our monkey is, the
statue will always be dropped into the center of the viewport.

The statues will now drop from the center of the screen as required, but there are still some refinements to be made to this behavior, and we'll work on them as we progress through this chapter.

Examining the scene instruction blocks

We have been learning how to use the `create Actor Type at …` block, which we found under the **Actors** category in the **Scene** section of the block palette.

Take this opportunity to examine the other instruction blocks that can be found in the **Scene** section of the block palette—particularly those in the **View** and **Game Flow** subcategories. Many of the more advanced blocks won't necessarily make sense yet, but there are some very interesting instruction blocks for which their purpose is immediately apparent. For example, in the **View** category, there is a `shake screen for 0 sec with intensity 0 %` block which, perhaps unsurprisingly, does exactly what it says, it shakes the screen for the specified time with the specified intensity.

Make a note of any interesting blocks, and consider how they might be useful in our game. Perhaps the scene could shake each time a statue hits the ground.

Preparing for future changes

We've created a problem for the future! What if we decide to change the screen size for our game? Perhaps we decide to target a different device for our game—the screen size of 640 pixels wide and 480 pixels high might not be appropriate. We've already learned that we can easily change these parameters in the **Game Settings** dialog box, but if we change the screen width, our game isn't going to work as planned. We've specified that the statue should be dropped at exactly 320 pixels from the left-hand edge of the screen, which is half the current screen width of 640. If, for example, we change the screen width to 800 pixels, then the statue won't drop in the center of the screen because half that width is 400 pixels. It will be dropped somewhere towards left of the center, which is not the desired location! Let's fix that problem.

Time for action – making the behavior more flexible

The game file that needs to be imported and loaded for this session is
`5961_06_07.stencyl`.

Ensure that the `Drop Actors Randomly` behavior is being displayed. Execute the
following steps in order to make the behavior more flexible

1. Delete the number `320` from the right-hand textbox in the green addition
   block (it's not strictly necessary to delete this, but it keeps everything neater).

2. Click on the drop-down arrow in the same textbox from which we just deleted
   the number.

3. In the **Math** section of the pop-up menu, click on the **0 x 0** block.

4. Click on the drop-down arrow in the left-hand textbox of the newly added
   green multiplication block.

5. Select **Scene** from the drop-down menu and then, in the **Basics** section of the
   next pop-up menu, click on the red **screen width** block.

6. In the right-hand textbox of the green multiplication block enter the number `0.5`.
   Your screen should like the following screenshot:

7. Test the game.

What just happened?

Nothing appears to have changed in the game because the statues are still dropping in
exactly the same location. However, we have ensured that, whatever the width of our
screen, the statue will always drop in the center of the screen rather than at the fixed
location that we originally entered. We have calculated the x position of the statue by
adding half the width of the screen; that is, `screen width x 0.5`, to `x of camera`.

This may seem a trivial change to make, but there is another benefit. Imagine that we had
20 different behaviors that referred to the width of the screen, and that the numbers had
been manually typed, as they were in our original version of the behavior. If we now imagine
that we have decided to change the screen width in the **Game Settings** dialog box, then
we'd have to work our way through all 20 behaviors and manually adjust the numbers!
This would be a very time-consuming process and, even worse, it would increase the risk
of introducing errors into our game.

Why did we multiply the screen width by 0.5, when we could have divided the screen width by 2, in order to achieve the same result? In theory, computer code can often multiply faster than it can divide, so some developers consider it to be a more optimized calculation. However, in practice, it's unlikely to have any effect on a game developed with Stencyl. The choice of whether to multiply or divide is entirely down to the developer.

 There is a potential disadvantage to calculating the x coordinate for the center of the screen, rather than manually typing the number into the instruction block. The computer has to calculate the x coordinate based on the width of the screen every time a statue is dropped, which uses processing power. This is unlikely to cause a problem for us, but it does demonstrate that game designers have a lot of issues to consider when building a game!

Introducing randomness into our game

We've now learned how to do calculations with Stencyl's instruction blocks, and we have also learned about the **screen width** block, which can be used to dynamically retrieve the width of the screen. However, earlier in this chapter, the issue of randomness was raised, but we haven't actually introduced that element of gameplay, so let's do that now.

Time for action – introducing randomness to our behavior

The game file that needs to be imported and loaded for this session is
5961_04_08.stencyl.

We're going to modify our instructions so that the statues are dropped at a random location, so ensure that the Drop Actors Randomly behavior is being displayed. Execute the following steps in order to introduce randomness to our behavior:

1. Click and drag the green multiplication block out of the addition block, and drop it onto the gray background, below the orange **do every 3 seconds** block, as shown in the following screenshot:

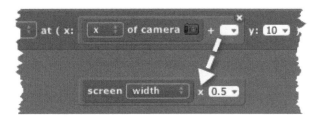

2. Click on the drop-down arrow in the now empty textbox in the green **x of camera + ...** block.

3. Select **Math** from the drop-down menu and then, in the **Operations** section of the pop-up menu, click on the **random number between ...** block.

4. Enter the number 0 into the textbox immediately after the word **between**.

5. Click on the drop-down arrow in the textbox immediately after the word **and**.

6. From the drop-down menu, select **Scene**, and then click on the **screen width** block:

7. Press *Ctrl + K* or, on Mac OS X press *Command + K*.

8. Test the game. Make the monkey run left and right, and watch as several statues fall from the sky.

What just happened?

The actors are now falling at a random location somewhere between the leftmost edge of the screen and the rightmost edge of the screen.

The first step was to drag the **screen width x 0.5** blocks out of the behavior because we no longer needed them. We then added the **random number between ... and ...** block, which allows us to specify a low number and high number, and then uses this information to generate a random number within that range. We specified a lower number of 0, which is the x coordinate for the left-hand side of the screen, and a higher number of **screen width**, which is the x coordinate for right-hand side of the screen. When our game is running, the **random number between 0 and screen width** instruction will automatically generate for us a random x position between zero and 640. The random number is then added to the x of camera to ensure that the statues always fall within the viewport.

Finally, we pressed the key combination of *Ctrl + K*, or *Command + K* on Mac OS X. This shortcut removes any unused blocks from the behavior designer, such as the ones that we dragged out of the behavior in the first step.

Unused blocks don't have to be removed from the behavior designer, they are ignored when the game is compiled, and they don't use any extra memory in our compiled game. However, it's a good idea to tidy up the behavior editor when the blocks are no longer required.

Optimizing the number of actors

Let's solve two more problems. The first problem is a technical one; depending on the speed of the computer's processor, after approximately 10 to 20 statues have been dropped, the game starts to lag, it slows down to an unacceptable speed because there are too many active actors on screen. Computers have limited resources and it is our job, as the game developer, to use these resources effectively.

The second problem is a gameplay issue; if too many statues have fallen, it can become impossible to complete the level, because the statues might block the monkey's path through the jungle. In some games, this may be the desired gameplay, but we want to create a game that is a little less stressful for our player on the first level, perhaps gameplay could become more difficult in later levels, but not just yet.

There are many ways to resolve such problems in a game, and it's usually down to the imagination of the developer to find a solution. We're going to solve both problems simultaneously, with a new behavior.

Time for action – making the statues disappear after a delay

The game file that needs to be imported and loaded for this session is
`5961_04_09.stencyl`.

Let's create a timer that will remove each statue from the scene after a specified delay, Now perform the following instructions:

1. If the **Drop Actors Randomly** tab is open, then close the tab.
2. On the **Dashboard**, click on **Actor Behaviors**.
3. Create a new actor behavior called **Manage Statues**.
4. Click on **+Add Event** and select **Time** from the menu.
5. Click on the **After N seconds** icon.
6. Change the name of the **After N Seconds** event to `Kill statues`.
7. In the **do after ... seconds** block, enter the number 5 into the textbox.
8. The **Actor** section button in the instruction block palette should already be selected, so click on the gray **Properties** category button in the palette.
9. Drag the blue **kill Self** block onto the orange **do after 5 seconds** block, as shown in the following screenshot:

10. Click on the green **Attach to Actor Type** button above the instruction block palette, and double-click on the **Stencyl Book Statue** in the **Choose an Actor Type** dialog box.

11. Test the game. Watch several statues fall and wait for at least five seconds.

What just happened?

We created a new actor behavior, which automatically kills the actor five seconds after it is created, and we attached the new behavior to the statue actor.

It was an easy behavior to create and it does a very straightforward job, however, the result is not very elegant—the statues just vanish! As with other aspects of the game, this may be the desired effect, but instantly vanishing actors might be rather confusing for players of a game. Perhaps we can implement a more elegant solution.

Implementing our first special effect

Rather than have our statues disappear instantly, we're going to make them gently fade away.

Time for action – making the statues disappear after a delay

The game file that needs to be imported and loaded for this session is `5961_04_10.stencyl`.

Ensure that the `Manage Statues` behavior is displayed on screen.

Towards the end of this *Time for action* section, there is a screenshot displaying the completed behavior, and this can be referred to while completing the following steps:

1. Drag the **kill Self** block out of the orange **do after 5 seconds** block, and drop it onto the gray background below the orange block.

2. Ensure that the **Actor** section button is selected at the top of the instruction block palette, and click on the gray **Tweening** category button.

3. Drag the **fade in Self over 0 sec using None** block into the **do after 5 seconds** block.

4. In the **fade in Self over ... sec using None** block, click on the **in** option and change it to **out**.

5. Enter the number 1 into the **over** textbox.

6. Display the flow instruction blocks by clicking on the **Flow** section button at the top of the instruction block palette, and click on the **Time** category button.

7. Drag the **do after 0 seconds** block from the instruction block palette and place it underneath the blue **fade out ...** block.

8. In the new **do after ... seconds** block, change the textbox to 1.

9. Drag the blue **kill Self** block into the new **do after 1 seconds** block:

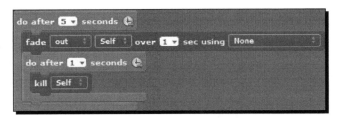

10. Test the game. Watch what happens to each statue after five seconds.

What just happened?

We have modified the behavior so that, instead of just killing the statue instantly, it will gently fade the statue out of view and then kill the actor.

It's important to note that when the statue has completely faded out of view, it still exists (it's just invisible!), which is why we need the **kill Self** block. We also need to understand that while the **fade out Self over 1 sec using None** block is doing its job, it does not wait for the fading to complete before the behavior moves on to the next instruction. That's why we have had to put the **kill Self** block inside an additional **do after 1 seconds** block. If we fail to delay the **kill Self** instruction, then the **fade out Self over 1 sec using None** block will start to fade the statue, but the **kill Self** block will instantly remove the statue after the fade process has started and before **the fade out Self over 1 sec using None** block has completed its work.

By introducing this new behavior, we have fixed two problems—the gameplay problem, whereby statues could block the monkey's path, and also the technical problem, which caused the game to lag when too many statues were on the screen. Lateral thinking such as this, will often help us to resolve gameplay and technical problems. So, bear this in mind in the cases when a difficult technical or gameplay issue occurs during the development process. Consider that there might be a straightforward solution that can also make the game more interesting and fun to play.

Experimenting with the timings

The game file that needs to be imported and loaded for this session is
`5961_04_11.stencyl`.

In the `Kill statues` event, we have three different timings to consider:

1. The main `do after 5 seconds` event block, which determines how long the event should wait after the creation of the statue and before triggering the enclosed instruction blocks.

2. The `fade out Self over 1 sec using None` block, which determines over how long the fade will occur.

3. The additional `do after 1 seconds` block, which specifies how long to wait before the statue is removed from the scene. In practice, for this effect, the delay should always be the same as the delay for the `fade out Self over 1 sec using None` block.

Experiment with the timings of the blocks to get a feel of how it affects the gameplay, and decide upon a set of timings that works well in the game.

Another interesting experiment would be to edit the `Drop Actors Randomly` scene behavior, so the statues appear more quickly. Reducing the `do every … seconds` delay in the `Drop statues` event will make the statues appear more frequently, and, if the fade and kill delays are sped up, the game becomes far more manic. Consider how changes to these arguments (the numbers and textual information that affect the way that some instruction blocks work) can change the gameplay. Often, an increase in difficulty in later levels can easily be achieved, simply by changing the timings in a behavior.

It might be a good idea to ask someone else to test the game in its current state, and listen to what they have to say about their first impressions of the game. Make a note of these comments and keep them. There will always be an opportunity to come back to this behavior at a later stage of the development to make further adjustments.

Ensure that, after experimenting, the game is tested thoroughly and is working correctly.

Have a go hero – making the fruit fade when collected

The game file that needs to be imported and loaded for this session is
`5961_04_11.stencyl`.

Earlier in this chapter, we created an actor behavior called `Manage Player Collisions`, in which the `Collides with Collectibles` event removes the fruit from the scene when the monkey collides with it.

Try modifying the `Collides with Collectibles` event so that it fades out the fruit rather than killing it instantly. Refer to the previous *Time for action – making the statues disappear after a delay* section, in which we changed the `Manage Statues` behavior to fade out the statues. The code is very similar.

Right-clicking on an existing instruction block in a behavior, and selecting **Copy** from the drop-down menu, places the block into the Stencyl clipboard. The copied blocks can then be pasted (right-click, **Paste**) into the gray background area of a different behavior, and then dragged and dropped into the required location.

Try different timings for the fading of the fruit and note that timings do not have to be whole numbers. It is acceptable to specify fractions of a second, for example, `do after 0.5 seconds`.

Understanding active actors

Stencyl does its best to assist us in optimizing our games. For example, if we have a moving actor in our scene, but it leaves our screen, Stencyl will make the actor **inactive**, so that it isn't wasting our computer's processing resources on unnecessary physics calculations. The actor will be made **active** again when it reappears in our scene.

Although this optimization feature is very useful, it can cause problems with certain forms of gameplay. For example, we may want our offscreen actors to remain active, even though they have left the screen. In our game, we may occasionally see that this built-in optimization becomes a problem if a statue falls at an angle, or on its side, at the very edge of the screen. The statue can freeze in midair.

In the following screenshot, the dotted rectangle represents the screen that we can see during gameplay. The statue is falling such that it is far enough away from the edge of the screen to make the actor inactive, but close enough that we can still see the corner of the statue, frozen onscreen.

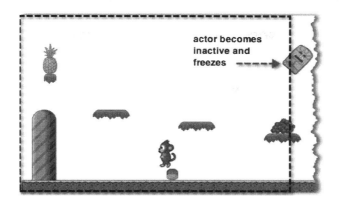

This phenomenon is difficult to see when testing our game. Our monkey has to be exactly in the right place on the screen, and running in the right direction, when the statue falls. While this might happen very infrequently, the chances are that it will happen eventually, and players of our game will not be impressed to see the game's actors freezing unexpectedly.

Experiencing a freezing statue

The game file that needs to be imported and loaded for this session is `5961_04_11_freeze_demo.stencyl`.

Rather than playing our game for an extended period, and hoping to see a statue freeze at the edge of the screen, we can see the problem by loading the demonstration file that has been provided.

The demonstration version of the game has been configured so that a frozen statue can be seen at the right-hand edge of the screen, as shown in the previous screenshot. Test the demonstration game, but do not press any keys. The corner of a statue will be seen hanging in midair.

If the monkey is then made to run to the right of the screen, so that the camera moves, the statue will become active again, and fall as expected.

After completing the previous experiment, do not use the demo game to continue development. The demo game has been configured specifically for the purpose of demonstrating how inactive actors can freeze and still be visible onscreen, and several other elements of the game have been deleted or modified in order to simplify the demonstration.

It is recommended that, once the experiment is complete, the demo game be closed and deleted.

The origin of the actors

Stencyl determines which actors are to become inactive based on the location of the origin of the actor. By default, the origin of an actor will be at its exact center; it's the central point around which the actor will rotate. Stencyl tries to take into account the size of the actor, so it can ensure that the actor is completely offscreen before making it inactive. However, if an actor is not in its original orientation, it may still be seen to freeze.

Our next task is to prevent the statue actors from becoming inactive.

Time for action – stopping the statues from becoming inactive

The game file that needs to be imported and loaded for this session is `5961_04_12.stencyl`.

Ensure that the `Manage Statues` actor behavior is on screen. We should be able to see the `Kill statues` event. Execute the following steps to stop the statue from becoming inactive:

1. Click on the **+ Add Event** button at the top of the left-hand panel.

2. Select **Basics**, then click on **When Creating**.

3. Rename the **Created** event to **Statues always active**.

4. Ensure that the **Actor** section button is selected in the instruction block palette.

5. Click on the **Properties** category button.

6. In the **Misc** subcategory, locate the blue **make Self always active** block, and drag it into the orange **when created** block, as shown in the following screenshot:

7. Test the game.

What just happened?

Although our game doesn't necessarily appear to behave any differently, the statues' physics properties are now still active, even when offscreen.

We have added a new **when created** event to the Manage Statues behavior, and we have renamed the new event to Statues always active. A **when created** event is triggered only once, when the actor is first created, and it's a very useful event into which one-off configuration blocks can be placed.

Because this behavior has been attached to the statue actor, the event will be carried out once for each statue actor as it is created, and then it will never be executed again for that actor.

Inside the **when created** event, we placed the make Self always active block, which ensures that the actor will never become inactive, even if it is not visible in the viewport. Now we can be sure that players of our game won't experience any unexpected frozen actors.

It's important to be aware that always active actors can have a serious impact on the performance of a game if they are not used carefully. Even when active actors are offscreen, they will still react to the game's physics requirements.

For this reason, care should be taken while deciding whether or not to make an actor always active. In our scene, we know that the statues are created every three seconds, and we know that the statues are killed after six seconds (a five second delay, then a one second fade-out). So, it is impossible for more than three statues to be active in our scene at any time.

Our earlier experiments have shown that we can have up to approximately 10 to 20 statues in a scene before the game's performance is adversely affected, and we must take this into consideration if we adjust the timings in the future. For example, if we add more playable levels to our game, which are more challenging, the number of active statues in the scene may increase.

There's more than one way

When developing games, there is almost always more than one way to achieve the same result and, very often, there are many ways! It's not necessarily a case of one method being better than the others, but sometimes different solutions can affect the gameplay or the performance of the game in different ways. For example, the game might lag, or there might be other consequences of using a particular solution.

Freezing actors is an example of a problem that has more than one solution. We chose to make the statue actors always active, which is a perfectly good solution for our game. However, there is at least one other equally good solution, which can be achieved using a Scene block called set offscreen bounds to ..., shown in the following screenshot:

This block can be found in the **Scene** section blocks under the **View** category.

Normally, the offscreen bounds are the same size as the screen. If the actor's origin moves outside the bounds of the screen, then the actor will become inactive. However, using a `set offscreen bounds to …` block allows us to specify bounds beyond the edges of the screen, in which our actors can remain active.

This could be perfect for our requirements because, if we set the offscreen bounds to an appropriate size, the statues would not freeze as they left the sides of the screen, but, if the monkey moved, leaving the statue far away and outside the edges of the screen where gameplay isn't affected, the statue would become inactive. This would free up resources without affecting the gameplay.

Have a go hero – using the offscreen bounds block

The game file that needs to be imported and loaded for this session is `5961_04_13.stencyl`.

Try replacing the `make Self always active` block with a `set offscreen bounds to …` block. Take care in deciding upon values for the arguments for this block.

 For detailed information relating to how to use a specific instruction block, right-click on the block and select **View Help** on the pop-up menu. This will open up a web browser at the relevant help page on the Stencyl website.

It will be helpful to know that the size of the statue is approximately 55 pixels wide and 80 pixels high.

Creating a countdown timer

Our game already has several challenges for players such as:

- Collecting fruit
- Avoiding dangerous animals
- Dodging falling statues

However, we're going to give our players another challenge, which doesn't involve other actors.

Time for action – creating a countdown timer

The game file that needs to be imported and loaded for this session is
`5961_04_14.stencyl`.

Ensure that the game has been saved, and close any open tabs, leaving only the **Dashboard**
tab visible. Now execute the following instructions to create the countdown timer:

1. Create a new Scene Behavior called **Score Management**.

2. Click on the **Attributes** section button in the instruction block palette.

3. Click on the **Create an Attribute** button, situated immediately below the
category buttons.

4. In the **Name** textbox, enter `Countdown`.

5. Select **Number** in the **Type** drop-down list.

6. Click on the **OK** button to close the dialog box.

7. In the left-hand panel, click on **+ Add Event**.

8. Select **Time**, then **Every N Seconds**.

9. Rename the **Every N Seconds** event to `Decrement Countdown`.

10. In the new **do every ... seconds** event, enter the digit `1` into the empty textbox.

11. Click on the **Numbers & Text** section button at the top of the instruction
block palette.

12. Drag the **increment number by 0** block into the **do every 1 seconds** event block.

 Note that the **Number** option automatically changes to **Countdown**.

13. Click on the **increment** option item and change it to **decrement**.

14. Enter the digit `1` into the **decrement Countdown by ...** textbox.

15. Click on the **Flow** section button at the top of the block palette.

16. Click on the **Debug** category button.

17. Locate the **print anything** block in the **Print to Console** subcategory, and drag
it below the **decrement Countdown by 1** block.

18. Select the **Attributes** section button at the top of the block palette, and click on the **Getters** category button.

19. Drag the blue **Countdown** block into the empty **print ...** textbox, as shown in the following screenshot:

20. Click on the green **Attach to Scene** button situated above the block palette, and select the **Jungle** scene.

21. In the **Attributes** window that appears in the main panel, enter the digit 10 into the **Countdown** textbox.

22. On the main Stencyl menu, select the **Log Viewer** option from **View**.

23. Test the game.

24. When the game has compiled and is being displayed on the screen, examine the contents of the **Log Viewer** window. Watch what happens after 10 seconds.

25. Close the game.

What just happened?

We've created a Score Management behavior, and have displayed the value of the game's countdown in Stencyl's **Log Viewer** window. We should see that the countdown starts with a value of nine, and reduces by a value of one each second. After 10 seconds, the countdown reached zero, but then it continued to count backwards to -1, -2, -3, and it would continue to count backwards infinitely if we allowed it to (and if we had enough time).

The first step was to create an attribute to store the value of the countdown. An attribute is a changeable value that is used to store a specific piece of information, and, in this case, we need to store a number; therefore, we created a number attribute that represents the number of seconds that we want to count down from. Our new number attribute, called Countdown, can now be used anywhere within the behavior. It can be added to, subtracted from, and tested to see if it equals another value. We can manipulate attributes in almost every way imaginable!

Within the Score Management behavior, we added the do every ... seconds event, which we renamed to Decrement Countdown. We then added the increment number by ... block, but since we want our attribute to count down, we changed it from increment to decrement. Because our behavior only has one attribute, the name of that attribute automatically replaced the **Number** option. Finally, for this block, we specified the value we wanted to decrement by, which is 1.

The decrement Countdown by 1 block will be executed once every second, thus providing us with a second-by-second countdown. However, we haven't told the game what to do when the countdown reaches zero. So, it will just carry on counting down until we end the game.

When we attached the behavior to the jungle scene, we were presented with the behavior configuration screen. Because we created an attribute for this behavior, we were given the opportunity to provide a starting value for Countdown, and we entered the number 10.

We don't yet have any way to display the value of the Countdown attribute within our game (that will be discussed in a later section). For now, we are temporarily using the print ... instruction block to display the value in the Log Viewer.

The Log Viewer is a very useful tool—we can use a print ... block to output information to the Log Viewer, so that we can see what is going on in our game at any time, without having to worry about displaying information on the game screen.

It's also a great tool for debugging because, if we have a problem and we're not sure why the problem is occurring, we can use a print ... block to see the values of our attributes, or other information that Stencyl makes available to us, for example, the coordinates of actors.

During the testing of the game, we could see the value of Countdown in the Log Viewer, but the countdown started from nine, not 10. Why? When creating instructions, it's vital to fully understand the sequence of events that will occur. When our Decrement Countdown behavior starts, the process is as follows, remembering that the starting value of the Countdown attribute is 10:

◆ Decrease the Countdown attribute by 1 (it's now equal to 9)
◆ Print the value of Countdown to the Log Viewer

The first time the value of `Countdown` is printed to the Log Viewer, it has already been reduced by one. This may appear to be a trivial point to note, but such issues can have unexpected consequences in behaviors. So, is certainly worth being aware of what can go wrong. For example, before the game starts, we may have advised the player that they will have 10 seconds to complete the task. They may be annoyed when it appears that they only have 9 seconds. Game players can be very unforgiving.

In this instance, the problem can be resolved very easily, if we wish to do so—simply display the `Countdown` attribute before it is decreased. We can just drag the `print Countdown` block so that it is above the `decrement Countdown by 1` block. Try it!

Examining the debug blocks

We have used a `print` ... debug block which, as we have discovered, is very useful for showing us values used in our game, without having to display them within the game itself.

There are several other debug blocks available to us. Take this opportunity to examine them, and consider how they might be useful to us as game developers.

To view the debug blocks, click on the **Flow** section button, then on the **Debug** category button in the block palette.

Remember that right-clicking any block will provide access to the **View Help** option.

Implementing decision making into our game

Now that we have the countdown working, we need to implement a solution that will kill the monkey when the counter reaches zero.

Time for action – listening for the countdown to reach zero

The game file that needs to be imported and loaded for this session is `5961_04_15.stencyl`.

Rather than allowing the countdown to continue beyond zero and into negative numbers, in the following steps we're going to create a behavior with an event that will react when the player runs out of time:

1. Create a new Actor Behavior **called Health**.
2. Add a new **Time** event, **Every N Seconds**, and rename it to **Countdown expired**.
3. Change the **do every ... seconds** textbox to 1 second.
4. Click on the **Flow** section button in the palette.

5. Ensure that the **Conditions** category button is selected.

6. Drag the orange **if** block into the **do every 1 seconds** event.

7. Click on the drop-down arrow in the **if** block, select **Comparison**, and, in the **Inequality** section, click on the **0 < 0** block.

8. In the right-hand textbox of the green **0 < 0** block, enter the number 1.

9. In the block palette, click on the **Behavior** section button and the **Attributes** category button.

10. In the **For Scene** subcategory of the block palette, locate the red **for this scene, get text from behavior text** block and drag it into the left-hand textbox in the **0 < 0** block.

11. Click on the drop-down arrow in the left-hand textbox of the **for this scene, get … from behavior …** block and select **Attribute Names** in the drop-down menu.

12. In the pop-up menu, move the mouse over the letter **S**, then select **Score Management** and then **Countdown**, as shown in the following screenshot:

13. Locate the **kill Self** block in the palette, and drag it into the **if for this scene, get countdown from behavior Score Management** block, as shown in the following screenshot:

14. Attach the behavior to the monkey actor.

15. Test the game.

16. When the game is being displayed on the screen, examine the contents of the **Log Viewer** window. Watch what happens to the monkey after 10 seconds.

17. Close the game and close the **Log Viewer** window.

What just happened?

We've attached the newly created `Health` behavior to the monkey and we should now be familiar with the main event block in this behavior—it will do something every one second, because we created a `do every` ... event block.

For the first time, we are introducing an `if` ... block, which allows the instruction blocks to make a decision based on some information in our game. We want to know when our countdown timer is less than one, or in other words, when our player is out of time!

When we use an `if` ... block, we must give it something to test and, in this case, we are comparing two numbers using the green less than block. The < symbol means less than and we're checking to see if something is less than the digit 1, which we entered into the second textbox.

The something that we're checking is decided by the red `for this scene, get _ Countdown from behavior Score Management` block shown in the following screenshot, which, at first, might look a little complicated. So, let's break it down:

This block will retrieve the value of an attribute that can be found in another behavior in the current scene. We used a very useful shortcut to populate the textboxes. We located the name of the attribute that we needed by using the drop-down menus. We could have typed the information into the boxes, and that works perfectly well—if we type all the information correctly! If we were to type any of the information incorrectly, then the instruction just won't work. So, why not just use the shortcut?

In plain English, our red `for this scene, get` ... block could be phrased as follows:

In the current scene, retrieve the value of the Countdown attribute that is used in the Score Management behavior.

We created the `Score Management` behavior in the *Time for action – listening for the countdown to reach zero* section, and we know that that there is an attribute called `Countdown`, which is decreased every second.

If we now look at our new `Countdown expired` event as a whole, we can phrase it in English as:

Every one second, check if the value of Countdown is less than one and, if it is, kill Self.

Because we attached this behavior to the monkey actor, Self refers to the monkey.

We have a timer that will count down second-by-second, and we now have an event that checks when the value of the countdown is less than one and, if the countdown is less than one, the monkey is killed!

As we discovered earlier, a kill block is somewhat abrupt, and our monkey actor just disappears without warning. We'll be giving our game some polish later on but, remember, for the time being, we're just getting our gameplay mechanics working correctly.

 There is a very important point to note when retrieving attribute values using the red attribute blocks. Note that the name of the attribute—in our case it is Countdown—is preceded with an underscore character so it appears as _Countdown. The underscore character is needed because these instruction blocks use Stencyl's **internal names** for the attributes, not the friendly names that we have given to them. For this reason, it is generally recommended, as we have done, to use the pop-up menus to populate the textboxes in these blocks.

What if? Otherwise...

We have used an if ... block to check for a specific condition, and to carry out actions if that condition is True. In our game, the actor is killed when the Countdown attribute has a value less than one.

However, what can we do if we need to respond when the condition is not True?

In the **Flow** section of the palette, in the **Conditions** category, there are two other instruction blocks alongside the **if ...** block in the **Conditionals** subcategory. Both of these alternative conditional blocks begin with the word **otherwise**.

Research what these blocks do, and consider how they might be useful when creating behaviors for a game.

Repositioning an actor during gameplay

We're going to give our player more than one chance to complete the level. When the monkey dies after colliding with an enemy actor, we're going to move it back to the start of the level.

Time for action – creating an event to relocate the monkey

The game file that needs to be imported and loaded for this session is
`5961_04_16.stencyl`.

Ensure that the `Health` behavior is being displayed. It currently contains a single event
called `Countdown expired`. Now perform the following steps:

1. Click on **+ Add Event | Advanced | Custom Event**.

2. Rename the **Custom Event** to **Relocate monkey**.

3. In the new orange **when … happens** event block, enter the name `RestartLevel`
   (note the capitalization and that there no spaces).

4. In the block palette, under **Actor**, click on **Position**, locate the **set x to 0 for Self**
   block, and drag it into the **when RestartLevel happens** block.

5. Hold down the *Alt* key on the keyboard (*Option* on Mac OS X), and drag the
   new **set x to … for Self** block so that a copy of it appears below the first one.

6. In the top **set x to … for Self** block, enter the number `200` into the textbox.

7. In the lower **set x to 0 for self** block, click on the **x** option and change it to **y**,
   then enter `175` in the textbox, as shown in the following screenshot:

8. Save the game. It's not ready for testing yet.

What just happened?

We've created a **Custom Event** called `Relocate monkey`. Custom events allow us to create
a set of instructions that will be started by a unique trigger that we can specify.

The behaviors we have created so far rely on built-in events, such as when the value of an
attribute is less than a specified number, or when actors belonging to the specified groups
collide with each other. Our new custom event will listen out for the triggering of an event
called `RestartLevel`, and we'll be creating an instruction to trigger that event in the next
section, *Time for action – triggering the custom event*.

Once our custom event has been triggered, it will execute the instructions inside the `when RestartLevel happens` block. In this case, the instructions specify a new x and y position for the monkey, the actor will be placed right back where it started.

How did we know which numbers to specify for the x and y positions? If we open up the jungle scene in the Scene Designer, we can find out the start position of the monkey by clicking on the monkey actor in the scene and looking down to the lower left-hand corner of the **Stencyl** window, where we will see the coordinates of the currently selected actor, as shown in the following screenshot:

> Stencyl Book Monkey 1 (ID: 1)   (200, 175)

> The x and y coordinates depend on exactly where the monkey actor was placed in the jungle scene, so have a look at the coordinates, and adjust the numbers in the blue `set x to ... for Self` and `set y to ... for Self` blocks accordingly.

Triggering custom events in our behaviors

We've created a custom event that will react to the `RestartLevel` trigger, so our next task is to put together the instructions that will trigger the custom event when required.

Time for action – triggering a custom event

The game file that needs to be imported and loaded for this session is `5961_04_17.stencyl`. Execute the following instructions:

1. Open the **Manage Player Collisions** actor behavior.

2. In the left-hand panel, click on the **Collides with Enemies** event title.

3. Right-click on the **kill Self** block and select **Remove** in the pop-up menu.

4. In the block palette, click on the **Behavior** section button and ensure that the **Triggers** category is selected.

5. Drag the **trigger event text in behavior text for self** instruction block into the orange **when Self hits a ...** block. Double-check that the correct instruction block has been selected (there are several blocks with similar names).

6. In the left-hand textbox of the **trigger event ... in behavior ... for Self** block, type `RestartLevel`—this must be typed so that it is identical to the name entered into the custom event block that we created previously, so check the capitalization.

7. In the right-hand textbox of the **trigger event RestartLevel in behavior ... for Self** block, click on the drop-down arrow and select **Behavior Name | H | Health** from the drop-down menu, as shown in the following screenshot:

8. Test the game. Observe what happens when the monkey collides with an enemy actor, such as the croc.

What just happened?

We have created a trigger for our custom `RestartLevel` event! When the monkey collides with an enemy actor, it is no longer instantly killed. It is relocated to its starting position in the scene, so the player can have another attempt at completing the level.

The first step was to remove the **kill Self** block, as we no longer needed it. We then inserted the new **trigger event ... in behavior ... for Self** block, which needs two pieces of information—the name of the event to trigger, and the name of the behavior that holds the event.

It's absolutely vital to ensure that the event name (the name of the trigger) is typed exactly the same as it is in the custom event, otherwise the trigger just won't work.

> Trigger names cannot have spaces, so it's often considered good practice to capitalize the first letter of each word in the trigger's name, so that they are easier to read.
>
> Another useful tip is to copy the name of the trigger from the custom event block, and paste it into a **trigger ...** block, so it can be guaranteed that the names match.

If we glance back to the block palette, where the various **trigger ...** blocks are currently on view, we can see that that there are two **trigger ...** blocks in the **For Actor** subcategory. We used the first block because we only have one custom event, called `RestartLevel`, and we know the name of the behavior that holds the event.

We could have been a little lazy and used the second block, which does not require us to specify the behavior name. There isn't really a problem with using that block; other than it having a trivial effect on the performance of the game, the player wouldn't notice anything slow down. However, it's a good idea to specify the behavior name when possible because, first, it helps us to understand what is happening right now and, secondly, if we need to review or modify the game in six months' time, it will remind us in which behavior to find the custom event.

Nevertheless, there is a very good reason for sometimes using the second **trigger ...** block, which does not require the behavior name, and that is because we can create multiple custom events with the same trigger name. Imagine that we have four different behaviors that need to do something when an actor dies, we could create a custom event in each of those behaviors, and give each custom event the same trigger name, such as PlayerDied. We could trigger all those custom events with a single **trigger ...** block, thus saving ourselves a lot of work.

Triggers and more triggers

In the section *Time for action – triggering the custom event*, we used the first **trigger ...** block, which can be found in the **For Actor** subcategory of the **Behaviors** section of the palette, and we also discussed the use of the second block in the same subcategory.

 Note that there are three other types of **trigger ...** blocks: two in the **For Scene** subcategory, and one in the **For Both** subcategory.

Consider how these additional **trigger ...** blocks could be used, and particularly when it might be beneficial to use the **For Both** trigger, which can trigger actor and scene events.

Taking time to learn the available blocks

It's impossible to master the tools that are available to us, without knowing which tools are available.

In this chapter, we have created some very useful behaviors, but we have only used a small subset of the instruction blocks that are available to us.

Take some time to methodically work through the instruction block palette, and examine each block carefully, for example, does it have a drop-down option menu such as the block shown in the following screenshot?

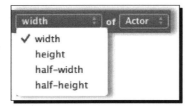

If it does have a drop-down option menu, discover what the available options are, and consider how they might be useful in game design. Don't worry if the purpose of each block and the options available don't make sense immediately, some of the features are quite advanced, and are rarely used. However, knowing that these features are available will help to solve game design problems as they arise in the future.

For the moment, concentrate on the following sections and categories in the block palette:

◆ **Actor**: **Position** and **Properties**

◆ **Flow**: **Conditional**, **Looping**, and **Time**

◆ **Flow**: **Debug** and **Commenting**

◆ **Numbers & Text**: **Math**, **Trig / Exponents**, and **Text**

Just being aware of all the blocks in the previously mentioned Sections and Categories is a great start to being able to solve many of the problems that we face when designing and creating computer games.

 If we're not sure what an instruction block is for, but we think it looks interesting, we can use the help system to learn more about the block. Just right-click on the block in the palette and select **View | Help**.

Learning from the provided behaviors

The behaviors that have been provided with Stencyl are an excellent source of information and inspiration. They can be edited and modified just like our own custom behaviors. In fact, the behaviors provided with Stencyl are just custom behaviors that have been created by someone else.

It's certainly a valuable exercise to examine the built-in behaviors that we have used in our game. The built-in behaviors that we have used are as follows:

- Cannot Exit Scene
- Camera Follow
- Jump and Run Movement

These behaviors can be located in the **Dashboard**, along with our behaviors that we have created—just double-click on the behavior's icon to view the instruction blocks that have been used to create the events.

Be aware that making changes to the built-in behaviors is very likely to cause problems in our game, so be careful to ensure they are not modified in any way.

Make a duplicate of the game, and experiment with it, rather than making experimental changes to our original game file. To make a duplicate of a game, save it first, to ensure that any recent changes have been saved to disk. Then, on the Stencyl menu, select **File | Save Game As**, and provide a name for the duplicate game. At this point, we can make changes without risk of affecting our original game.

Summary

We've reached the end of this chapter and, once again, we have made amazing progress. Over only three practical chapters, we have completed almost all of the gameplay-mechanics for our game.

We still have quite some way to go before we can say that our game is complete, there's a lot of polishing to do before we get there. However, we have, so far, covered many of the vital skills that we'll need to create numerous different types of games. It's important to remember that these skills are transferable to other genres of game. Many games will need the counters, decision making `if` ... blocks, and triggers that we have learned about in this chapter!

The skills we have learned in this chapter include:

- Creating a custom behavior that carries out actions, and attaching it to an actor
- Using random numbers to introduce the element of surprise in our game
- Making a timer event in a behavior that is attached to a scene
- How and why actors should or shouldn't be always active
- Our first special effect—fading an actor until it disappears
- Positioning an actor at any desired location during gameplay
- Creating custom events and triggering them from other behaviors

We've also benefited from learning many game design skills and techniques, such as:

- The difference between screen size and scene size
- How to use the instruction block palette
- Basic optimization techniques, such as reducing the number of active actors onscreen at any one time
- Understanding that there is often more than one way to solve a problem, and how different solutions can be beneficial or disadvantageous to gameplay

We've reached the stage of development where the vast majority of gameplay is in place, and most of our future tasks will involve fine-tuning and polishing our game to make it more presentable to our players.

In *Chapter 5, Animation in Stencyl*, we're going to learn about some of the different types of animation that can be implemented within Stencyl, and we'll use these skills to add some interesting visual effects into our game.

5
Animation in Stencyl

Now that we have much of the gameplay in place, our game has started to become more interesting and playable, but it is still missing some sparkle!

While playing video games, we will often take many of the subtle animations and visual effects for granted, but without them, a game can seem soulless. So, the next stage in the development of our game is to implement some animations and effects that will help bring our game to life.

Often, very subtle effects have a great impact on a game player's experience, so we're going to implement some animations and features that will add interest to the actors in our game.

A very useful trick is to add seemingly trivial animations to a static character, and this is one of the effects that we'll be implementing in this chapter — our mysterious sleeping statue is going to awaken before it fades away!

In this chapter we will be:

- Creating an actor using an imported image file
- Understanding Stencyl's animation terminology
- Importing a ready-made sprite sheet
- Editing animation frames
- Using instruction blocks to control animations
- Implementing **tweening** with instruction blocks

Creating an actor using an imported image file

In *Chapter 3, Detecting Collisions*, we used the Animation Editor to create and modify collision shapes for several of the actors in our game. However, up to this point, all the actor animations in our game have been provided for us in the form of downloads from StencylForge.

If we want to use graphics that have been created outside the Stencyl development environment, we need to know how to import them into Stencyl.

Time for action – importing an image into the Animation Editor

The game file to import and load for this session is `5961_05_01.stencyl`.

Before proceeding with the following steps, we must ensure that we have downloaded the file `5961_05_monkey_angel_actor.png` from this book's download page on the Packt Publishing website at `www.packtpub.com`, and have saved it into a folder on our hard disk so that we can easily locate it when required.

 Some of the smaller buttons used in this session are represented by onscreen icons and are not labeled with a text description. Hovering the mouse over any button will display a tooltip stating the button's function.

1. Display the monkey actor in the Animation Editor by clicking on the **Dashboard** tab, then selecting **Actor Types**, and double-clicking on the **Stencyl Book Monkey** icon.

2. Ensure that the **Appearance** button at the upper-center of the main panel (shown in the following screenshot) is selected; we should see the existing monkey animations in the **Animations** panel on the left of the screen:

3. Click on the icon for the `Dead` monkey animation; it may already be selected, but click it again just to be sure because we're going to delete it!

4. Locate the Remove Animation button, shown as follows, at the bottom of the **Animations** panel, and click on it:

5. Click on the **Remove** button in the confirmation dialog box.

6. Locate the Create Animation button, shown as follows, and click on it:

7. Ensure that the newly created `Animation 7`, in the **Animations** panel is selected (it should be highlighted with an orange border).

8. In the main panel, click on the **Click here to add a frame** icon to display the **Import Frames from Image Strip** dialog box.

9. When the dialog box is displayed, ensure that the **Scale** option is set to **Standard (1x)**.

10. Click the blue **Choose Image...** button.

11. Locate the `5961_05_monkey_angel_actor.png` file that we downloaded prior to starting these steps, and double-click on it to open the file.

12. Click on the **Add** button.

13. In the **Properties** section of the main panel, change the contents of the **Name** text box from `Animation 7` to `Angel`.

What just happened?

We have imported a single image of an angel monkey, which is now available to use in our game.

Our first step was to delete the existing `Dead` monkey animation because we no longer needed it. We then created a new, blank animation into which we imported the image of the angel monkey that we had previously saved to disk.

Before selecting the file to import, we checked to ensure the **Scale** option of the imported image was **Standard (1x)** because we didn't want Stencyl to change the scale (size) of the image for us. Stencyl has the ability to output games designed for mobile devices with very high-resolution screens, such as the iPad retina display, so we can import images that have been created at a very high resolution, and Stencyl will scale them for us as required. However, the images that we are using have been designed for use in our lower-resolution game, so we are importing them at their original scale. For more information about image scaling, review the relevant topic at `www.stencyl.com/help`.

Finally, we changed the name of the animation from the default of `Animation 7` to `Angel`.

 Thanks to Conrad of `www.omgparticle.com` for designing the angel actor, which is based on an original image created by Vicki Wenderlich of `www.vickiwenderlich.com` and made available under the Creative Commons Attribution license.

Understanding Stencyl's animation terminology

Although we've already used animations within our game, it's probably a good idea to review the terminology relating to animations within Stencyl.

In Stencyl, an **animation** is a collection of all the information required to be able to display a particular **state** for our actor. For example, our monkey actor has eight different animations, or states, that are listed below:

◆ Angel
◆ Idle Left
◆ Idle Right
◆ Jump Left
◆ Jump Right
◆ Run Left
◆ Run Right
◆ Waiting

The information contained in each animation includes the individual **frames** that make up the animation and collision shape information, together with some additional animation settings that can be configured as required.

Animation frames

Each animation must contain one or more frames — the individual images that are used to give the impression of movement within an animation. For example, our monkey actor has an animation called `Run Left`, which contains two separate frames as shown in the following screenshot:

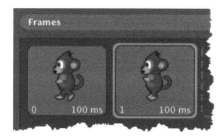

We can see that, in each frame, in addition to an image, there are two other pieces of information. The number shown at the lower-left corner of each frame is the frame number, and the number in the lower-right corner is the duration for which each frame will be shown before moving onto the next frame. In our example, the frames are numbered 0 and 1, and the duration of each frame is 100 milliseconds, or one-tenth of a second.

Frame timings can be adjusted by double-clicking on the frame and changing the duration in the **Edit Frame** dialog box. Lowering the duration makes the animation appear to run more quickly, and increasing the duration makes the animation appear to run more slowly.

Animation settings

In the Animation Editor, we can see that there are various properties that we can specify for each animation, as shown in the following screenshot:

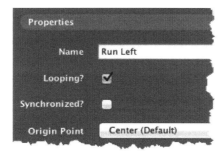

Name

We have already made use of the first option, **Name**, which allows us to specify an easily recognizable name for each animation. While it is often tempting to leave the default name in place, for example, Animation 1, it is good practice to always provide a relevant name, even if the actor has only a single animation. This will help us to easily identify a specific animation within the Animation Editor, but it is also useful to be able to refer to an animation, by name, from within our behaviors' instruction blocks, as we'll learn later in this chapter in the section entitled, *Using instruction blocks to control animations*.

Note that the animations are ordered alphabetically in the **Animations** panel. However, if the name of an animation is changed, the list will not be reordered until the Animation Editor for the actor is closed and then reopened. Currently, our Angel animation appears at the end of the list of animations because we have just created it.

Pressing *Ctrl + R* (*Command + R* on Mac OS X) refreshes (saves and reloads) all the open tabs. Doing this right now will save and reload the **Stencyl Book Monkey** tab, thus placing the monkey animations in alphabetical order. Try it!

Looping

The second option shown in the above screenshot is **Looping?**, which allows us to specify whether or not the frames are shown repeatedly — looping back to the first frame after the final frame has been displayed. If we remove the check mark from this option, the animation will display each frame only once, and will then stop on the final frame. Our Run Left animation has two frames, which we would like to display repeatedly, so the **Looping?** option is checked for this animation. If there is only one frame within an animation, then this option will have no effect!

Synchronized

The **Synchronized?** option ensures that every instance of the same actor within a scene will display the same animation frames simultaneously. For example, if we have a power-up in our game, which is represented by a spinning coin, then checking the **Synchronized?** option will make all the coins spin in time with each other.

Origin Point

The final option available to us in the **Properties** section of the Animation Editor is **Origin Point**. In *Chapter 4, Creating Behaviors*, we learned that the origin point of an actor is the point around which it will rotate. The origin point is also used by Stencyl to position the actor at its x and y coordinates, and to determine when an actor has left the screen or scene.

By default, the origin point of an actor is set at its center, but if required, we can change the origin point to another location on the animation, by selecting an option from the drop-down list.

Default animation

The default animation is the animation that will initially be displayed when the actor appears in a scene when the game is running. The first frame of the default animation is the frame that will be displayed when the actor is placed into a scene during editing with the Scene Editor.

Our monkey's default animation is Waiting and, if we look at this animation's icon in the **Animations** panel, we can see that a star, shown as follows, denotes its default status:

When we play our game, we might notice that the monkey's Idle Right animation is displayed, and not the default Waiting animation as specified in the Animation Editor. This is because the monkey's Jump and Run Movement behavior immediately displays the Idle Right animation before players of our game can see the default Waiting animation.

In our current game, the default animation is not relevant, but the first animation we create for an actor will always be set as the default animation, and one animation for each actor must be specified as the default.

If we need to specify a different animation as the default, we can click on the icon for the animation in the **Animations** panel of the Animation Editor, then click the **Set as Default Animation** button at the bottom of the left-hand panel, as highlighted in the previous screenshot.

Have a go hero

Currently, each of the frames for the monkey's Run Left and Run Right animations has a display duration of 100 ms.

Experiment to see if the visualization of the movement of the monkey in the game can be improved by changing the duration of the frames.

Also, try changing the default animation for the monkey and note that regardless of which animation we select as the default, it will make no difference when the game is played because the Jump and Run Movement behavior immediately changes it!

Importing a ready-made sprite sheet

A **sprite sheet** or **image strip**, is a single graphics file that contains all the frames required for a single Stencyl animation, an example of which is shown as follows:

Let's import this sprite sheet into our game.

Time for action – importing a sprite sheet

The game file to import and load for this session is 5961_05_02.stencyl.

Before proceeding with the following steps, we must ensure that we have downloaded the file 5691_05_06_blinking_statue_sheet.png from this book's download page on the Packt Publishing web site at www.packtpub.com, and have saved it into a folder on our hard disk so that we can easily locate it when required:

1. Open the **Stencyl Book Statue** actor in the Animation Editor so that we can see the single animation of the statue.

2. Click on the **Create Animation** button, represented by the + (plus) symbol, at the bottom of the **Animations** panel.

3. In the **Animations** panel, click on the red warning triangle icon for the new Animation 1.

4. In the main panel, in the **Properties** section, change the animation's **name** to Blinking Statue.

5. Ensure that the **Looping?** option has a check mark in the box.

6. Leave all the other animation settings as they are.

7. In the **Frames** section of the main panel, click on the **Click here to add a frame** icon to display the **Import Frames from Image Strip** dialog box.

8. Ensure that the **Scale** option at the upper center of the dialog box is set to **Standard (1x)**.

9. Click on the **Choose Image…** button.

10. Locate the image file `5691_05_blinking_statue_sheet.png` that we downloaded and saved at the start of this session, and double-click on it to open it.

11. Change the **Columns** setting to `8`, and ensure that **Rows** is currently set to `1`.

12. Click on the **Add** button to complete the import.

13. In the left-hand panel, click on the icon for `Animation 0`.

14. Click on the **Remove Animation** button at the bottom of the **Animations** panel.

15. Test the game; watch the statues blink!

What just happened?

We have imported a sprite sheet containing a series of frames for our statue's animation, and when we tested the game, we should have seen that our statue repeatedly opened and closed its eyes very quickly.

The animation doesn't look quite right yet, but we'll be making some adjustments to the frame durations in the next section, *Time for action – modifying the animation's frame durations*.

Our first step was to create a new empty animation in the Animation Editor, but because there were no frames, a default warning triangle was used as the icon for the new animation. Once the new animation had been created, we renamed it, and we also ensured that the **Looping?** option was checked, so that the animation will repeatedly display all the frames for the statue.

We then moved on to importing the image strip into the Animation Editor — it was important at this point to ensure that we had the **Scale** option set to **Standard (1x)**, so that Stencyl did not attempt to rescale the image. In the **Import Frames from Image Strip** dialogue box, we set **Columns** to `8` and checked that **Rows** was set to `1`. We chose these numbers because our image strip is configured with eight images horizontally, but only one row. It is possible to import image strips that are configured as a grid with multiple rows and columns; we just have to enter the correct information when importing the image strip!

If necessary, we could also have changed the **X Spacing**, **Y Spacing**, **X Border**, and **Y Border** settings in the dialog box, depending on how the individual images were presented in the graphics file; for example, some image strips include gaps or borders around each frame, which need to be removed prior to use in Stencyl's Animation Editor.

Finally, after confirming the new animation's settings, we removed the old statue animation named `Animation 0` because we no longer needed it. Note that our new `Blinking Statue` animation is now the default animation for the statue actor; when there is only a single animation, it is always the default.

We can now clearly see the eight statue images that have been combined to create the blinking animation of the statue!

 The author's Blinking Statue image strip is based on an original image created by Vicki Wenderlich of www.vickiwenderlich.com, made available under the Creative Commons Attribution license.

Fine-tuning an animation's frame durations

Having tested our game, we have seen that the statue is opening and closing its eyes, but it is doing it very quickly, which looks rather manic! We'd like to present the statue actor to our players as a sleepy, mysterious character. So let's make some changes to the statue's frame durations.

Time for action – modifying an animation's frame durations

The game file to import and load for this session is 5961_05_03.stencyl.

1. Ensure that we can see the new frames for the Blinking Statue animation by clicking on the **Dashboard** tab, then selecting **Actor Types** and double-clicking on the **Stencyl Book Statue** icon.

2. In the **Animations** panel, note that we can see the miniature animation for the Blinking Statue looping through each frame very quickly.

3. In the main panel, double-click on the statue with frame number **0** (zero) to open the **Edit Frame** dialog box.

4. Change **Duration (in milliseconds)** from 100 to 1000.

5. Click on the **OK** button.

6. In the **Animations** panel, note that we can immediately see the change in the statue's frame duration for the frame that we changed.

7. Change the duration of frame number **4** to 1000.

8. Test the game!

What just happened?

We have changed the display duration for two specific frames within the animation.

Firstly, we modified frame **0** to have a duration of 1000 milliseconds, which is equal to one second, and then we repeated the process for frame **4**.

As soon as we closed the **Edit Frame** dialog box by clicking the **OK** button, the miniature representation of the animation in the **Animations** panel was updated, so that we could see how our changes had affected the animation.

Because we were only modifying two of the frames, it was a quick process to change them one at a time. However, if we need to change multiple consecutive frames, we can click on the first frame in the sequence, hold the *Shift* key on the keyboard, and then click on the last frame in the sequence, which will select the series of frames. We can then click on the **Edit Frame** button at the lower-center of the screen to display the **Edit Duration (Multiple Frames)** dialog box. At this point, we can enter a new duration for all of the selected frames, and they will all be updated immediately when the **OK** button is clicked.

Have a go hero

The game file to import and load for this session is `5961_05_04.stencyl`.

We've changed the frame duration for frames **0** and **4**, and we have also learned how to select and modify the duration of multiple consecutive frames.

Have a go at using these skills to make the statue open its eyes slowly once, then close them again before it fades away.

It may take some experimentation to get the timing just right, so be patient. When the task is complete, ask someone to provide feedback on whether or not they think the effect is successful.

Editing animation frames

All the images that we have used in our game have been provided for us. Some of them were downloaded from StencylForge in earlier chapters and in this chapter, we have imported a single frame for use in an animation (the angel monkey). We have also imported an image strip that contains eight ready-made images, which were converted into a single animation.

In Stencyl, it is possible to create new frames or edit existing frames using the provided graphics package called `Pencyl`. While Pencyl is a basic graphics creation and editing software package, it has some useful features for making minor edits to an image, and can be used in the event when a more sophisticated graphics package is unavailable. Pencyl is also useful if we just need to make a quick modification to an existing image, without waiting for large, complex graphics software to load.

Let's have a look at how we can edit an existing image with Pencyl!

Time for action – editing an existing frame with Pencyl

The game file to import and load for this session is 5961_05_05.stencyl.

Note that, when using the Pencyl graphics editor, hovering the mouse cursor over any of the tools in the toolbar will display a tooltip detailing the name of the tool.

1. Display the **Stencyl Book Snake** actor in the Animation Editor; the snake actor has only one animation, with a single frame.

2. In the main panel, in the **Frames** section, the first and only frame for the snake actor should be highlighted with an orange border; if it is not, click on frame **0** to select it.

3. Locate the **Edit Frame (External)** button at the bottom of the main panel and click on it. Be sure not to click on the **Edit Frame** button; that's the option for changing frame durations!

4. In a few moments, the Pencyl image editor will be displayed on the screen with the snake actor in the editing window.

5. Click on Zoom Tool, represented by a magnifying-glass icon, in the toolbar at the left edge of the screen.

6. With Zoom Tool selected, click in the gray area of the snake's fangs.

7. Click on the Dropper tool in the toolbar.

8. Click on the light gray area of one of the fangs.

9. Click on the Pencil tool in the toolbar.

10. Using the Pencil tool, click to paint the fangs, so that they appear longer, as shown in the following image:

11. If required, use the Undo feature to correct any mistakes by selecting **Edit | Undo** on Pencyl's main menu, or use the shortcut keys *Ctrl + Z*, or *Command + Z* on Mac OS X.

12. In Pencyl's main menu, click on **File | Save**.

13. Click on **File | Quit**.

14. When Pencyl quits, observe that the changes to the snake's fangs are immediately represented in the frame's icon in the main Animation Editor panel.

What just happened?

We have used the Pencyl image editor to make a modification to the snake actor's graphic.

Clicking the **Edit Frame (External)** button in the Animation Editor automatically loaded the snake actor's graphic into the Pencyl graphics editor.

We then zoomed into the image to allow us finer control over the changes, and used the Dropper tool to select the color of the snake's fangs. Once the correct color had been selected, we used the Pencil tool to make the fangs longer.

Finally, saving the changes and quitting Pencyl automatically updated the actor's image within Stencyl's Animation Editor.

Using an alternative graphics tool

Some Stencyl users may wish to use an alternative graphics tool — perhaps one with which they are more familiar, or which provides more advanced features than Pencyl.

Time for action – changing the default graphics editor

Note that this section is optional, and is only achievable if an alternative graphics editor is available on the computer on which Stencyl is installed.

We can specify an alternative graphics editor using the following steps:

1. Click on **File | Preferences** (**Stencyl | Preferences** on Mac OS X).
2. In the **Preferences** dialog box, click on the **Editors** icon.
3. In the **Image Editor** section, click on the current setting, **Pencyl (Built-In Editor)** and select **Choose Application...** from the drop-down menu.
4. Use the displayed file browser to locate the preferred graphics editor and double-click on the filename of the application.
5. The location and name of the new graphics application will now be shown in the **Image Editor** section of the **Preferences** dialog box.
6. Click on **Apply Changes** to return to confirm the settings.

What just happened?

We have changed the default settings in Stencyl so that the graphics editor of our choice will now be used whenever we use the **Edit Frame (External)** option within the Animation Editor.

Note that, the settings in the **Preferences** dialog box are all global settings; they will affect how Stencyl works every time we use it and not just for the current game!

Have a go hero

We have used several of the Animation Editor's features in this chapter, but there are several other useful, time-saving tools available to us.

Take this opportunity to become familiar with the other option buttons at the bottom of the main panel in the Animation Editor, and consider how they could help speed up the process of creating multiframe animations.

Using instruction blocks to control animations

We have learned that each actor can have several animations that are used to represent the actor's various states within a game. Often, only one animation is required, such as the single animation for the Blinking Statue. However, in many cases, several animations are required, and we need to know how to tell Stencyl which animation should be used at a particular point in the game.

Our monkey actor has eight different animations to represent the states of running, jumping, standing still, and so on, and earlier in this chapter, we added a new single-frame animation called Angel, which will be used to show the player that the monkey actor has died.

Let's see how we can instruct Stencyl to display a different animation for our monkey actor.

Time for action – switching animations with instruction blocks

The game file to import and load for this session is 5961_05_06.stencyl.

1. Ensure that the Health actor behavior is displayed on the screen — click on the **Dashboard** tab, then click on **Actor Behaviors**, and double-click on the **Health** behavior's icon in the main panel.

2. Click on the **+ Add Event** button at the top of the left-hand panel.

3. Select **Advanced**, and then **Custom Event**.

4. Rename the new **Custom Event** to Show Angel in the left-panel.

5. In the new event's **when ... happens** block, enter the text ShowAngel (note that there is no space).

6. In the instruction block palette, click on the **Behavior** section button, then click on the **State** category button.

7. Drag the **Enable behavior text for Self** instruction block into the orange **when ShowAngel happens** block.

8. In the new **Enable behavior ... for Self** block, click on **Enable** and change it to **Disable**.

9. In the same block, click on the drop-down arrow after the word **behavior**, select **Behavior Names** in the pop-up menu, then select **J | Jump and Run Movement**.

10. Drag another **Enable behavior text for Self** instruction block from the palette and drop it below the one that we just added.

11. Change **Enable** to **Disable** and using the drop-down menu, change the empty textbox to `Manage Player Collisions`.

12. Click on the **Actor** section button in the palette, and then click on the **Draw** category button.

13. Locate the **switch animation to anim attribute for Self** block, and drag it beneath the **Disable behavior Manage Player Collisions for Self** block.

14. In the **switch animation to** block, type `Angel` in the text box.

15. In the palette, under **Scene | Game Flow**, locate the **Fade Out for 0 secs, then reload and Fade In for 0 secs** block and drag it underneath the **switch animation to Angel for Self** block. Be certain to select the correct block from the palette in this step; there is another similarly-named block in the same subcategory!

16. In the red block that we just added, enter the number 1 in the text box after the words **Fade out for**.

17. Enter the number 1 in the text box after the words **Fade in for**.

18. Ensure that the new **Show Angel** custom event looks like the following screenshot:

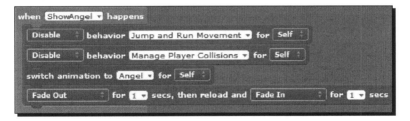

19. In the left-hand panel, click on the title of the **Countdown expired** event to display the **do every 1 seconds** instructions.

20. Right-click on the **kill Self** block and select **Remove** from the drop-down menu.

21. In the **Behavior | Triggers** section of the palette, locate the **trigger event text in behavior text for Self** block, and drag it into the orange **if** block.

22. Enter the text `ShowAngel` (without spaces) in the textbox after the words **trigger event**.

23. Click on the drop-down arrow in the textbox after the word **behavior**, and select **Behavior Names | H | Health** from the pop-up menu.

24. Ensure that the updated **Countdown expired** event looks like the following screenshot:

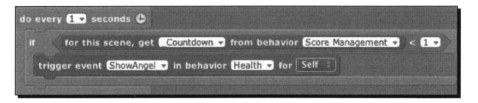

25. Test the game. Wait for the countdown to reach zero while watching the monkey actor.

What just happened?

We have created a new custom event that switches to the monkey's Angel animation, and is triggered when the countdown timer expires.

Our new custom event utilizes two new instruction blocks that we haven't used previously in our game. The first block that we introduced, in the Show Angel event, disables the Jump and Run Movement behavior, and we need to do this for two reasons: firstly, to prevent the player from continuing to control the monkey after the countdown has completed, and secondly, because the Jump and Run Movement behavior continuously updates the monkey actor. If we failed to disable the movement behavior, it would automatically switch from the Angel animation, straight back to one of the monkey's idle animations, before we even had time to see the Angel animation onscreen! We also added a block to disable the Manage Player Collisions behavior. When the countdown expires, we don't want the player to be able to collect any items, which could happen if the monkey was falling down towards one of the collectibles just as the countdown expired. Disabling this behavior will also prevent the monkey switching to the Angel animation if it falls onto an enemy at the same moment the countdown expires.

Note that we don't need to reenable the behaviors at any time, because we are reloading the scene, which puts the behaviors back into their original enabled state.

Beneath the blocks to disable the behaviors, we introduced a **switch animation to ... for Self** block. This block allows us to specify which animation we want to display, and we must supply the exact name of the animation, as it appears in the Animation Editor, including any capitalization and spaces.

The last step in creating our custom event was to add the instruction to fade out the scene and reload it. Reloading a scene puts it back to how it was right at the start of the game – it is completely reset as though it has never been played. This is the desired behavior for our game – when the countdown expires, the player must restart the scene. Don't worry; we'll be increasing the countdown to a more achievable value, later in the development process!

As we learned in Chapter 4, *Creating Behaviors*, custom events must be triggered so they can carry out the required actions. We placed the trigger instruction into the existing `Countdown expired` event that checks every one second to determine if the countdown has reached zero. Originally, when the countdown reached zero, we simply killed the monkey, so we had to remove the `kill Self` block before inserting the `trigger event...` instruction.

Have a go hero

We have used the `switch animation to` instruction, which we found in the **Animation** subcategory of the **Actor | Draw** section of the palette.

There are several other instruction blocks in the **Animation** subcategory that can be used in behaviors to find information about and control animations associated with a particular actor.

Review these instruction blocks and consider how they might be useful when developing a game, remembering that right-clicking on any block and selecting **View | Help** will display some useful information.

Implementing tweening with instruction blocks

So far, in this chapter, we have learned about managing an actor's animations with the Animation Editor, and also how to select specific animations using instruction blocks from the palette.

We are now going to learn about some of the instruction blocks that can be used to change how actors appear to players of our game. Although these are not strictly tools relating to Stencyl's animation features, they do relate to the way in which we can instruct Stencyl to manipulate the way actors appear on the screen.

Time for action – using the grow instruction block

The game file to import and load for this session is `5961_05_07.stencyl`.

1. Ensure that the **Manage Player Collisions** behavior is displaying the `Collides with Collectibles` event; click on the **Dashboard** tab, select **Actor Behaviors**, and double-click on the **Manage Player Collisions** icon in the main panel.

2. Holding the *Shift* key on the keyboard, drag the **fade out of group over 0.25 sec using None** block and drop it onto the icon of the trashcan at the upper-right of the center panel. Only the blue block should move during this process. If the other blocks are dragged with the blue block, place the blocks into their original position, release the *Shift* key, and try again!

3. In the **Actor | Tweening** category of the instruction-block palette, locate the **grow self to (w: 0%, h: 0%) over 0 sec using None** block and drag it, so that it snaps into place above the orange **do after 0.25 seconds** block.

4. Drag the blue **... of group** block from the **when Self hits a ... of Collectibles** block, and drop it onto the word **Self** in the new **grow** block.

5. In the new blue block enter 0 into the **w:** textbox and 0 into the **h:** textbox.

6. Enter 0.5 in the textbox that appears after the word **over**.

7. In the orange **do after 0.25 seconds** block, change the timing to 0.5 seconds.

8. Ensure that the **Collides with Collectibles** event now looks like the previous screenshot and then test the game; move the monkey so that it collides with some collectibles.

What just happened?

We have modified the `Collides with Collectibles` event in the `Manage Player Collisions` behavior so that the collectible items shrink away to nothing when the monkey collides with it.

Originally, when a collision occurred between the monkey and a collectible, the collectible would fade away, but we dragged the original `fade out...` block into the trashcan to remove it from the event. Holding down the *Shift* key when dragging a block ensures that only a single block is dragged.

We then located the `grow...` instruction block in the palette, dragged it into the event, and changed the timing of the grow effect to `0.5` seconds. The **w:** and **h:** textboxes in the `grow...` instruction specify the final width and height of the actor when the effect has completed. In our case, we set both the **w:** and **h:** settings to 0, because we want the actor to shrink so that it is no longer visible. If we needed an actor to grow, we could specify the final **w:** and **h:** sizes to be greater than 100 percent; for example, setting the size to 200 percent would make the actor grow to twice its original size.

The final step was to modify the timing in the `kill... of group` block, so that the actor will not be removed from the scene until the grow effect has completed.

Have a go hero

We have now used both a `fade...` block (which we have now removed) and a `grow...` block in our game.

Experiment with the grow effect option (currently set to `None`) and the timings of the `grow...` block in the `Collides with Collectibles` event, remembering also to change the timing of the `do after...` block.

Also, take this opportunity to review the available **Tweening** blocks in the palette, and consider how they may be used to make interesting special effects in our game. We've only touched on how to use the effects that are available to us, so go ahead and try various combinations of effects; some will look great, and some may be a little over-the-top, but have some fun while learning!

Summary

In the first part of this chapter, we learned how to import images from a graphics file into an actor's animation. We found that we can import either a single image into a frame, or we can specify a sprite sheet that contains several images, and import it into a series of frames for an actor's animation.

We also learned how to use Stencyl's built-in graphics editor, Pencyl, to make changes to existing frames in an animation, and we then looked at how we can change the preferences in Stencyl, so that our preferred graphics editor could be used instead.

The next step in learning about using animations in Stencyl was to change an existing behavior, so that it switched to the actor animation of our choice just at the right time. We then moved on to implement one of the tweening effects available to us in the instruction block palette.

Although we haven't made any major changes to our game in this chapter, we have learned some very important features that can make a game far more visually interesting for our players.

In *Chapter 6, Managing Information*, we're going to learn how to manage lives, keep score, and display useful information for players of our game.

6

Managing and Displaying Information

The gameplay mechanics are in place, we've added some nice visual effects, and our game is starting to look great, but there is still an important element missing; players of our game have no indication of how they are progressing. We need to let our players know how well (or badly) they are doing, otherwise there will be no incentive for them to continue playing the game!

There are many different pieces of information that might be useful to a player during gameplay, but we need to be careful not to overwhelm them, otherwise they'll be distracted from the game. Currently, we are keeping track of the time that is available for the player to complete the task of collecting all the fruit, but we're also going to be adding a count of the lives that the player has left.

In order to present this information to the player, we need to display it on the screen, but we're not only going to implement text messages for our players to read — we're also going to introduce a graphical method of displaying some of the information.

We'll also be monitoring how many lives the player has remaining, and because we'll be creating additional levels for the game in Chapter 7, Polishing the Game, we must also keep track of the current level.

The last piece of information that we will need to work with is how many pieces of fruit have been collected; we need to know when players of our game have successfully completed a level!

In order to realize these goals, in this chapter, we'll be doing the following:

- Displaying a countdown timer on the screen
- Configuring fonts
- Creating a game attribute to count lives
- Using graphics to display information
- Counting collected actors
- Keeping track of the levels

Prior to continuing with the development of our game, let's take a little time out to review what we have achieved so far, and also to consider some of the features that our game will need before it can be published.

A review of our progress

The gameplay mechanics are now complete; we have a controllable character in the form of a monkey, and we have some platforms for the monkey to jump on and traverse the scene.

We have also introduced some enemy actors, the croc and the snake, and we have Aztec statues falling from the sky to create obstacles for the monkey. Finally, we have the fruit, all of which must be collected by the monkey in order to successfully complete the level.

With regards to the scoring elements of the game, we're currently keeping track of a countdown timer (displayed in the debug console), which causes the scene to completely restart when the monkey runs out of time. When the monkey collides with an enemy actor, the scene is not reloaded, but the monkey is sent back to its starting point in the scene, and the timer continues to countdown.

Planning ahead – what else does our game need?

With the gameplay mechanics working, we need to consider what our players will expect to happen when they have completed the task of collecting all the fruits. As mentioned in the introduction to this chapter, our plan is to create additional, more difficult levels for the player to complete!

We also need to consider what will happen when the game is over; either when the player has succeeded in collecting all the fruits, or when the player has failed to collect the fruits in the allocated time. The solution that we'll be implementing in this game is to display a message to advise the player of their success or failure, and to provide options for the player to either return to the main menu, or if the task was completed successfully, continue to the next level within the game.

We'll be creating the introduction screen and additional levels in *Chapter 7, Polishing the Game*, but first, we need to implement a structure so that the game can keep track of information, such as how many lives the player has left and which level of the game is currently being played.

Let's put some information on the screen so that our players can keep track of the countdown timer.

Displaying a countdown timer on the screen

In *Chapter 4, Creating Behaviors*, we created a new scene behavior called Score Management, which contains the **Decrement Countdown** event, shown as follows:

Currently, as we can see in the previous screenshot, this event decrements the Countdown attribute by a value of 1, every second.

We also have a debug print instruction that displays the current value of Countdown in the debug console to help us, as game developers, keep track of the countdown. However, players of the game cannot see the debug console, so we need to provide an alternative means of displaying the amount of time that the player has to complete the level.

Let's see how we can display that information on the screen for players of our game.

Time for action – displaying the countdown timer on the screen

The game file to import and load for this session is 5961_06_01.stencyl.

1. Ensure that the **Score Management** scene behavior is visible: click on the **Dashboard** tab, select **Scene Behaviors**, and double-click on the **Score Management** icon in the main panel.

2. Click **+ Add Event | Basics | When Drawing**.

3. Double-click on the title of the new **Drawing** event, and rename it to Display Countdown.

4. Click on the **Drawing** section button in the instruction block palette.

5. Drag a **draw text anything at (x: 0 y: 0)** block into the orange **when drawing** event block in the main panel.

6. Enter the number `10` into the **x:** textbox and also enter `10` into the **y:** textbox.

7. Click on the drop-down arrow in the textbox after **draw text** and select **Text | Basics**. Then click on the **text & text** block.

8. In the first textbox in green, **... & ...** block, enter the text `COUNTDOWN:` (all uppercase, followed by a colon).

9. In the second textbox, after the **&** symbol, click on the drop-down arrow and select **Basics**, then click on the **anything as text** block.

10. Click on the drop-down arrow in the **... as text** block, and select **Number | Attributes | Countdown**.

11. Ensure that the new **Display Countdown** event looks like the following screenshot:

12. Test the game.

What just happened?

When the game is played, we can now see in the upper-left corner of the screen, a countdown timer that represents the value of the Countdown attribute as it is decremented each second.

First, we created a new Drawing event, which we renamed to Display Countdown, and then we added a `draw text anything at ( x: 0 y: 0 )` block, which is used to display the specified text in the required location on the screen.

We set both the **x:** and **y:** coordinates for displaying the drawn text to `10` pixels, that is, 10 pixels from the left-hand side of the screen, and 10 pixels from the top of the screen.

The next task was to add some text blocks that enabled us to display an appropriate message along with the value of the Countdown attribute. The `text & text` block enables us to concatenate, or join together, two separate pieces of text. The Countdown attribute is a number, so we used the `anything as text` block to convert the value of the Countdown attribute to text to ensure that it will be displayed correctly when the game is being played.

In practice, we could have just located the `Countdown` attribute block in the **Attributes** section of the palette, and then dragged it straight into the `text & text` block. However, it is best practice to correctly convert attributes to the appropriate type, as required by the instruction block. In our case, the `number` attribute is being converted to text because it is being used in the text concatenation instruction block. If we needed to use a text value in a calculation, we would convert it to a number using an `anything as number` block.

Configuring fonts

We can see, when testing the game, that the font we have used is not very interesting; it's a basic font that doesn't really suit the style of the game!

Stencyl allows us to specify our own fonts, so our next step is to import a font to use in our game.

Time for action – specifying a font for use in our game

The game file to import and load for this session is `5961_06_02.stencyl`.

Before proceeding with the following steps, we need to locate the `fonts-of-afrika\ Afritubu.TTF` file in this chapter's code files, which can be downloaded from the Packt Publishing website at `www.packtpub.com`.

Place the file in a location where it can easily be located, and continue with the following steps:

1. In the **Dashboard** tab, click on **Fonts**.
2. In the main panel, click on the box containing the words **This game contains no Fonts. Click here to create one**.
3. In the **Name** textbox of the **Create New...** dialog box, type `HUD Font` and click on the **Create** button.
4. In the left-hand panel, click on the **Choose...** button next to the **Font** selector.
5. Locate the file `Afritubu.TTF` and double-click on it to open it.
6. Note that the main panel shows a sample of the new font.
7. In the left-hand panel, change the **Size** option to `25`.
8. Important: save the game!
9. Return to the **Display Countdown** event in the **Score Management** scene behavior.
10. In the instruction block palette, click on the **Drawing** section button and then the **Styles** category button.

11. Drag the **set current font to Font** block above the **draw text** block in the **when drawing** event.

12. Click on the **Font** option in the **set current font to Font** block, and select **Choose Font** from the pop-up menu.

13. Double-click on the **HUD Font** icon in the **Choose a Font...** dialog box.

14. Test the game. Observe the countdown timer at the upper-left corner of the game.

What just happened?

We can see that the countdown timer is now being displayed using the new font that we have imported into Stencyl, as shown in the following screenshot:

The first step was to create a new blank font in the Stencyl dashboard and to give it a name (we chose HUD Font), and then we imported the font file from a folder on our hard disk.

Once we had imported the font file, we could see a sample of the font in the main panel. We then increased the size of the font using the **Size** option in the left-hand panel. That's all we needed to do in order to import and configure a new font in Stencyl! However, before progressing, we saved the game to ensure that the newly imported font will be available for the next steps.

With our new font ready to use, we needed to apply it to our countdown text in the Display Countdown behavior. So, we opened up the behavior and inserted the **set current font to Font** style block. The final step was to specify which font we wanted to use, by clicking on the **Font** option in the font style block, and choosing the new font, **HUD Font**, which we configured in the earlier steps.

 Heads-Up Display (HUD) is often used in games to describe either text or graphics that is overlaid on the main game graphics to provide the player with useful information.

Using font files in Stencyl

Stencyl can use any **TrueType** font that we have available on our hard disk (files with the extension TTF); many thousands of fonts are available to download from the Internet free of charge, so it's usually possible to find a font that suits the style of any game that we might be developing. Fonts are often subject to copyright, so be careful to read any licensing agreements that are provided with the font file, and only download font files from reliable sources. For more information about locating game resources, see *Appendix, Planning, Resources & Legal Issues*.

Have a go hero

The game file to import and load for this session is `5961_06_03.stencyl`.

When we imported the font into Stencyl, we specified a new font size of `25`, but it is a straightforward process to modify further aspects of the font style, such as the color and other effects.

Click on the **HUD Font** tab to view the font settings (or reopen the Font Editor from the **Dashboard** tab) and experiment with the font size, color, and other effects to find an appropriate style for the game. Take this opportunity to learn more about the different effects that are available, referring to Stencyl's online help if required.

Remember to test the game to ensure that any changes are effective and the text is not difficult to read!

Creating a game attribute to count lives

Currently, our game never ends. As soon as the countdown reaches zero, the scene is restarted, or when the monkey collides with an enemy actor, the monkey is repositioned at the starting point in the scene. There is no way for our players to lose the game! In some genres of game, the player will never be completely eliminated; effectively, the same game is played forever. But in a platform game such as ours, the player typically will have a limited number of chances or lives to complete the required task.

In order to resolve our problem of having a never-ending game, we need to keep track of the number of lives available to our player. So let's start to implement that feature right now by creating a **game attribute** called `Lives`!

Time for action – creating a Lives game attribute

The game file to import and load for this session is `5961_06_03.stencyl`.

1. Click on the **Settings** icon on the Stencyl toolbar at the top of the screen.
2. In the left-hand panel of the **Game Settings** dialog box, click on the **Attributes** option.
3. Click on the green **Create New** button.
4. In the **Name** textbox, type `Lives`.
5. In the **Category** textbox, change the word **Default** to `Scoring`.
6. In the **Type** section, ensure that the currently selected option is **Number**.
7. Change **Initial Value** to `3`.
8. Click on **OK** to confirm the configuration.
9. We'll leave the **Game Settings** dialog box open, so that we can take a closer look.

What just happened?

We have created a new game attribute called `Lives`. If we look at the rightmost panel of the **Game Settings** dialog box that we left open on the screen, we can see that we have created a new heading entitled **SCORING**, and underneath the heading, there is a label icon entitled **Lives**, as shown in the following screenshot:

The **Lives** item is a new game attribute that can store a number. The category name of **SCORING** that we created is not used within the game. We can't access it with the instruction blocks; it is there purely as a memory aid for the game developer when working with game attributes. When many game attributes are used in a game, it can become difficult to remember exactly what they are for, so being able to place them under specific headings can be helpful.

Using game attributes

The attributes we have used so far, such as the `Countdown` attribute that we created in the `Score Management` behavior, lose their values as soon as a different scene is loaded, or when the current scene is reloaded. Some game developers may refer to these attributes as **local** attributes, because they belong to the behavior in which they were created. Losing its value is fine when the attribute is just being used within the current scene; for example, we don't need to keep track of the countdown timer outside of the Jungle scene, because the countdown is reset each time the scene is loaded.

However, sometimes we need to keep track of values across several scenes within a game, and this is when game attributes become very useful.

Game attributes work in a very similar manner to local attributes. They store values that can be accessed and modified, but the main difference is that game attributes keep their values even when a different scene is loaded. Currently, the issue of losing attribute values when a scene is reloaded is not important to us, because our game only has one scene. However, when our players succeed in collecting all the fruits, we want the next level to be started without resetting the number of lives. So we need the number of lives to be remembered when the next scene is loaded.

We've created a game attribute called `Lives`, so let's put it to good use.

Time for action – decrementing the number of lives

The game file to import and load for this session is `5961_06_04.stencyl`.

1. If the **Game Settings** dialog box is still open, click on **OK** to close it.

2. Open the **Manage Player Collisions** actor behavior.

3. Click on the **Collides with Enemies** event in the left-hand panel.

4. Click on the **Attributes** section button in the palette.

5. Click on the **Game Attributes** category button.

6. Locate the purple **set Lives to 0** block under the **Number Setters** subcategory and drag it into the orange **when** event so that it appears above the red **trigger event RestartLevel in behavior Health for Self** block.

7. Click on the drop-down arrow in the **set Lives to ...** block and select **0 - 0** in the **Math** section.

8. In the left textbox of the **... - ...** block, click on the drop-down arrow and select **Game Attributes | Lives**.

9. In the right-hand textbox, enter the digit `1`.

10. Locate the **print anything** block in the **Flow** section of the palette, under the **Debug** category, and drag it below the **set Lives to Lives – 1** block.

11. In the **print ...** block, click on the drop-down arrow and select **Text | Basics | text & text**.

12. In the first empty textbox, type `Lives remaining:` (including the colon).

13. Click on the drop-down arrow in the second textbox and select **Basics | anything as text**.

14. In the **... as text** block, click on the drop-down arrow and select **Number | Game Attributes | Lives**.

15. Ensure that the **Collides with Enemies** event looks like the following screenshot:

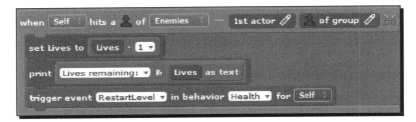

16. Test the game; make the monkey collide with an enemy actor, such as the croc, and watch the debug console!

What just happened?

We have modified the `Collides with Enemies` event in the `Manage Player Collisions` behavior so that it decrements the number of lives by one when the monkey collides with an enemy actor, and the new value of `Lives` is shown in the debug console.

This was achieved by using the purple game attribute setter and getter blocks to set the value of the `Lives` game attribute to its current value minus one. For example, if the value of `Lives` is 3 when the event occurs, `Lives` will be set to 3 minus 1, which is 2!

The `print` ... block was then used to display a message in the console, advising how many lives the player has remaining. We used the `text & text` block to join the text `Lives remaining:` together with the current value of the `Lives` game attribute. The `anything as text` block converts the numeric value of `Lives` to text to ensure that it will display correctly.

Currently, the value of the `Lives` attribute will continue to decrease below 0, and the monkey will always be repositioned at its starting point. So our next task is to make something happen when the value of the `Lives` game attribute reaches 0!

No more click-by-click steps!

From this point onwards, click-by-click steps to modify behaviors and to locate and place each instruction block will not be specified! Instead, an overview of the steps will be provided, and a screenshot of the completed event will be shown towards the end of each *Time for action* section.

The search facility, at the top of the instruction block palette, can be used to locate the required instruction block; simply click on the search box and type any part of the text that appears in the required block, then press the *Enter* key on the keyboard to display all the matching blocks in the block palette.

Time for action – detecting when Lives reaches zero

The game file to import and load for this session is `5961_06_05.stencyl`.

1. Create a new scene called `Game Over` — Select the **Dashboard** tab, select **Scenes**, and then select **Click here to create a new Scene**. Leave all the settings at their default configuration and click on **OK**.

2. Close the tab for the newly created scene.

3. Open the **Manage Player Collisions** behavior and click on the **Collides with Enemies** event to display the event's instruction blocks.

4. Insert a new **if** block under the existing `print` block.

5. Modify the **if** block to if **Lives > 0**.

6. Move the existing block, **trigger event RestartLevel in behavior Health for Self** into the **if Lives > 0** block.

7. Insert an **otherwise** block below the **if Lives > 0** block.

8. Insert a **switch to Scene and Crossfade for 0 secs** block inside the **otherwise** block.

9. Click on the **Scene** option in the new block, then click on **Choose Scene** and select the **Game Over** scene.

10. Change the **secs** textbox to `0` (zero).

11. Ensure that our modified **Collides with Enemies** event now looks like the following screenshot:

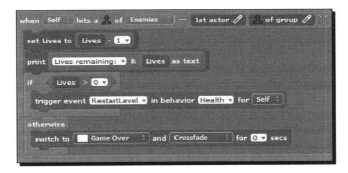

12. Test the game; make the monkey run into an enemy actor, such as the croc, three times.

What just happened?

We have modified the `Collides with Enemies` event so that the value of the `Lives` game attribute is tested after it has been decremented, and the game will switch to the `Game Over` scene if the number of lives remaining is less than zero.

If the value of `Lives` is greater than zero, the `RestartLevel` event in the monkey's `Health` behavior is triggered. However, if the value of `Lives` is not greater than zero, the instruction in the `otherwise` block will be executed, and this switches to the (currently blank) `Game Over` scene that we have created.

If we review all the instructions in the completed `Collides with Enemies` event, and write them in English, the statement will be:

When the monkey collides with an enemy, reduce the value of Lives by one and print the new value to the debug console. Then, if the value of Lives is more than zero, trigger the RestartLevel event in the monkey's Health behavior, otherwise switch to the Game Over scene.

Before continuing, we should note that the `Game Over` scene has been created as a temporary measure to ensure that as we are in the process of developing the game, it's immediately clear to us (the developer) that the monkey has run out of lives. In *Chapter 7, Polishing the Game*, we'll be introducing a more appropriate and visually appealing game over message for our players!

Have a go hero

The game file to import and load for this session is `5961_06_06.stencyl`.

- Change the `Countdown` attribute value to `30` — open the Jungle scene, click on the **Behaviors** button, then select the **Score Management** behavior in the left panel to see the attributes for this behavior.

 The following tasks in this *Have a go hero* session are optional — failure to attempt them will not affect future tutorials, but it is a great opportunity to put some of our newly learned skills to practice!

In the section, *Time for action – displaying the countdown timer on the screen*, we learned how to display the value of the countdown timer on the screen during gameplay.

Using the skills that we have acquired in this chapter, try to complete the following tasks:

- Update the `Score Management` behavior to display the number of lives at the upper-right corner of the screen, by adding some new instruction blocks to the `Display Counter` event.
- Rename the `Display Counter` event to `Display HUD`.
- Remove the `print Countdown` block from the `Decrement Countdown` event also found in the `Score Management` behavior.

 Right-click on the instruction block and review the options available in the pop-up menu!

- Remove the `print Lives remaining: & Lives as text` instruction block from the `Collides with Enemies` event in the `Manage Player Collisions` behavior.

 The suggested modifications along with comments can be viewed in the downloadable files that accompany this book, in the file named `5961_06_07.stencyl`.

Removing debug instructions

Why did we remove the debug `print` ... blocks in the previous *Have a go hero* session? Originally, we added the debug blocks to assist us in monitoring the values of the `Countdown` attribute and `Lives` game attribute during the development process. Now that we have updated the game to display the required information on the screen, the debug blocks are redundant!

While it would not necessarily cause a problem to leave the debug blocks where they are, it is best practice to remove any instruction blocks that are no longer in use. Also, during development, excessive use of debug print blocks can have an impact on the performance of the game; so it's a good idea to remove them as soon as is practical.

Using graphics to display information

We are currently displaying two on-screen pieces of information for players of our game: the countdown timer and the number of lives available. However, providing too much textual information for players can be distracting for them, so we need to find an alternative method of displaying some of the information that the player needs during gameplay.

Rather than using text to advise the player how much time they have remaining to complete the level, we're going to display a timer bar on the screen.

Time for action – displaying a timer bar

The game file to import and load for this session is `5961_06_07.stencyl`.

1. Open the **Score Management** scene behavior and click on the **Display HUD** event.

2. In the **when drawing** event, right-click on the blue block that draws the text for the countdown timer and select **Activate / Deactivate** from the pop-up menu. Note that the block becomes faded.

3. Locate the **draw rect at (x: 0 y: 0) with (w: 0 h: 0)** instruction block in the palette, and insert it at the bottom of the **when drawing** event.

4. Click on the **draw** option in the newly inserted block and change it to **fill**.

5. Set both the **x:** and **y:** textboxes to `10`.

6. Set the width (**w:**) to **Countdown x** `10`.

7. Set the height (**h:**) to `10`.

8. Ensure that the **draw text ...** block and the **fill rect at ...** block in the **Display HUD** event appear as shown in the following screenshot (the **draw text LIVES: ...** block may look different if the earlier *Have a go hero* section was attempted):

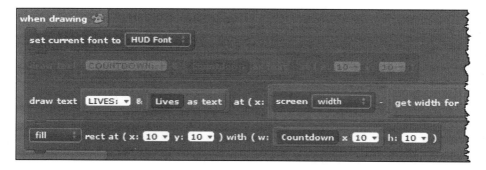

9. Test the game!

What just happened?

We have created a timer bar that displays the amount of time remaining for the player to collect the fruit, and the timer bar reduces in size with the countdown!

First, in the **Display HUD** event we deactivated, or disabled, the block that was drawing the textual countdown message, because we no longer want the text message to be displayed on the screen.

The next step was to insert a `draw rect` ... block that was configured to create a filled rectangle at the upper-left corner of the screen and with a width equal to the value of the `Countdown` timer multiplied by `10`. If we had not multiplied the value of the countdown by `10`, the timer bar would be very small and difficult to see (try it)!

We'll be making some improvements to the timer bar later in this chapter.

Activating and deactivating instruction blocks

When we deactivate an instruction block, as we did in the **Display HUD** event, it no longer functions; it's completely ignored! However, the block remains in place, but is shown slightly faded, and if required, it can easily be reenabled by right-clicking on it and selecting the **Activate / Deactivate** option.

Being able to activate and deactivate instruction blocks without deleting them is a useful feature — it enables us to try out new instructions, such as our timer bar, without having to completely remove blocks that we might want to use in the future. If, for example, we decided that we didn't want to use the timer bar, we could deactivate it and reactivate the `draw text ...` block!

 Deactivated instruction blocks have no impact on the performance of a game; they are completely ignored during the game compilation process.

Have a go hero

The game file to import and load for this session is `5961_06_08.stencyl`.

 The tasks in this *Have a go hero* session are optional; failure to attempt them will not affect future tutorials.

Referring to Stencyl's online help if required at `www.stencyl.com/help/`, try to make the following improvements to the timer bar:

◆ Specify a more visually appealing color for the rectangle

◆ Make it thicker (height) so that it is easier to see when playing the game

◆ Consider drawing a black border (known as a **stroke**) around the rectangle

◆ Try to make the timer bar reduce in size smoothly, rather than in big steps

Ask an independent tester for feedback about the changes and then modify the timer bar based on the feedback.

 To view *suggested* modifications together with comments, review the `Display HUD` event in the downloadable files that accompany this book. The file that contains the modifications suggested above is named `5961_06_09.stencyl`.

Counting collected actors

With the number of lives being monitored and displayed for the player, and the timer bar in place, we now need to create some instructions that will enable our game to keep track of how many of the fruit actors have been collected, and to carry out the appropriate action when there is no fruit left to collect.

Time for action – counting the fruit

The game file to import and load for this session is `5961_06_09.stencyl`.

1. Open the **Score Management** scene behavior and create a new number attribute (not a game attribute) with the configuration shown in the following screenshot (in the block palette, click on **Attributes**, and then click on **Create an Attribute...**).

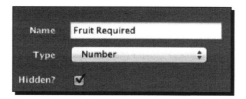

2. Add a new **when created** event and rename it to `Initialize Fruit Required`.

3. Add the required instruction blocks to the new **when created** event, so the `Initialize Fruit Required` event appears as shown in the following screenshot, carefully checking the numbers and text in each of the blocks' textboxes:

4. Note that the red **of group** block in the **set actor value ...** block cannot be found in the palette; it has been dragged into place from the orange **for each ... of group Collectibles** block.

5. Test the game and look for the **Fruit required** message in the debug console.

What just happened?

Before we can create the instructions to determine if all the fruit have been collected, we need to know how many fruit actors there are to collect. So we have created a new event that stores that information for us in a number attribute called `Fruit Required` and displays it in the debug console.

We have created a `for each ... of group Collectibles` block. This very useful **looping** block will repeat the instructions placed inside it for each member of the specified group that can be found in the current scene. We have specified the `Collectibles` group, and the instruction that we have placed inside the new loop is `increment Fruit Required by 1`. When the loop has completed, the value of the `Fruit Required` attribute is displayed in the debug console using a `print ...` block. When constructing new events, it's good practice to insert `print ...` blocks so we can be confident that the instructions achieve the results that we are expecting. When we are happy that the results are as expected, perhaps after carrying out further testing, we can remove the debug printing from our event.

We have also introduced a new type of block that can set a value for an actor; in this case, we have `set actor value Collected for ... of group to false`. This block ensures that each of the fruit actors has a value of `Collected` that is set to `false` each time the scene is loaded; remember that this instruction is inside the `for each ...` loop, so it is being carried out for every `Collectible` group member in the current scene.

Where did the actor's `Collected` value come from? Well, we just invented it! The `set actor value ...` block allows us to create an arbitrary value for an actor at any time. We can also retrieve that value at any time with a corresponding `get actor value ...` block, and we'll be doing just that when we check to see if a fruit actor has been collected in the next section, *Time for action – detecting when all the fruit are collected*.

Translating our instructions into English, results in the following statement:

> *For each actor in the Collectibles group, that can be found in this scene, add the value 1 to the Fruit Required attribute and also set the actor's Collected value to false. Finally, print the result in the debug console.*

Note that the `print ...` block has been placed after the `for each ...` loop, so the message will not be printed for each fruit actor; it will appear just once, after the loop has completed!

If we wish to prove to ourselves that the loop is counting correctly, we can edit the **Jungle** scene and add as many fruit actors as we wish. When we test the game, we can see that the number of fruit actors in the scene is correctly displayed in the debug console. We have designed a flexible set of instructions that can be used in any scene with any number of fruit actors, and which does not require us (as the game designer) to manually configure the number of fruit actors to be collected in that scene! Once again, we have made life easier for our future selves!

Now that we have the attribute containing the number of fruit to be collected at the start of the scene, we can create the instructions that will respond when the player has successfully collected them all.

Time for action – detecting when all fruits have been collected

The game file to import and load for this session is `5961_06_10.stencyl`.

1. Create a new scene called `Level Completed`, with a **Background Color** of yellow. Leave all the other settings at their default configuration.

2. Close the tab for the newly created scene.

3. Return to the **Score Management** scene behavior, and create a new custom event by clicking on **+ Add Event | Advanced | Custom Event**.

4. In the left-hand panel, rename the custom event to `Fruit Collected`.

5. Add the required instruction blocks to the new **Fruit Collected** event, so it appears as shown in the following screenshot, again carefully checking the parameters in each of the text boxes:

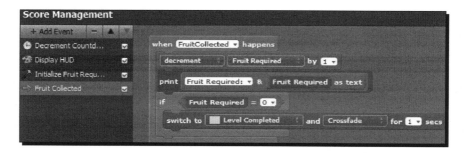

6. Note that there is no space in the **when FruitCollected happens** custom event name.

7. Save the game and open the **Manage Player Collisions** actor behavior.

8. Modify the `Collides with Collectibles` event so it appears as shown in the following screenshot. The changes are listed in the subsequent steps:

9. A new **if get actor value Collected for ... of group = false** block has been inserted.

10. The existing blocks have been moved into the new **if ...** block.

11. A **set actor value Collected for ... of group to true** block has been inserted above the **grow ...** block.

12. A **trigger event FruitCollected in behavior Score Management for this scene** block has been inserted above the **do after 0.5 seconds** block.

13. An **if ... of group is alive** block has been inserted into the **do after 0.5 seconds** block, and the existing **kill ... of group** block has been moved inside the newly added **if ...** block.

14. Test the game; collect several pieces of fruit, but not all of them!

15. Examine the contents of the debug console; it may be necessary to scroll the console horizontally to read the messages.

16. Continue to test the game, but this time collect all the fruit actors.

What just happened?

We have created a new Fruit Collected event in the Score Management scene behavior, which switches to a new scene when all the fruit actors have been collected, and we have also modified the Collides with Collectibles event in the Manage Player Collisions actor behavior in order to count how many pieces of fruit remain to be collected.

When testing the game we can see that, each time a piece of fruit is collected, the new value of the Fruit Required attribute is displayed in the debug console, and when all the fruit actors have been collected, the yellow Level Completed scene is displayed.

The first step was to create a blank Level Completed scene, which will be switched to when all the fruit actors have been collected. As with the Game Over scene that we created earlier in this chapter, it is a temporary scene that enables us to easily determine when the task of collecting the fruit has been completed successfully for testing purposes.

We then created a new custom event called Fruit Collected in the Score Management scene behavior. This custom event waits for the FruitCollected event trigger to occur, and when that trigger is received, the Fruit Required attribute is decremented by 1 and its new value is displayed in the debug console. A test is then carried out to determine if the value of the Fruit Required attribute is equal to zero, and if it is equal to zero, the bright yellow, temporary Level Completed scene will be displayed!

Our final task was to modify the `Collides with Collectibles` event in the `Manage Player Collisions` actor behavior. We inserted an `if...` block to test the collectible actor's `Collected` value; remember that we initialized this value to `false` in the previous section, *Time for action – counting the fruit*. If the `Collected` value for the fruit actor is still `false`, then it hasn't been collected yet, and the instructions contained within the `if` ... block will be carried out. Firstly, the fruit actor's `Collected` value is set to `false`, which ensures that this event cannot occur again for the same piece of fruit. Next, the `FruitCollected` custom event in the `Score Management` scene behavior is triggered. Following that, the `do after 0.5 seconds` block is executed, and the fruit actor will be killed.

We have also added an `if ... of group is alive` check that is carried out before the collectible actor is killed. Because we are killing the actor after a delay of `0.5` seconds, it's good practice to ensure that the actor still exists before we try to kill it! In some games, it may be possible for the actor to be killed by other means during that very short `0.5` second delay, and if we try to kill an actor that does not exist, a **runtime error** may occur, that is, an error that happens while the game is being played. This may result in a technical error message being displayed to the player, and the game cannot continue; this is extremely frustrating for players, and they are unlikely to try to play our game again!

Preventing multiple collisions from being detected

A very common problem experienced by game designers, who are new to Stencyl, occurs when a collision between two actors is repeatedly detected. When two actors collide, all collision events that have been created with the purpose of responding to that collision will be triggered repeatedly until the collision stops occurring, that is, when the two actors are no longer touching. If, for example, we need to update the value of an attribute when a collision occurs, the attribute might be updated dozens or even hundreds of times in only a few seconds!

In our game, we want collisions between the monkey actor and any single fruit actor to cause only a single update to the `Fruit Required` attribute. This is why we created the actor value `Collected` for each fruit actor, and this value is initialized to be `false`, not collected, by the `Initialize Fruit Required` event in the `Score Management` scene behavior. When the `Collides with Collectibles` event in `Manage Player Collisions` actor behavior is triggered, a test is carried out to determine if the fruit actor has already been collected, and if it has been collected, no further instructions are carried out. If we did not have this test, then the `FruitCollected` custom event would be triggered numerous times, and therefore the `Fruit Required` attribute would be decremented numerous times, causing the value of the `Fruit Required` attribute to reach zero almost instantly; all because the monkey collided with a single fruit actor!

 Using a Boolean value of `True` or `False` to carry out a test in this manner is often referred to by developers as using a **flag** or **Boolean flag**.

Note that, rather than utilizing an actor value to record whether or not a fruit actor has been collected, we could have created a new attribute and initialized and updated the attribute in the same way that we initialized and updated the actor value. However, this would have required more effort to configure, and there is no perceptible impact on performance when using actor values in this manner. Some Stencyl users never use actor values (preferring to always use attributes instead), however, this is purely a matter of preference and it is at the discretion of the game designer which method to use.

In order to demonstrate what happens when the actor value `Collected` is not used to determine whether or not a fruit actor has been collected, we can simply deactivate the `set actor value Collected for … of group to true` instruction block in the `Collides with Collectibles` event. After deactivating the block, run the game with the debug console open, and allow the monkey to collide with a single fruit actor. The `Fruit Required` attribute will instantly be decremented multiple times, causing the level to be completed after colliding with only one fruit actor!

 Remember to reactivate the `set actor value` … block before continuing!

Keeping track of the levels

As discussed in the introduction to this chapter, we're going to be adding an additional level to our game, so we'll need a method for keeping track of a player's progress through the game's levels.

Time for action – adding a game attribute to record the level

The game file to import and load for this session is `5961_06_11.stencyl`.

1. Create a new number game attribute called `Level`, with the configuration shown in the following screenshot:

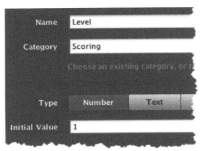

2. Save the game.

What just happened?

We have created a new game attribute called `Level`, which will be used to record the current level of the game.

A game attribute is being used here, because we need to access this value in other scenes within our game; local attributes have their values reset whenever a scene is loaded, whereas game attributes' values are retained regardless of whether or not a different scene has been loaded.

We'll be putting this game attribute to good use in *Chapter 7, Polishing the game*!

Fixing the never-ending game!

We've finished designing and creating the gameplay for the Monkey Run game, and the scoring behaviors are almost complete. However, there is an anomaly with the management of the `Lives` game attribute. The monkey correctly loses a life when it collides with an enemy actor, but currently, when the countdown expires, the monkey is simply repositioned at the start of the level, and the countdown starts again from the beginning!

If we leave the game as it is, the player will have an unlimited number of attempts to complete the level — that's not much of a challenge!

Have a go hero

The game file to import and load for this session is `5961_06_12.stencyl`.

> The recommended tasks in this *Have a go hero* session should be attempted, as *Chapter 7, Polishing the Game*, relies on some of these modifications.
>
> Suggested solutions together with comments, can be found in the `Health` and `Manage Player Collisions` behaviors in the download file named `5961_06_13.stencyl`.

- (Recommended) In the `Countdown expired` event, which is found in the `Health` actor behavior, modify the test for the countdown so that it checks for the countdown timer being exactly equal to zero, rather than the current test, which is for the `Countdown` attribute being less than 1. We only want the `ShowAngel` event to be triggered once when the countdown equals exactly zero!

- (Recommended) Update the game so that the `Show Angel` event manages the complete process of losing a life, that is, either when a collision occurs between the monkey and an enemy, or when the countdown timer expires. A single event should deduct a life and restart the level.

◆ (Optional) If we look carefully, we can see that the countdown timer bar starts to grow backwards when the player runs out of time! Update the `Display HUD` event in the `Score Management` scene behavior, so that the timer bar is only drawn when the countdown is greater than zero.

There are many different ways to implement the above modifications, so take some time and plan the recommended modifications!

Test the game thoroughly to ensure that the lives are reduced correctly and the level restarts as expected, when the monkey collides with the enemy, and when the countdown expires. It would certainly be a good idea to review the download file for this session, compare it with your own solutions, and review each event carefully, along with the accompanying comment blocks. There are some useful tips in the example file, so do take the time to have a look!

Summary

Although our game doesn't look vastly different from when we started this chapter, we have made some very important changes.

First, we implemented a text display to show the countdown timer, so that players of our game can see how much time they have remaining to complete the level. We also imported and configured a font and used the new font to make the countdown display more visually appealing.

We then implemented a system of tracking the number of lives that the player has left, and this was our first introduction to learning how game attributes can store information that can be carried across scenes.

The most visible change that we implemented in this chapter was to introduce a timer bar that reduces in size as the countdown decreases. Although very few instruction blocks were required to create the timer bar, the results are very effective, and are less distracting for the player than having to repeatedly look to the top of the screen to read a text display.

The main challenge for players of our game is to collect all the fruit actors in the allocated time, so we created an initialization event to count the number of fruit actors in the scene. Again, this event has been designed to be reusable, as it will always correctly count the fruit actors in any scene. We also implemented the instructions to test when there are no more fruit actors to be collected, so the player can be taken to the next level in the game when they have completed the challenge. A very important skill that we learned while implementing these instructions was to use actor values as Boolean flags to ensure that collisions are counted only once.

Finally, we created a new game attribute to keep track of our players' progress through the different levels in the game, and we'll be using this game attribute in *Chapter 7, Polishing the Game*, where we'll also be adding the finishing touches to our game!

7

Polishing the Game

We now have a gameplay framework in place for our Monkey Run game, which means that the game is playable, and the scoring mechanisms are in place.

We have also introduced a system whereby the player can succeed in completing the one and only level in the game, at which point a temporary success scene is displayed. Alternatively, the player can fail the level and will be presented with a temporary game over scene.

With these elements in place, we have completed the main part of the game development process, and we can now concentrate on applying the finishing touches to make the game presentable and ready to publish for the world to see!

We'll be adding some polish to the gameplay in this chapter, but a game also needs many features that are outside the scope of gameplay. We need to consider what players will see immediately after the game has loaded. We'll also need to think about what players will experience when they are transitioning between levels and when they have completed the game.

By the end of this chapter, we will have implemented the above elements, and we'll have completed our game with the exception of audio, which we'll be introducing in *Chapter 8, Implementing Sounds*.

Let's look at the tasks that we'll be completing in this chapter—the tasks that will take us through to completion of the visual aspects of our game.

We will be:

◆ Adding a background and foreground

◆ Creating a visual special effect

◆ Creating additional levels

◆ Adding a pause feature

◆ Implementing a level progression routine

◆ Creating a Game Over message

◆ Creating a Main Menu scene

◆ Finalizing the game-completed scene

Let's start polishing!

Adding a background and foreground

Currently, the colors in our game are themed appropriately—jungle greens and browns—but the background is looking rather plain. So let's brighten up our game with a more realistic jungle scene.

Time for action – adding a background to the Jungle scene

The game file to import and load for this session is `5961_07_01.stencyl`.

Before proceeding, locate the file entitled `jungle_background_1920x480.png`, which is provided with the downloadable files that accompany this book, and place it in a folder so that it can be easily located.

1. In the **Dashboard** tab, click on **Backgrounds**.

2. In the main panel, click inside the dotted box containing the text **This game contains no Backgrounds. Click here to create one**.

3. In the **Create New...** dialog box, enter a name of **Jungle Background** and then click on the **Create** button.

4. In the left-hand panel, click on **Create here to add a frame**.

5. In the **Add Frame** dialog box, ensure that the **Scale** option is set to **Standard (1x)**.

6. Click on the **Choose Image...** button.

7. Locate the file `jungle_background_1920x480.png` and double-click on it.

8. When the jungle image appears in the **Add Frame** dialog box, click on the **Add** button and wait a few moments for the thumbnail of the image to appear in the left-hand panel.

9. Open the **Jungle** scene (via the **Dashboard** tab).

10. Click on the **Background** button in the row of buttons at the upper-center of the screen:

11. In the **Backgrounds** section in the left-hand panel, click on the **+** button:

12. In the **Choose a Background** dialog box, double-click on the thumbnail for the **Jungle Background** image.

13. Test the game and make the monkey run along the scene so the screen scrolls.

What just happened?

We have added a jungle-themed background to the Jungle scene and we can see that, as the monkey runs along the scene, the background scrolls in time with the camera, giving the impression of movement through the jungle:

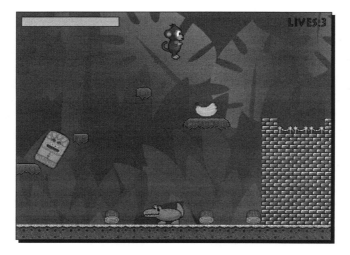

Adding a background requires two main steps. Firstly, we needed to create a new background by importing an image file. In our case, we selected the file that had been provided with the downloadable files for this book.

Once we had imported the background into our game, we then opened the Jungle scene, and specified which background to use.

 The background image for our jungle scene was created by Vicki Wenderlich (www.vickiwenderlich.com), and is available under the Creative Commons Attribution license. The original image has been cropped to meet the size requirements for our game.

Importing the image as a Stencyl background enables us to reuse it within any scene in our game without having to import it for each scene.

It is also useful to note that, although we imported an image as a background, which is displayed behind all the other elements in the scene, it is also possible to import an image as a background and add it to our scene as a foreground that is displayed in front of all the other objects in a scene! This may appear to be a little confusing, but if we want to add a foreground to our game, we must first import it using the **Backgrounds** panel in the **Dashboard** tab—we then add it to our scene as a foreground. For example, we could have a foreground of jungle flora.

Have a go hero

The game file to import and load for this session is `5961_07_02.stencyl`.

An image file named `jungle_foreground_1920x480.png` has been provided for the jungle foreground, and this can be found in the downloadable files for this chapter.

Import and specify the image, `jungle_foreground_1920x480.png`, as a background, then add it as a foreground for the Jungle scene.

The steps to complete this task are almost identical to those in the previous section, *Time for action – adding a background to the Jungle scene*. However, note that the terminology can be a little confusing because as discussed in the previous *What just happened* section, even when we want to add a foreground to a scene, we still have to import it as a new background!

The important differences are to ensure that the correct filename is selected for the image file, and when adding the new foreground to the scene, add it as a foreground rather than a background (previous step 11)—at this step, look at the bottom half of the left-hand panel and add the jungle foreground!

Don't forget to test the game—note how the monkey runs behind the foreground flora, and that, although the tiles we placed for the floor of the jungle are now completely obscured, they are still doing the job of preventing the monkey from falling off the bottom of the scene!

 The results of this *Have a go hero* session can be seen in the download file `5961_07_03.stencyl`.

Viewing foregrounds and backgrounds in the Scene Editor

By default, when viewing a scene in the Scene Editor, background and foreground images are not displayed. Open up the Jungle scene in the Scene Editor right now, and have a look. The plain sea-green background is still visible, and our new jungle background and flora foreground are nowhere to be seen!

Having the foreground and background hidden can help us more easily work with the actors and tiles within the Scene Editor. However, if we do wish to preview the scene along with the foreground and background, we can do so quite easily.

If we look at the toolbar at the top-right of the **Scene Editor** panel, we can see some icons shown as follows:

The two icons highlighted in the previous screenshot are toggles that are used to display or hide the background and foreground respectively.

Using these tools enables us to edit the scene with or without being able to see the foreground or background, which is useful for previewing the completed scene and for assisting in placing actors and tiles appropriately using the editing tools. Click on these icons now to show and hide the foreground and background.

More about foregrounds and backgrounds

We are not using all the foreground and background features that are available to us in Stencyl as the static images work well for our game design. However, if required, it is very easy to implement **parallax** scrolling in a Stencyl game, so it is certainly worth investigating these features.

 Parallax scrolling is a special technique that scrolls the foreground and background images at different speeds to give an impression of greater depth to the scene.

Be sure to read the Stencyl help pages to learn more about the available foreground and background techniques that can be used in games. Judicious use of these effects can make a game shine!

We have now seen how the straightforward process of introducing an interesting static background into our game, along with a well-designed foreground, has really brought our game to life. It immediately looks more fun to play, and the foreground has provided the illusion of depth to the game.

It is design elements such as these that can make the difference between a game that is quite good (but which is only played once) and a game that players keep coming back to for more fun!

Creating a visual special effect

Although visual special effects don't necessarily make any difference to the gameplay, they can add further interest and immersion into the game for our players. We're going to add a very striking special effect into the game.

Making the ground shake

With just a few instruction blocks, we can make the jungle shake each time one of the stone statues "land"!

Time for action – making the ground shake

The game file to import and load for this session is `5961_07_03.stencyl`.

1. Open the **Manage Statues** actor behavior and create a new **When Creating** event.

2. Rename the new event to `Initialize statue`.

3. Add the instruction block to the new event, as shown in the following screenshot:

4. Create a new **When Updating** event and rename it to `Check if stopped`.

5. Add the required instruction blocks, so the new event looks like the following screenshot:

6. Create a new **When this actor collides with... Something Else** event and rename it to `Shake screen on collision`.

7. Modify the new collision event using the instruction blocks shown in the following screenshot:

8. Test the game; watch as the statues land on any object!

What just happened?

We have implemented the instructions to make the screen shake when a statue lands, either on a tile, such as the ground, or on an actor.

The instructions for this effect comprise of three separate parts. The first part required us to specify an actor value for the statue when it is created; remember that actor values will apply uniquely to each statue actor as it is created. We called the actor value `Stopped` and set it to `false`, because the actor is moving the instant it enters the scene. In other words, it has not stopped!

We then implemented the second part of the instructions in the statue's `when updating` event, which we renamed to `Check if stopped`. This section checks the x and y speed of the statue and if both are less than `0.1`, which effectively means that the statue is not moving, we set the actor value `Stopped` to be `true`.

Why don't we test for an x and y speed of zero? Due to the design of the physics engine that Stencyl uses, waiting for an actor to reach a speed of absolute zero can take a while (and sometimes never happens!), causing the screen to shake excessively.

Try changing the `Check if stopped` event to test for a speed of zero, retest the game and wait for several statues to fall. Don't forget to change the values back once the test is complete!

Finally, we created the third part; a `when this actor hits something else` event, which checks the status of the actor value, `Stopped`, and if it is `false`, the `shake screen...` block is executed.

If we write the instructions for all three parts in English, the result will be as follows:

> *When a statue actor is created, give it an actor value called Stopped, and set it to false. While the game is running, if the statue stops moving, set the value of Stopped to true. While the game is running, if the statue collides with anything, and its Stopped value is false, shake the screen.*

The implementation for the shaking effect might appear to be more complicated than required! Why do we need an actor value, and why do we need to check whether or not the statue has stopped moving?

The answer lies in how the collision detection works in Stencyl. When using the `when this actor hits something else` block or any other type of collision, a collision is occurring for the whole time when the two objects are touching. In the case of our statues, they might collide with a platform causing the screen to shake once, but then the statue might fall onto the tiles that represent the ground, and just lie there, apparently motionless. However, while the statue is lying on those tiles, a collision is still occurring, so the screen will shake continuously until the statue disappears. Such an effect will cause an eye-popping experience for players of our game, because there is always at least one statue onscreen at any time!

If we cast our minds back to *Chapter 6, Managing and Displaying Information*, when we implemented the instructions for counting the collected fruit in the section entitled *Counting collected actors*, we used an actor value as a Boolean flag to determine whether or not a fruit actor had been collected. This enabled us to ensure that each fruit actor was only collected once, thus avoiding an incorrect count. The use of the actor value, `Stopped`, in our new screen-shaking instructions follows the same principle. We are using the actor value as a flag to determine whether or not we still want the statue to cause the shaking effect.

To see what happens if we do not test the value of the `Stopped` actor value, we can carry out a basic test.

Temporarily change the `Shake screen on collision` event in the `Manage Statues` behavior, so it looks like the following blocks:

Now, if we test the game, we can clearly see the problem. The screen starts to shake as soon as a statue hits any object and it rarely stops shaking because there is almost always at least one statue colliding with another object!

Don't forget to revert to the correct code! If required, review the previous section *Time for action – making the ground shake*, step 7, to ensure that the correct instruction blocks are in place.

The instructions for making the screen shake work well, but there is definitely room for improvement. For example, test the game and when a statue lands on a platform and stops moving, make the monkey push the statue off the platform so the statue lands on the ground. It may take some time for a statue to fall in the right place to carry out this experiment but if we are patient, we will see that the screen does not shake when the statue collides with any other objects after being pushed by the monkey. This is because, after the statue lands on a platform and stops moving, the `Stopped` actor value is immediately set to `false`; the statue can never shake again!

Have a go hero

The game file to import and load for this session is `5961_07_04.stencyl`.

For our purposes, we may be happy with the way that the screen shaking is experienced by the user. However it will be an interesting challenge to improve the current effect:

◆   Consider how it might be possible to ensure that the statue does not shake the screen when it is stationary, but also reactivates its shaking ability if it is pushed or falls off a platform.

Please be aware that this is quite a difficult challenge, and there are numerous solutions! Be sure to save the game, and perhaps give the saved game a new name (**File | Save Game As...**), before attempting to modify the events. If things go terribly wrong (and sometimes things do go terribly wrong when experimenting), it's much easier to load an earlier version of the game, than it is to recreate the behavior!

As noted, this is a comparatively a difficult challenge; the game will work perfectly well as it is. There's no harm in skipping this challenge and returning to it at a later time if desired.

A suggested solution is provided in the download file `5961_07_05.stencyl`, along with comments in the `Check if stopped` and `Shake screen on collision` events of the `Manage Statues` actor behavior.

Creating additional levels

In *Chapter 6*, *Managing and Displaying Information*, we paved the way for creating additional levels by creating a temporary scene called `Level Completed`, which is displayed when all the fruit actors have been collected in the jungle scene.

In this section, we're going to create a second jungle scene for the player to progress to when the first scene has been completed successfully, and in the following Time for action section, in step 7, we will be designing a new level. Bear in mind the following points during the design and testing process:

◆ This is just a quick prototype level to enable us to progress with the game design

◆ Ensure that the green domes at each end of the level are kept in the same position in the new level

◆ For testing purposes, keep level 2 quite easy to complete within the allocated 30 seconds; it will make testing much easier

◆ If necessary, review *Chapter 2*, *Let's Make a Game!*, in which we learned how to use the scene editor tools

Time for action – renaming, duplicating, and modifying a level

The game file to import and load for this session is `5961_07_05.stencyl`.

1. In the **Dashboard** tab, click on **Scenes**, double-click on the **Jungle** scene, then click on the **Properties** button in the row of gray buttons at the upper-center of the screen.

2. Change the name of the scene to `Level1` (the word *Level* followed by the digit one, without any spaces).

3. Click on **OK** to confirm the change, then close the tab for the jungle scene (now called `Level1`).

4. In the **Scenes** panel, in the **Dashboard** tab, right-click on the jungle scene (now called `Level1`) and select **Duplicate** from the pop-up menu.

5. In the main panel, double-click on the **Copy of Level1** scene thumbnail to open the scene.

6. Click on the **Properties** button at the top of the Scene Designer, and rename the scene to `Level2` (the word *Level* followed by the digit two, without any spaces).

7. Make the desired changes to the new scene; add tiles and move tiles as required. Reposition the fruit, remembering that additional fruit actors can be added from the palette.

8. When the scene is ready do not test the game.

9. If we save the game, then look at the **Scenes** panel in the **Dashboard** tab (don't close the **Level2** tab), we should see the following configuration:

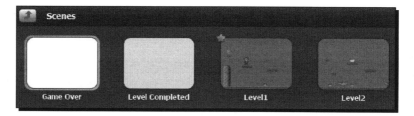

10. Switch back to the **Level2** tab, and click on the green **Test Scene** button found above the palette in the right-hand panel.

What just happened?

We've created a new jungle scene for our players to complete!

Firstly, we renamed our original jungle scene, so it is now called Level1. We then made a copy of Level1 using the **Duplicate** feature, and renamed the new scene to Level2. The final step was to modify the newly created scene, Level2, so that it presents a new challenge for our players. For testing purposes, we have ensured that the second level is not too difficult to complete, and this will enable us to continue with the development of the game without becoming too distracted by the small details relating to the challenges in the new scene.

It's important to understand that when we duplicate a scene, an exact copy of the scene is made with not only its tiles and actors, but also with all its behaviors! This is why the Drop actors randomly and Score Management behaviors work exactly as expected in the newly duplicated Level2 scene.

When testing the new scene, we took advantage of the **Test Scene** button, which enables us to test the scene that is currently being designed in the Scene Editor. This is an incredibly useful button; without it, we would have to play the whole game, starting with Level1 and successfully complete it, before we could test Level2. Testing our game in this manner would be a very tedious and time-consuming process with only two levels; imagine if our game had 10 levels to test!

Progressing through the levels

If we tested the game from the start, we would find that upon completion of Level1, the player would still be presented with the temporary **Level Completed** scene. Clearly, the desired action upon completion of scene Level1 is to allow the player to progress to Level2!

The good news is that we've already put much of the framework in place for this task. Firstly, in *Chapter 6*, *Managing information*, we created a game attribute for storing the current level, and secondly, we have recently given our two jungle scenes sensible names so that our game will be able to display them in the correct order.

Time for action – implementing level progression

The game file to import and load for this session is 5961_07_06.stencyl.

Remember to use the instruction block search facility if required; it's at the top of the palette!

1. Open the **Score Management** scene behavior.

2. Click on the **Fruit Collected** event in the left-hand panel, and modify the event by inserting a **set Level to…** instruction block (found in the palette under **Attributes | Game Attributes**) so that it looks like the highlighted blocks in the following screenshot:

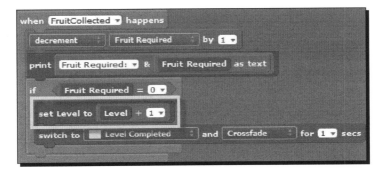

3. Modify the **switch to...** block so that the red **switch to...** block appears as shown in the highlighted section of the following screenshot:

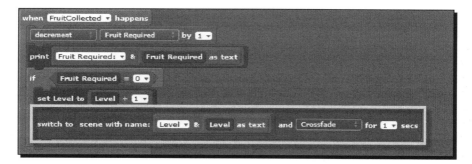

4. Review the previous steps 2 and 3 to ensure that the math plus block **... + ...** and the text concatenation block **... & ...** have been implemented as shown.

5. Switch back to the **Scenes** panel in the **Dashboard** tab, open the yellow **Level Completed** scene, and rename it to Level3 (no space).

6. Save the game (this is important!) and view the **Scenes** panel in the **Dashboard** tab. We should now see the following configuration:

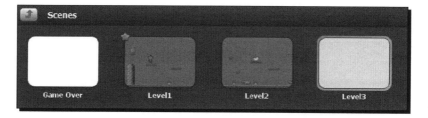

7. Test the game and play the first scene to completion by collecting all the fruit actors. Then, continue to play the game as it progresses through the scenes!

What just happened?

We have implemented the instructions that allow the player to progress through the scenes as each one is completed successfully.

Because we already have most of the game's framework in place, we didn't have much work to do! The main changes we have made take place inside the if Fruit Required = 0 block, because this is the routine that determines when all the fruit in a scene have been collected.

Our first step was to insert the `set Level to...` block and modify it, so that it increased the value of the game attribute `Level` by 1 when all the fruit has been collected. Once this instruction has been carried out, `Level` will be equal to the number of the next level that is to be played.

We then modified the existing `switch to...` scene block, so that instead of switching to a scene that we have hardcoded into the instructions, the scene name will be calculated at the time that the last piece of fruit has been collected. The scene name is calculated by taking the text **Level** and appending the text value of the `Level` game attribute using the text concatenation block.

The very last step was to rename the **Level Completed** scene (currently a temporary, blank yellow scene) to `Level3`. This ensures that when our final playable level (`Level2`) has been completed, the next scene to be displayed will be a scene that lets our player know that they have completed the game. Even though our game only has two playable levels, we need to create a `Level3`, so that the instructions have somewhere to take us when we have completed the second level. We could have given the yellow scene a more appropriate name, such as `All Levels Completed`, but this would have required more complex sequence of instructions. Sometimes, pragmatism can save a lot of development work!

It's great to see that the preparations we made in *Chapter 6*, *Managing and Displaying Information*, have now come to fruition (is that a terrible pun?) with the addition of a single instruction, and the modification of just one other instruction!

Adding even more levels

Because we have now completed all the hard work, and implemented a good design for the process of allowing the player to progress through levels, adding new game levels is now an incredibly easy process.

All we need to do is duplicate any scene that contains an existing level, and rename the new scene and the final, level completed scene, so that levels are numbered consecutively. We don't need to change any of the game instructions or make any other modifications to the design of the game!

An important point to note is that, when testing levels using the **Test Scene** button in the Scene Editor, on successfully completing the level, the game will not progress correctly through the later levels. This is because the game attribute `Level` is always set to a value of 1 when the game starts, even during the testing process. If we click on the **Test Scene** button to test, for example, a new `Level10`, the next level to be displayed on completion of that level will always be `Level2`!

Have a go hero

The game file to import and load for this session is `5961_07_07.stencyl`.

Have a go at adding a new level, just to prove how easy it is!

It is recommended that only one additional level is created for test purposes only; adding further levels at this stage of development will cause some additional work that can be avoided, as we'll discover later in this chapter!

As always, it's a good idea to test the game thoroughly, preferably obtaining input from independent testers.

Adding a pause feature

Currently, our player has no choice other than to play the whole game from start to finish without a break. While some games work in this way as a planned feature, this method of play is not appropriate for our game, so we're going to introduce a feature that will allow players to pause the game at any time.

Preparing the pause banner framework

Before implementing the instructions to pause the game, we're going to put an appropriate framework into place.

Time for action – creating the pause framework

The game file to import and load for this session is `5961_07_08.stencyl`.

1. Locate and download the actor called **Stencyl Book Paused Banner** from StencylForge.

2. When the **Stencyl Book Paused Banner** actor has downloaded, click on the **Physics** button in the row of buttons at the upper-center of the screen.

3. In the **General** section, which is currently displayed in the main panel, change the **What kind of actor type?** setting to **Cannot Move**.

4. Click on the **Advanced** icon at the top of the panel, and change the **Can be Paused?** setting to **No**.

5. Close the tabs for the **Stencyl Book Paused Banner** actor and **StencylForge**.

6. Create a new scene behavior called `Pause Management`.

7. Using the green **Attach to Scene** button at the upper-right corner of the screen, add the new behavior to the scene called **Level1**.

8. Switch back to the **Pause Management** behavior, then repeat step 7, attaching the behavior to **Level2** and **Level3** (but not **Level4**, which is the yellow, completed scene).

9. Close the tabs for **Level1**, **Level2**, and **Level3**.

10. In the new **Pause Management** behavior, create an actor attribute called `Paused Banner`, by clicking on the **Attributes** section button in the block palette, then the **Create an Attribute...** button below the category buttons. Ensure that the new attribute is configured with **Type** as **Actor** as shown in the following screenshot:

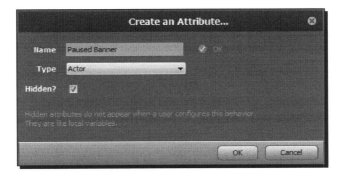

11. Add a new **when created** event to the **Pause Management** behavior and rename it to `Create Pause Banner`.

12. Add the required blocks to the newly created **when created** event, as shown in the following screenshot:

13. Do not test the game yet; we have some more work to do before the pause feature is ready!

What just happened?

We have put in place the framework for placing a pause message on the screen.

The first step was to download the **Paused Banner** actor from StencylForge; when we add the instructions for pausing the game, this message banner will be displayed so players of our game will have a clear indication that the game has been paused. Because we do not want the banner to move under any circumstances, we configured its **What kind of actor type?** setting to **Cannot Move**. Because by default, all actors are configured to pause when the game is paused, we have specified that the banner cannot be paused. This will ensure that the banner is displayed correctly when all the other actors in the scene have been paused.

We then created a new scene behavior called `Pause Management`, and we attached it to the three existing game levels, but not the scene named **Level4**. In the previous *Have a go hero* section, it was suggested that only one additional level should be added in order to avoid additional work later in the development process. Because we are still developing our game, we will almost certainly be adding additional scene behaviors that will be required for each of the game levels, and when we do add those behaviors, we must remember to add them to each and every level that already exists in the game. For this reason, it's a good idea to leave the design and creation of additional levels until the development process has been finalized. This allows us to simply duplicate existing levels along with all the behaviors that are attached to the original scene.

However, because we already have three levels in our game, the next step was to attach the new `Pause Management` behavior to each of those levels. We could have done this after completing the design of the events in this behavior, but it's a good idea to attach it as soon as the behavior has been created, so that we don't forget to do it at a later stage!

The next step was to create an actor attribute called `Paused Banner`, and this attribute will be used to store the instance of the `Stencyl Book Paused Banner` actor that we have just created, so that we can access it easily from any other events with the `Pause Management` behavior. We'll be accessing this attribute in the `when created` event.

We then added the required instructions to the `when created` event. The first block creates an instance of the `Stencyl Book Paused Banner` actor with an `x` and `y` position of zero.

The second instruction in the `when created` event, `set Paused Banner to Last Created Actor`, sets the value of the `Paused Banner` actor attribute that we created earlier, to the value of `Last Created Actor`, which must be the newly created `Stencyl Book Paused Banner`, because that actor was created in the immediately-preceding instruction block! This ensures that, as long as the scene is active, we can always easily refer to the banner using the `Paused Banner` actor attribute; without this attribute, it would be very difficult to access and make changes to the banner.

We then inserted an instruction to hide the banner actor that we just created; this ensures that it cannot be seen by the player when the scene is first displayed. Note that we have just hidden the banner actor, so it cannot be seen; we have not killed it, so we can now manipulate it as required!

Implementing the pause feature

Now that we have the framework in place, we can create the main pause routine.

Time for action – implementing the main pause routine

The game file to import and load for this session is `5961_07_09.stencyl`.

1. Click on the **Settings** button on Stencyl's main toolbar, then click on the **Controls** icon in the left-hand panel of the **Game Settings** dialog box.

2. Scroll to the bottom of the **Controls** panel and click on the **Click here to add a new control** box to display a new control as shown in the following screenshot:

3. Change the **Name** option of the control from **Key 0** to `pause`.

4. Click in the **Key** box (next to the letter **A**), and press the *P* key on the keyboard (it will display onscreen as a capital P).

5. Click on **OK** to confirm the changes and close the **Game Settings** dialog box.

6. In the **Pause Management** behavior, add a new keyboard event by clicking on **+ Add Event | Input | Keyboard**, then change the event name to `Pause clicked`.

7. Click on the **Control** option in the new **when Control is pressed** block and select **Choose Control | pause**, then click on **OK**.

8. Change the **pressed** option to **released**.

9. The empty input event block should now appear as shown:

10. Add the instructions to complete the new keyboard event, as shown in the following screenshot. Note that the **Paused Banner** option in the blue blocks in this event can be found by clicking on the **Actor** option that initially appears in these blocks and then selecting **Choose Attribute** from the pop-up menu:

11. Double-check to ensure that each of the options and numbers in the instruction blocks appear exactly as shown in the previous screenshot.

12. Test the game and press the *P* key on the keyboard to pause and resume the game!

What just happened?

We have created a routine that enables players of our game to pause and resume the game at any point!

Firstly, we created a new **control key** for pausing the game, using the **Controls** configuration panel in Stencyl's main **Game Settings** dialog box. Although it's quite a long process to explain in detail, it is simply a matter of creating a new control, giving it a friendly name to use in the game (in our case, we called it `pause`), and then specifying the keyboard key that will cause the control to trigger the input event (we chose the letter P). We can now refer to the control by name, anywhere in our game instructions, without having to remember which key we assigned to the control. It's interesting to note that we can assign more than one key to a single control, so we can offer more flexibility to players of our game; for example, many players prefer to use the *W*, *A*, *S*, and *D* keys for directional control within a game, rather than using the arrow keys.

We then added a new input event that is triggered when the player releases the pause control (which we have specified as being the *P* key on the keyboard). Although we could have specified for the event to be triggered when the key was pressed rather than when it is released, for this type of control, a better user experience is usually provided by detecting when the key is released. However, this is a matter of opinion, so experiment by changing the option to pressed, and make a decision as to which provides a better response from a player's point of view. Again, perhaps obtaining some feedback from other players might be appropriate!

Once we had created an event that will respond to a specific key press, we were able to add the important instructions that will manage the pausing and resuming of the game.

The instructions that we added into the when pause is released block are split into two sections.

The first section is enclosed in the if game is paused block, and these instructions are only carried out if the game is already paused—the sprite (another name for the actor's image) for the Paused Banner actor will be hidden, and then the game is resumed, or unpaused. The second section, enclosed in the otherwise block is only executed if the game is not paused. In this case, the game will be paused, the x and y positions for the Pause Banner actor will be set, and then the actor will be displayed with the Show sprite for Paused Banner instruction. Immediately prior to showing the banner, we used the Send Paused Banner to front block; this ensures that the banner will always appear in front of any other actors that are currently onscreen.

Let's have a closer look at the set x to ... and set y to ... instructions that we have placed in the otherwise block: the set x to ... block sets the x position of Paused Banner to the x of camera + 200 pixels. The figure of 200 pixels was manually calculated to ensure that the banner will appear in an approximately central horizontal position, based on the fixed width of the banner actor (which is approximately 95 pixels wide). We need to add x of camera to take account of the fact that the monkey may have been moved, thus causing the screen to scroll to the left or right. If we failed to take the camera position into account, then the banner would be displayed at 200 pixels from the left-hand edge of the scene, and not 200 pixels from the left-hand edge of the screen! The set y ... instruction is straightforward; it simply positions the banner 100 pixels from the top of the screen.

If we translate the Pause clicked event into English, it could be stated as follows:

When the pause control key is released, check if the game is already paused. If it is already paused, then hide the banner actor and resume the game. If the game is not paused, then pause the game, position the banner actor at the specified location, in front of all other actors, and show the banner actor.

Summary of the pause routine configuration

We can see that, in essence, the pause routine is relatively straightforward; we have been able to distil it into three sentences in the above English translation. However, it took us several steps to reach the point of having a fully-functioning pause feature, so let's review the steps that we took to create it. We did the following:

◆ Downloaded the banner actor from StencylForge

◆ Configured the physics settings for the banner actor

◆ Created the scene behavior and attached it to all the existing game levels

◆ Created an actor attribute for the banner actor

◆ Added an event to create and immediately hide the banner when the scene is created

◆ Configured the control key in the **Game Settings** dialog box

◆ Created a keyboard event that is triggered by the pause control key

◆ Inserted the instruction blocks to hide the banner and resume if the game is already paused

◆ Inserted the instructions to pause the game, and to position and show the banner if the game is not already paused

The previous points can now be used as a template for a pause feature in any game that we create!

Have a go hero

The game file to import and load for this session is `5961_07_10.stencyl`.

We now have a functioning pause feature that works very well. However, as always, there is room for improvement.

Remembering that we have hardcoded the positioning of the `Paused Banner` actor attribute in the `Pause clicked` event of the `Pause Management` behavior, consider what would happen to the positioning of the banner if we changed the height or width of the game's screen!

◆ Modify the instructions so that the positioning of the banner automatically takes into account the height and width of the screen.

◆ Consider that we might want to use a different size of banner; how could we ensure that it is always positioned appropriately regardless of size?

Note that this *Have a go hero* task is optional; the game will continue to function if the previous exercise is not completed.

A suggested solution is provided along with comments, in the download file `5961_07_11.stencyl`. The suggested modifications can be found in the `Pause Clicked` event of the `Pause Management` scene behavior.

Implementing a level progression routine

Although the transitioning between levels currently does its job quite well (the next level is automatically displayed when all the fruit has been collected), there is definitely room for improvement. The main problem with the current configuration is that the transition to the next level happens without any warning, so it would be a good idea to allow the player to pause and take a breath before continuing with the game.

We're going to implement a system that displays a message for the player, and which offers the opportunity to either progress to the next level or return to the main menu scene by clicking on the appropriate buttons. We haven't created the main menu scene yet, we'll be doing that later in this chapter!

Although implementing the success message is not difficult, it requires quite a few steps, so we'll break the process down into the following two *Time for action* sessions:

- Displaying the message and buttons
- Responding to the player's selection

Displaying the message and buttons

Let's start with a framework for displaying the message and buttons.

Time for action – displaying the message and buttons

The game file to import and load for this session is `5961_07_11.stencyl`.

1. Download the following three actors from StencylForge:

   - **Stencyl Book Success Banner**
   - **Stencyl Book Menu Button**
   - **Stencyl Book Next Button**

2. For each of the above three actors, change the two physics settings specifying that the actor cannot move and cannot be paused, then close the tabs for StencylForge and for each of the three actors.

3. Open the **Score Management** scene behavior and create three new `Hidden Actor` attributes with the following names:

- ❏ `Success Banner`
- ❏ `Menu Button`
- ❏ `Next Button`

4. Again, in the **Score Management** behavior, view the **Fruit Collected** event and deactivate the **set Level to...** and **switch to...** blocks (right-click and select **Activate / Deactivate**).

5. Immediately above the deactivated **set Level to...** block, insert a **trigger event ...** instruction block as shown in the following screenshot:

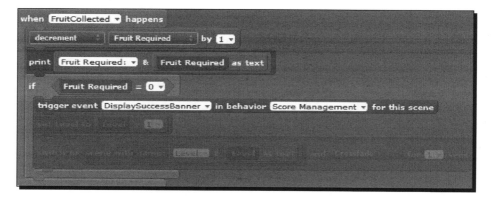

6. Add a new custom event to the **Score Management** behavior, and rename it to `Display Success Banner`.

7. Add the instruction blocks to the new custom event as shown in the following screenshot, ensuring that the event's trigger name is entered as `DisplaySuccessBanner` (no spaces):

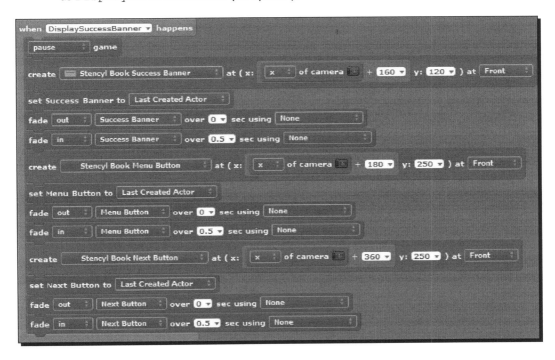

8. Ensure that each of the options in the blocks is configured correctly, as shown in the previous screenshot.

9. Test the game and collect all the fruit in the first level (but first, read the following *testing tip*)!

Testing tip: when testing routines such as the one we have just created, it can be very frustrating and time-consuming to have to play the level through to completion in order to see the finished result! In such cases, it is a good idea to make a temporary change to the instructions so that the new routine can be tested easily. For example, one option is to increase the time allowed to complete the level, because we will have less of a chance of losing all our lives before the message is displayed. However, this change still requires us to play through the whole level. An alternative temporary modification, which will allow very quick testing of the new routine, is to modify the `Fruit Collected` event so that only one piece of fruit must be collected in order to display the message, as highlighted in the following screenshot:

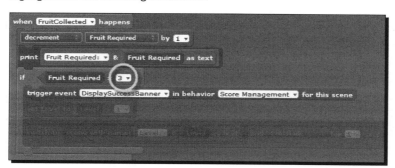

For the purposes of this test, the `DisplaySuccessBanner` trigger will occur when there are three pieces of fruit remaining. In the first level, there are four pieces of fruit, so as soon as we have collected just one fruit actor, the event will be triggered and our message will be displayed! If the level contains a different number of fruit actors, change the `if Fruit Required` ... block to specify one less piece of fruit that exists in the level.

Once the testing has been completed and we are happy that the routine is working as expected, it is important to remember to return any test values to their original values—in this case, change the number of fruit actors required back to zero. It's also very important to run some tests by completing the entire level, just to ensure that we haven't missed any problems!

What just happened?

We have created a new custom event that creates a success message, along with the two option buttons, and displays it to the player when all the pieces of fruit have been collected, as shown in the following screenshot:

The first step required was to download (from StencylForge) the actors for the success message - the **Success** banner, the **Menu** button, and the **Next** button, and to configure the physics settings for all three actors, so that they cannot be paused and will not move when they are placed in the game.

We then created three new hidden actor attributes for each of the new actors that we downloaded. These attributes will make it much easier to manipulate the message and button actors elsewhere in the behavior.

The next step required us to deactivate two of the instruction blocks in the Fruit Collected event. We're going to use these two blocks in the following section, *Time for action – responding to the player's selection*, which is why we deactivated them rather than deleting them. There is no point in making additional work for ourselves when we already have the required ready-to-use blocks!

The final change we made in the Fruit Collected event was to add a trigger for a custom event called DisplaySuccessBanner. The DisplaySuccessBanner custom event didn't exist at this point; we were just putting the required framework in place ready for the next steps.

With the above additions and modifications in place, we then moved on to the main instructions for displaying the message to the player, which required us to create a new custom event that we renamed to Display Success Banner. We then ensured that we put the correct trigger name, DisplaySuccessBanner, in the when ... happens event block.

The first task for the custom event is to pause the game, so the action stops and the player can no longer control the monkey. This was achieved by inserting the pause game instruction block.

Although it took quite a bit of work to complete the rest of the Display Success Banner custom event, we have simply carried out the same actions three times for the three actors that are required to display the completed message. Let's examine the first group of blocks that refers to Stencyl Book Success Banner.

The first instruction (the red create ... block) creates the actor at a central location on the screen, taking into account the x position of the camera to ensure that the actor's position is centered horizontally, regardless of whether or not the screen has scrolled. The next instruction block, set Success Banner to Last Created actor, places a reference to the newly created actor into an attribute, so that we can access and manipulate the actor with ease. We immediately refer to this Success Banner attribute in the next block, fade out Success Banner over 0 sec using None. This instruction instantly fades the banner to zero transparency so the player cannot see it. The next block, fade in Success Banner over 0.5 sec using None, fades the banner into view over 0.5 seconds.

> It might be tempting to consider use of the Hide sprite for Self block in place of the fade out ... block. However, the Hide sprite ... block explicitly requires use of the corresponding Show sprite ... block, in order to bring the actor back into view!

We then repeat the process of creating, instantly fading-out, then fading-in the actors for the two option buttons, ensuring that the x and y coordinates are specified appropriately.

Why have we gone to the trouble of instantly fading-out, and then gently fading-in each of the actors required for the banner? It's simply a matter of presenting a more pleasant experience for players of our game! We could remove all of the fade ... instruction blocks from the DisplaySuccessBanner custom event, but the result would be a message that suddenly jolts onto the screen. Try temporarily deactivating each of the fade ... instruction blocks to get a feel for the difference in presentation. Was it worth the extra work of inserting and configuring the six blocks? That's a personal decision, and it's probably a good idea to elicit some feedback from independent testers.

Responding to the player's selection

Now that we have put a framework in place for displaying the success message, we need to implement the instructions to react appropriately when the player clicks on one of the buttons.

Time for action – responding to the player's selection

The game file to import and load for this session is `5961_07_12.stencyl`.

1. Create a new scene called `Main Menu`, with a background of blue; any blue will do as we'll be changing it later!

2. Close the new scene.

3. In the **Dashboard** tab, under **Actor Types**, double-click on the **Stencyl Book Menu Button** thumbnail to display the Animation Editor, then click on the **Events** button in the row of gray buttons at the upper-center of the screen.

4. Click on **+ Add Event | Input | On Actor**.

5. Change the event name to `Clicked`.

6. Modify the **when the mouse enters Self** block to **when the mouse is released on Self**.

7. Add the instruction blocks to resume the game and switch to the **Main Menu** scene as shown in the following screenshot:

8. Repeat steps 3 through 6 for **Stencyl Book Next Button**; remember to stop after completing step 6, and then continue with the following steps.

9. Double-check to ensure that the **Clicked** events in both the **Stencyl Book Menu Button** and **Stencyl Book Next Button** tabs state **when the mouse is released on Self**.

10. Insert an **unpause game** block into the new event for **Stencyl Book Next Button**, so it looks like the following screenshot:

11. Leaving the **Stencyl Book Next Button** actor tab open, return to (or open, if it is closed) the **Fruit Collected** event of the **Score Management** behavior.

12. Click-and-drag on the deactivated **set Level to ...** block, and drop it onto the gray background as shown in the following screenshot. Note that the deactivated **switch to ...** block will also be dragged.

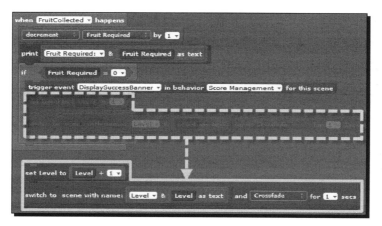

13. Right-click on **set Level to** and select **Copy**.

14. Return to the **Stencyl Book Next Button** actor tab, where we should see the **Clicked** event that we created earlier.

15. Right-click somewhere on the gray background below the orange **when the mouse is released on Self** block and select **Paste**.

16. Drag the newly pasted **set Level to ...** block (the **switch to ...** block will move with it) into the orange event block and reactivate both blocks, so the completed event looks like the following screenshot:

17. Return to the **Fruit Collected** event in the **Score Management** behavior and press the *Ctrl + K* keys on the keyboard (*Command + K* on Mac OS X) to remove the unused instruction blocks.

18. Test the game; collect all the fruit actors on Level 1 and click on the **Next** button when the success banner is displayed, and then continue to complete Level 2.

19. When Level 2 has been completed, click on the **Menu** button.

What just happened?

We have implemented the required instructions to enable our game to respond appropriately, based upon which button the player pressed when they completed a level.

Firstly, we created a temporary **Main Menu** scene, which is displayed when the player clicks on the **Menu** button.

The next step was to attach an event directly to the **Stencyl Book Menu Button** actor. We did not create a behavior and attach it to the actor, or place the instruction block in an existing behavior that was already attached to the actor. When an instruction block (or series of instruction blocks) is only relevant to a specific actor, it can be useful to attach the instructions directly to the relevant actor as an event, rather than specially creating a behavior that will only be used once. In this case, the **Stencyl Book Menu Button** actor is only going to be used for a single purpose—switching to the **Main Menu** scene. So we simply attached that instruction to the actor. We also inserted an **unpause game** instruction block into the **Clicked** event for the **Stencyl Book Menu Button** actor, because the **Display Success Banner** event that creates the success banner, pauses the game. If we don't use the **unpause game** instruction at this point, then the game will not function correctly when the next level starts!

We then followed a similar process for the **Stencyl Book Next Button** actor, but this time we copied and pasted the two required instruction blocks from the Score Management behavior's Fruit Collected event. We did this not just to save the trouble of rebuilding the two instruction blocks, but mainly because we have already tested these instructions in an earlier version of game, and we know that they work as required!

Have a go hero

The game file to import and load for this session is `5961_07_13.stencyl`.

In the previous two sections, *Time for action – displaying the message and buttons* and *Time for action – responding to the player's selection*, we implemented a system whereby, on completion of a level, the player is presented with a success message and two options: **Menu** and **Next**. We have tested the game, and we can now be confident that this newly implemented feature is working as required. However, there are some refinements that can be made to the behaviors and events that we have created:

◆ Modify the required instructions in the `Display Success Banner` event, so that the positioning of the banner and buttons is not hardcoded; the relevant instructions should take into account the screen size.

◆ Currently, when the monkey collects the last piece of fruit on each level, the fruit does not appear to have been collected, because the game pauses before the instruction to shrink the fruit has completed. Make the required modifications to the `Fruit Collected` event to allow time for the fruit to disappear before the success banner is displayed.

◆ When the success banner is on display, the pause feature can still be activated and deactivated by pressing the *P* key on the keyboard. Try it! It really doesn't look very professional! The addition of a single instruction block to the `Display Success Banner` event can resolve this problem.

Suggested solutions to the above modifications along with comments have been implemented in the download file named `5961_07_14.stencyl`.

 Note that the previous section (*Have a go hero*) tasks are optional. The game will continue to function if the above modifications are not completed.

Creating a game over message

In its current state, our game is simply displaying a temporary scene when the player has no more lives left. Our next polishing task is to create a routine that will advise the player when the game is over and offer the appropriate options to the player.

The message will consist of a **Game Over** banner and two option buttons: one to allow the player to return to the game's main menu scene, and the other to allow the player to immediately restart the game. When completed, the **Game Over** banner will be presented to the player as shown in the following screenshot:

Let's jump right in and build the instructions to create the **Game Over** banner.

STOP!

Haven't we already created a very similar information banner? Our game over banner is almost identical to the success banner that we created in the previous section, *Improving the level progression routine*, so this is a great opportunity to save ourselves some work!

Reusing the existing banner event

We have two options available to us when we have an existing event that we want to reuse. The first option is to duplicate the event, give it a new name, and then work through the event methodically by updating any instruction blocks that need to be changed for the new, slightly different event. While this can be quite a quick process and can be a reasonable solution, it does have its pitfalls, the main one being that, if in the future we need to make any changes to the way the original event works, we will also have to make those changes in all other versions of the event. This not only leads to additional, repetitive work, but can also lead to the introduction of errors.

Although we only need one other banner for our game, we're going to take the second, smarter option, which is to modify the existing banner event so that it is completely reusable. In practice, we might have planned to create a multipurpose banner behavior right from the start, but the idea of using banners was not something that we had considered in the earlier stage of game development.

Time for action – modifying the existing banner event

The game file to import and load for this session is `5961_07_14.stencyl`.

1. Open the **Score Management** scene behavior and rename the **Display Success Banner** event name in the leftmost panel to `Display Banner`.

2. In the newly renamed **Display Banner** event, change the trigger name for the event from **DisplaySuccessBanner** to `DisplayBanner`, as shown in the following screenshot:

3. At the bottom of the rightmost panel, click on the **Attributes** tab to display the attributes panel. At the top of the panel, we can see the basic settings for all the attributes that are being used in the **Score Management** behavior, as shown in the following screenshot:

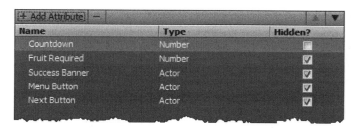

4. Click on the **+ Add Attribute** button at the top of the attribute panel and create a new attribute called `Required Banner`, using the configuration in the following screenshot, noting that the **Type** option of the attribute is **Actor Type**:

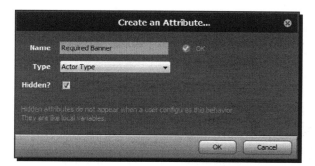

5. Ensure that the bottom of the lower section of the attribute panel is visible (if necessary, either scroll down or use the horizontal splitter-bar to increase the size of the lower panel), so that the **Default Value** box is visible, as highlighted by the dotted-line in the following screenshot:

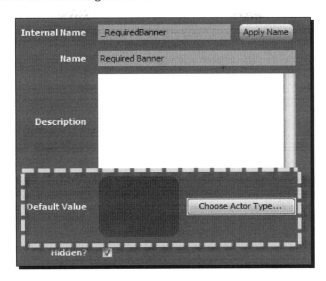

6. Click on the **Choose Actor Type...** button and double-click on the thumbnail for the **Stencyl Book Success Banner** actor.

7. Add another attribute called `Required Option Button`, again with a **Type** option as **Actor Type** and with the **Hidden?** option checked.

8. Click on the **Choose Actor Type...** button in the lower-half of the attribute panel, then double-click on the thumbnail for the **Stencyl Book Next Button** actor.

9. In the upper-half of the attribute panel, click once on the **Success Banner** attribute name.

10. In the lower-half of the attribute panel, change the **Internal Name** option of the attribute from **_SuccessBanner** to `_Banner` (noting the leading underscore) and change the **Name** option from **Success Banner** to `Banner`, shown as follows:

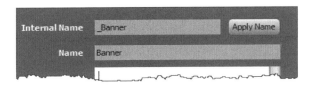

11. Click on the **Apply Name** button next to the **Internal Name** setting to display the **Requires a Refresh** dialog box.

12. Click on **Continue** to update the settings. Don't panic when the screen updates and the event that we're working on seems to disappear—it's normal behavior when updating attribute names!

13. In the upper-half of the attributes panel, select the **Next Button** attribute and change the **Internal Name** option to **_OptionButton** and the **Name** option to **Option Button**. Note that there is no space character in the internal name and it requires a leading underscore.

14. Click on the **Apply Name** button and click on **Continue** when the **Requires a Refresh** dialog box is displayed.

15. Click on the name of the **Display Banner** event in the left-hand panel and note that all references to the **Success Banner** attribute in the instruction blocks have automatically been replaced with **Banner**, and all references to the **Next Button** attribute have changed to **Option Button**.

16. In the **Display Banner** event, locate the red **create Stencyl Book Success Banner at...** block and click on the option that is currently set to **Stencyl Book Success Banner**, so the pop-up menu is displayed.

17. Select **Choose Attribute** and double-click on **Required Banner** in the **Choose Attribute** dialog box.

18. Locate the red **create Stencyl Book Next Button at ...** instruction block and click on the option that is currently set to **Stencyl Book Next Button** so the pop-up menu is displayed.

19. Select **Choose Attribute** and double-click on **Required Option Button** in the **Choose Attribute** dialog box.

20. In the left-hand panel, click on the **+ Add Event** button, create a new custom event, and rename it to `Display Success Banner`.

21. Click on the **Palette** tab at the bottom of the rightmost panel, and update the newly created event so that it looks like the following screenshot:

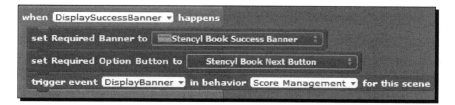

22. Test the game; collect all the fruit actors!

What just happened?

When we have collected all the fruit, the success banner is shown exactly as it was prior to making all the above changes, but our hard work was definitely worthwhile.

We have converted our single-purpose Display Success Banner event into a reusable event called Display Banner, which can display any banner that we specify based on two new attributes: one for specifying the banner and the other for specifying the option button. We then created a new Display Success Banner event that sets the two relevant attributes for the banner and option button, and then triggers the general-purpose Display Banner event.

Let's examine the steps that we took to complete the conversion.

Our first task was to rename the Display Success Banner event to give it a less specific name of Display Banner. This event will be able to display any banner, as long as we provide it with the relevant information! As well as renaming the event in the leftmost column, we also specified a new trigger name for the event, DisplayBanner, so that we can trigger the event using an appropriate name.

Currently, the event is creating a banner based on the Stencyl Book Success Banner actor and the option button Stencyl Book Next Button, that we have hardcoded into the instructions. In order to make the event reusable, we needed to provide the event with the ability to create a banner and option button that will be specified when the game is being played. So, instead of directly specifying the type of actor, we created two new attributes: Required Banner and Required Option Button, which are **actor type** attributes. An actor type attribute does not store an actual actor, but it stores the type of actor. By using actor type attributes, we can specify at run-time which banner actor and which button actor we want to use. Actor type attributes must have a default value set, so we did this by using the **Choose Actor Type...** button in the lower-half of the attribute panel.

We then used the attribute panel to rename two of the attributes in the Score Management behavior. The original attributes were called Success Banner and Next Button, which were names that were specific to the original task of displaying the success banner with a **next** button. However, our reusable event needs to display any banner and any option button that we specify, so we renamed the attributes to something more appropriate: Banner and Option Button. Although the event would have worked perfectly well without renaming these attributes, it's worthwhile specifying appropriate names. If we need to make changes to our game in the future, it will be difficult to remember what the attributes are used for, if they are not named appropriately!

When we renamed the attributes, we renamed both the internal name and the friendly names that we use when building events—a reminder of the configuration screen is shown in the following screenshot:

The friendly name (the **Name** field in the above screenshot) is the name used in Stencyl's instructions, such as the blocks that set and get the values of the attribute, as shown in the following screenshot:

We don't really need to understand why internal names are used by Stencyl. We just need to know that the internal name is automatically created using the friendly name that we have chosen, and Stencyl does this by removing all the spaces from the friendly name and preceding the whole name with an underscore character. If we change the friendly name, the internal name is not changed automatically, and while this will not cause our game to malfunction, it may cause confusion for us (as the developer), when using advanced Stencyl development features, such as hand-coding. For this reason, it is a good idea, when changing an attribute's friendly name, to also manually change its internal name so that it conforms to Stencyl's naming conventions—after all, it only takes a few seconds!

The following section entitled *Understanding internal attribute names* explains internal attribute names in more detail.

After changing the internal name of the relevant attributes, we clicked on the **Apply Name** button, which updated all references to the attribute's name throughout the behavior. This is why, when we examined the `Display Banner` event in step 15, all references to the `Success Banner` and `Next Button` attributes had been automatically changed to `Banner` and `Option Button`. The **Requires a Refresh** warning was displayed because Stencyl must close the behavior in order to process the modification and update all the instructions that refer to the changed attribute name. This process only takes a few seconds, after which the behavior is reopened.

 Note that many of the screens in Stencyl can be refreshed to ensure that changes are reflected in all behaviors and events – the shortcut key for refreshing is *Ctrl + R* (*Command + R* on Mac OS X).

The final stage of making our event truly reusable was to ensure that it was not hardcoded to create `Stencyl Book Success Banner` and `Stencyl Book Next Button`, so we changed the two `create` ... instruction blocks so that they created an actor of type `Required Banner` and an actor of type `Required Option Button`.

At this point we had created a completely reusable event that will display any banner and any option button that we specify using the actor type attributes that we have created. So, our final task was to create a new `Display Success Banner` event that will be able to use our multipurpose `Display Banner` routine.

The new `Display Success Banner` routine simply consists of the custom event called `DisplaySuccessBanner`, which will be triggered when all the fruit actors have been collected. The first instruction block sets the `Required Banner` actor type to the `Stencyl Book Success Banner` type of actor, and the second block sets the `Required Option Button` actor type of actor to the `Stencyl Book Next Button` type of actor.

The final instruction block triggers the new `DisplayBanner` event, which then uses the two attributes that we have just specified to display the required banner and option button!

Remember that the `Fruit Collected` event already triggers the `DisplaySuccessBanner` event, so we don't need to make any further modifications in order to trigger this event.

Understanding internal attribute names

Although it is not vital to understand the behind-the-scenes processes of attributes' internal names, it can be useful to learn a little more about the internal workings of Stencyl, in order to understand why we were working with the internal names of attributes in the previous section, *Time for action – modifying the existing banner event*.

We create all the instructions for Stencyl by selecting instruction blocks from the palette and placing them into events. However, when our game is compiled, Stencyl converts it to code. An example of some code that creates the attributes for our `Score Management` behavior is shown as follows (don't worry as we don't need to understand this code; it's just helpful to see what Stencyl is doing in the background):

```
public var _Countdown:Float;
public var _FruitRequired:Float;
public var _Banner:Actor;
public var _MenuButton:Actor;
public var _OptionButton:Actor;
public var _RequiredBanner:ActorType;
public var _RequiredOptionButton:ActorType;
```

If we look at the code that Stencyl has generated, we might recognize all of the attribute names that we created in the Score Management behavior, but we can see that the spaces have been removed from the names, and each name is preceded by an underscore character. The reason for this naming method is that traditional programming languages do not allow spaces in attribute names (attributes are called **variables** in traditional programming, but they do the same job). The preceding underscore character is not a requirement of traditional programming languages, but it is a programming convention used within Stencyl.

Although it is not vital to do so, it's a good idea to update attributes' internal names when changing the friendly names, because if the internal attribute names do not match the friendly names, it can be difficult to understand the code that is generated by Stencyl. While we are not working with the code that Stencyl generates, we may wish to do so in the future when we develop more advanced skills using the Stencyl toolset.

Updating attribute names

In the previous section, *Time for action – modifying the existing banner event*, we renamed two attributes and used the **Apply Name** button to update all references to the attribute in the behavior. However, it's important to note that only references to the renamed attribute within the current behavior are automatically updated.

For example, our Score Management behavior has an attribute called Countdown (internal name _Countdown). If we changed the internal name of the Countdown attribute, then any references to it outside of our Score Management behavior will not be updated; we will have to manually locate those references and modify them ourselves. For example, we have made a reference to the Countdown attribute in the monkey's Health behavior, part of which is shown in the following screenshot:

If we modify the internal attribute name, _Countdown, in the Score Management behavior, and click on the **Apply Name** button, the reference to the _Countdown attribute name in the Health behavior will not be updated!

For this reason, some Stencyl developers choose not to change the internal names of attributes. As with all decisions such as this, the choice belongs to the developer.

Displaying the game-over banner

We now have a reusable event that can display a banner and an option button of our choice, and we have used the event to display a success banner when the player completes each level in our game.

Let's put the reusability of the new banner event to the test, and use it to display a game over banner when the monkey loses his last life.

Time for action – displaying the game over banner

The game file to import and load for this session is `5961_07_15.stencyl`.

1. Download the **Stencyl Book Game Over Banner** and the **Stencyl Book Play Button** actors from StencylForge.

2. Set the physics properties for both the actors so that they cannot be moved or paused.

3. Ensure that the **Stencyl Book Play Button** tab is currently selected, and click on the **Events** button in the row of gray buttons above the Animation Editor panel.

4. Click on **+ Add Event | Input | On Actor** to add a new input event and rename it to `Clicked`, then modify the event so that it appears as shown in the following screenshot, remembering that the purple blocks are game attributes:

5. Open the **Score Management** scene behavior, and in the left-hand panel, right-click on the **Display Success Banner** event name and select **Duplicate**, then rename the newly duplicated event to `Display Game Over Banner`.

6. Modify the new **Display Game Over Banner** event as shown in the
   following screenshot, ensuring that the event's trigger name is changed to
   `DisplayGameOverBanner`, and both of the **set...** instructions are updated:

7. Open the actor behavior named `Health` and select the **Show Angel** event
   in the left-hand panel.

8. Deactivate the **switch to Game Over...** instruction block in the orange
   otherwise block at the bottom of the event, and insert the trigger block
   shown in the following screenshot:

9. Test the game; make the monkey lose all its lives and test the **Play** button!

What just happened?

We have utilized the reusable `DisplayBanner` event to display a game over banner when
the player loses all their lives.

In order to create our customized banner, we downloaded the two actors from StencylForge
that contained the required images for the game over banner and the play option button,
and we configured their physics settings so that they will always remain onscreen and cannot
be paused. We also attached a custom event to `Stencyl Book Play Button`, which,
when clicked, resumes the game with the `unpause game` block, resets the lives to 3 and
level number to 1, then switches to the `Level1` scene so that the game restarts.

We then duplicated the `DisplaySuccessBanner` event, renamed the duplicate to `DisplayGameOverBanner`, and modified the duplicated event to specify `Stencyl Book Game Over Banner` as `Required Banner`, and `Stencyl Book Play Button` as `Required button`. We could have created the `DisplayGameOverBanner` event manually block-by-block, but as we had an existing event that did a very similar job, it made sense to duplicate it and then modify its settings—after all, we know that the original `DisplaySuccessBanner` event already worked perfectly!

The next step was to update the `Show Angel` event to display the game over banner when the monkey runs out of lives. Previously, when the monkey ran out lives, we immediately switched to the `Game Over` scene. But we no longer want to do that, so we deactivated the `switch to Game Over…` block, and added an instruction to trigger the `DisplayGameOverBanner` custom event in the `Score Management` scene behavior.

Now, when our monkey runs out of lives, the `DisplayGameOverBanner` event is triggered and it specifies the correct banner and option button, and then triggers the general-purpose `DisplayBanner` event. The `DisplayBanner` event displays the correct banner and option button; in this case, it's the `Stencyl Book Game Over Banner` and `Stencyl Book Play Button`. When the **Play** option button is clicked, the `Lives` and `Level` game attributes are reset, and the game switches to `Level1`, so the player can start over from the beginning!

Creating a Main Menu scene

Our game can now be played from start to finish, and it neatly displays the relevant success or game over banner at the right time, allowing the player to control the flow of the game. However, we still have one last task to carry out before the visual presentation of our game is complete.

Time for action – displaying the introduction scene

The game file to import and load for this session is `5961_07_16.stencyl`.

When the game first loads up and appears onscreen, it starts immediately without giving the player any warning! We have already created a temporary **Main Menu** scene, which is displayed when the player clicks on the menu option button on either the success or the game over screen, but we should really spruce up the **Main Menu** scene and display it as an introduction to the game when it is first loaded:

1. Download the following actors from StencylForge:

   ❑ **Stencyl Book Title Banner**

   ❑ **Stencyl Book Title Credits**

   ❑ **Stencyl Book Start Button**

2. Click on the **Scenes** option in the **Dashboard** tab.

3. Click on the thumbnail for the **Main Menu** scene once, then click on the blue **Mark as Starting Scene** button at the lower-right corner of the screen; a gold star should appear on the upper-left corner of the **Main Menu** scene's thumbnail.

4. Open the **Main Menu** scene and click on the gray **Background** button at the upper-center of the screen.

5. Click on the **+** (plus) button found at the bottom of the **Backgrounds** panel and double-click on the **Jungle Background** thumbnail in the **Choose a Background** dialog box.

6. Press *Ctrl + R* (*Command + R* on Mac OS X) and the screen will refresh.

7. Click on the **Scene** button at the upper-center of the screen.

8. Click on the **Show Background** button at the upper-right of the Scene Editor's horizontal toolbar, as highlighted in the following screenshot:

9. Add the **Stencyl Book Title Banner**, **Stencyl Book Title Credits**, and **Stencyl Book Start Button** actors to the **Main Menu** scene as shown in the following screenshot:

10. Add an **On Actor** input event to the **Stencyl Book Start Button** actors and add the instruction blocks as shown in the following screenshot:

11. Test the game; make sure the **Start** button works!

What just happened?

We have customized the **Main Menu** scene so that it presents the name of the game to the user, along with the game credits and a functioning **Start** button, on an appropriate background.

Firstly, we added three new assets to the game: **Stencyl Book Title Banner**, **Stencyl Book Title Credits**, and **Stencyl Book Start Button**. Note that we didn't need to specify the physics properties for these actors because the scene has no gravity settings, and there is no movement occurring in the scene—the actors will happily stay exactly where we placed them without further configuration!

Up until this point in development, the **Level1** scene had been the starting scene for the game, but now that we have a functioning **Main Menu**, we have set it to be the starting scene, so that it is displayed when the game loads.

A plain background for our introductory scene doesn't provide a very good first impression for our game, so our next task was to add the **Jungle Background** to the scene. By default, backgrounds are not displayed in the scene editor, so we needed to click on the **Show Background** button to show the image, but before showing the background in the scene view, we refreshed the scene using the keyboard shortcut *Ctrl + R* (*Command + R* on Mac OS X). Refreshing the screen forces the changes to the background to be saved, so that it will be visible in the scene editor.

We could have designed and imported a different image for the **Main Menu** background, but for our purposes, the existing background looks the part. Another advantage of reusing existing assets, such as backgrounds, is that the file-size of the game will be smaller than if we added additional assets.

With the background visible, we were then able to position the required actors onscreen. In the screenshot of the example **Main Menu** scene shown in the previous step 9, it can be seen that the title actor showing the **Monkey Run** image has been positioned at an angle. This was achieved by placing the actor into the scene, then moving the cursor slightly outside any corner of the selection area for the actor, at which point the rotation cursor is displayed. Clicking-and-dragging the mouse when the rotation cursor is displayed will rotate the actor around its rotation point; usually the center of the actor. The following screenshot shows the rotation cursor (highlighted by a circle) positioned just outside the corner of the selection box for the **Stencyl Book Title Banner** actor.

The actor has also been stretched to make it larger, and this can be accomplished simply by clicking-and-dragging one of the corner handles for the actor—the handles are the miniature boxes displayed at the corners and sides of a selection box, also visible in the previous screenshot.

 Holding the *Shift* key on the keyboard while stretching an actor ensures that the width and height remain proportional to each other, rather than being distorted.

With the design of the **Main Menu** scene completed, the final step was to add a custom event to the **Stencyl Book Start Button** actor to make it do its job of starting the game. The event resets the Lives game attribute to 3 and switches to the Level1 scene, using the specified transition effect of Slide Right, when the actor is clicked.

Have a go hero

The game file to import and load for this session is 5961_07_17.stencyl.

Our **Main Menu** scene is perfectly adequate for a sample game, but it would benefit from a little more attention to the design and theme of the game!

Consider implementing the following:

- Introduce the monkey character to the scene—he's the main character in the game
- Include some of the other characters—perhaps positioned to give a new player a hint about some of the challenges in the game
- Implement some animation or movement to the scene
- Animate the **Start** button so that it grows when the mouse moves over it

The previous suggestions are the type of additional features that can really bring a game to life, immediately arouse interest in the game, and raise it from the realms of okay to excellent!

Research other games—what do they have in their introductory scenes to make them interesting and engaging to players before the game has even started?

The above suggestions have not been implemented in the sample game—this is a challenge to put into practice many of the skills that we have learned throughout this book. It's a great opportunity to review the various techniques that we have covered, and to consider how they can be used together to achieve different goals.

 Need help implementing some of the above suggestions? Visit the official Stencyl forums at `community.stencyl.com`. Before starting a new topic and asking for help, try searching the forums to see if other Stencyl users have asked similar questions and have already had them answered!

Finalizing the game-completed scene

When our player successfully completes the game, we need to show them an appropriate congratulatory message and provide a button for them to replay the game. Currently, we have a blank yellow scene, so let's get working on the final visual element of our game.

Time for action – implementing the game-completed scene

The game file to import and load for this session is `5961_07_17.stencyl`.

1. Download the **Stencyl Book Game Completed** actor from StencylForge.

2. Open the **Level4** scene (the yellow final level scene) and add the **Jungle Background**, remembering to press *Ctrl + R* (*Command + R* on Mac OS X) to refresh the scene with the new background configuration.

3. Switch to the scene view (click on the gray **Scene** button) and ensure that the background is on display (click on the **Show Background** icon on the toolbar).

4. Position the **Stencyl Book Game Completed** actor onscreen, and also add the **Stencyl Book Start Button** actor, as shown in the following screenshot:

5. Click on the green **Test Scene** button, and ensure that the completion scene appears as required and the **Start** button works as expected.

What just happened?

We've created a fully-functioning game-completed scene!

We simply added the **Jungle Background**, the **All levels completed** message, and the existing **Start** button actor!

The only required functionality in this scene is for the **Start** button to restart the game at `Level1`, and we had already configured it to carry out that function in the previous section, *Time for action – displaying the introduction scene*!

Have a go hero – improving the game-completed scene

The game file to import and load for this session is `5961_07_18.stencyl`.

Although the game-completion scene that we have created is functional, a game's final scene needs to be far more interesting to reward the player for their efforts!

Consider how this final scene can be improved and introduce:

◆ An animation for the **Start** button when the mouse moves over it

◆ Characters that appear in the game

◆ Other features to make the scene more interesting and rewarding

Remember to test any new features that are implemented, and try to obtain feedback from other testers. The suggested features have not been implemented in the sample game—this is another opportunity to experiment and be creative!

Summary

It's time to stop and review the results of our hard-work. Although this chapter is just about polishing our game, it's probably clear that once the basic game development has been completed, there is a very large amount of polishing to complete.

In fact, taking care of the polishing can take as long as, if not longer than, creating the main game! However, the time spent improving and honing a game can make all the difference between a game being playable and a game being addictive.

In this chapter, we have taken our bare-bones game and implemented many of the features that we would expect to find in a professional, published game.

We've added a themed foreground and background to the game, and added an interesting visual special effect that occurs during gameplay—the jungle now shakes when each statue lands! Our game now has more levels, and the players are presented with a helpful banner to advise when each level has been completed and to allow them to progress to the next level or return to the main introduction screen. We've also added a `pause` feature, so the player can have a break at any time without losing any lives, and we also present players with an information banner when the game is over.

The final visual elements, which we improved in our game, were the main introduction scene, which now includes credits and a **Start** button for the player to click, and the scene that is displayed when the game is completed successfully.

All the visual elements of our game have now been completed, but there is still one final essential element to introduce into our game before we can consider it to be complete! This final piece of polishing deserves a chapter of its own, so let's finish our game by introducing some sound effects and a soundtrack.

8
Implementing Sounds

In Chapter 7, Polishing the Game, we implemented the final visual-presentation elements for our game, which can now be played from start to finish.

Although players can now experience all the required gameplay mechanics, level transitions, and various other in-game essentials, there is one, final (and very important) element missing; our game is completely silent!

Our final task, to bring the development process of our game to completion, is to add some atmosphere to our game, by adding sound effects and a soundtrack.

Sounds form a vital part of the immersive experience of our game, so it's important to choose them carefully.

The two types of sounds that we will be implementing are **sound effects** and a **soundtrack**. In the process of learning about using sounds in Stencyl we will be doing the following:

- Adding a jumping sound effect
- Examining the `Play Sound` instruction blocks
- Organizing sounds in the game
- Adding a pickup sound effect
- Adding a soundtrack
- Understanding sound types in Stencyl
- Importing sounds into Stencyl

Let's start by implementing our first sound effect.

Adding a jumping sound effect

Rather than adding the instruction blocks for the various sound effects into many locations within our behaviors, we're going to create a single scene behavior that will be used to manage all the sounds in our game. We'll then trigger the relevant sound effects as required.

Our first task is to create a sound effect whenever the monkey jumps.

Time for action – implementing a jumping sound effect

The game file to import and load for this session is `5961_08_01.stencyl`.

1. Before we create the behavior to manage the sound effects, let's remove the redundant **Game Over** scene from the game (right-click on the scene's thumbnail in the **Scenes** panel and select **Remove**).

2. Download **Stencyl Book Jump Effect** from StencylForge and close the tabs for the jump sound effect and StencylForge.

3. Create a new scene behavior called `Sound Management`.

4. Click on the **Attach to Scene** button, and select **Level1**.

5. Close the tab for **Level1** to return to the **Sound Management** behavior.

6. Attach the behavior to all the other scenes in our game, including the **Main Menu** scene.

7. Close the tabs for all the open scenes and return to the **Sound Management** behavior.

8. Add a new custom event called `Jump SFX` and configure the event as shown in the following screenshot, ensuring to set the event's trigger name to `JumpSFX`:

9. Open the actor behavior named **Jump and Run Movement**, add a new keyboard input event (**+ Add Event | Input | Keyboard**), rename it to `Trigger Jump SFX`, and configure it as shown in the following screenshot, ensuring that **Control** is set to **up**. Note that the blue **Jumping** block is an attribute that is used in the **Jump and Run Movement** behavior (**Attributes | Getters** in the palette):

10. Test the game; make the monkey jump!

What just happened?

We've just added a jumping sound effect to the game!

The very first task was to remove the **Game Over** scene, because our game no longer uses it. Then, after downloading the sound effect from StencylForge, we created a new scene behavior called `Sound Management`, and attached it to all the scenes in our game; we may need to have sounds playing in scenes other than the playable levels.

 To check which scenes use a specific behavior, right-click on the behavior's thumbnail in the **Scene Behaviors** panel in the **Dashboard** tab, and select **Who uses this?** from the pop-up menu. This feature is also available in the **Actor Behaviors** panel.

We then created a new custom event called `Jump SFX` in the `Sound Management` scene behavior, which simply plays the specified sound effect on channel 1 when it is triggered. Further information about sounds and channels can be found in the following section entitled, *Examining the play sound instruction blocks*.

Our next step was to open the `Jump and Run Movement` behavior and add a new keyboard event. This event called `Trigger Jump SFX` waits for the `up` control to be pressed, and when that happens, it triggers the `JumpSFX` custom event in the `Sound Management` behavior. However, we placed the trigger inside an instruction that checks `if not Jumping`; this is shorthand for `if Jumping is not = true`, and is just a different way of carrying out the same test.

Why are we checking to see if the `Jumping` attribute in the `Jump and Run Movement` behavior is not true? Because we didn't create this behavior (it is one of the ready-made behaviors that is provided with Stencyl), a little research was required to find out how the jumping routines worked! It isn't necessary to fully understand the behavior in detail, but if we examine the main `always` (**when updating**) event in the `Jump and Run Movement` behavior, we can see that there is an attribute called `Jumping` that is set when (surprise!) the actor is jumping. We can also see attributes called `Jump` and `On Ground`, as shown in the following screenshot, which is an excerpt from the `Jump and Run Movement` behavior:

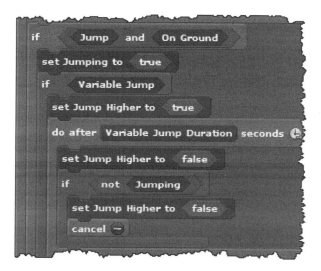

With this information, we might surmise that the `Jumping` attribute is set to `true` when the actor is jumping, and that it is set to `false` when the actor is no longer jumping.

We only want the jumping sound effect to be played when the player presses the `up` control and the actor is not already jumping, otherwise repeated presses of the `up` control will cause the sound effect to play, even when the monkey is already in the air, and that will just be annoying for players of our game!

Testing the game demonstrates that, however many times the player presses the `up` control, the jumping sound effect will only be played if the monkey is not already jumping. Perfect!

Have a go hero

The game file to import and load for this session is `5961_08_02.stencyl`.

Currently, the jumping sound effect will still play when the game is paused and the player presses the `up` control.

◆ Modify the `Jump SFX` custom event, so the sound effect will not occur when the game is paused

A suggested solution is provided in the download file `5961_08_03.stencyl`, along with comments in the `Jump SFX` event of the `Sound Management` scene behavior.

Examining the play sound instruction blocks

In Stencyl, we have two main options for playing sounds, as shown in the following screenshot:

The first option, **Play Sound**, does exactly what it states. Sounds played with this instruction can have their volume and fading controlled by the general-purpose sound-control instructions, **set volume to … %** and **Fade In over … secs**, which can be seen in the following screenshot:

These general-purpose sound controls work well in many circumstances, but the disadvantage is that all sounds played with the `Play Sound` instruction will simultaneously be altered using the volume and fade instructions; every sound currently being played will fade, or will have its volume changed at the same time and at the same level.

The second option, **Play Sound on channel ...**, provides additional flexibility; we can play any sound on any one of 32 channels. This provides us with the opportunity, if required, to control different sounds depending on our requirements. We can see that, using the two instruction blocks shown as follows, we can stop sounds on any channel, and we can also fade sounds in and out on any channel:

For example, we may want to have a soundtrack playing at a fixed volume throughout the game, but we may also want to fade in certain special effects at the same time, without affecting the volume of the main soundtrack. Playing the soundtrack and the special effects on different channels provides us with the required flexibility.

Currently, we don't need to vary the volumes of different sounds in our game, but we're going to play all our standard special effects on **channel 1**, so we can control them separately if we need to in the future.

It's useful to note that the Play Sound and Play Sound on channel ... instruction blocks can have the **Play** option changed to **Loop**, so the sound will repeat indefinitely, until we tell it to stop playing. This can be useful for repeating soundtracks, or for repeatedly playing a sound effect until we explicitly tell it to stop.

Organizing sounds in the game

Developers implement sounds into Stencyl games in many different ways. For example, to implement our jumping sound effect, we could simply have added a new keyboard event in the Jump and Run Movement behavior that reacted to the up control being pressed, and then played the required special effect within that event.

There is nothing wrong with implementing sounds in this way, but it can make life difficult for the developer when modifying a game in the future. For example, if we had implemented 50 different sound effects in our game, and we later decided that we wanted to play them on a different sound channel, we would have to locate all 50 of the Play Sound instruction blocks in our game. These blocks could be spread across several different behaviors and even in events that are attached directly to actors; locating them all would be a huge task which is time-consuming and error prone!

We have chosen to create a single behavior dedicated to managing sounds within the game, which makes it much easier to locate and modify the effects and their related instructions, when required. When we want to play a sound, all we need to do is use a single instruction block to trigger the required sound effect event!

We should note that there are always trade-offs when deciding how to implement features in a game. One disadvantage of using a single behavior for managing sounds is that we must attach the behavior to every scene in our game, as we discovered when we first created the Sound Management behavior. If we had implemented the jumping sound effect in one of the monkey actor's behaviors, then the sound event would be associated with the monkey, which appears in every level; therefore, we would not have had to attach a behavior to each level in the game. As we have discussed in various sections of this book, these design decisions are at the discretion of the developer.

Adding a pickup sound effect

We've already added one sound effect to our game, and it's now time to add a second sound effect that will be played when the monkey collects the fruit.

Time for action – implementing a pickup sound effect

The game file to import and load for this session is 5961_07_03.stencyl.

1. Download **Stencyl Book Pickup Effect** from StencylForge, and then close the tabs for the sound effect and StencylForge.

2. In the **Sound Management** behavior, add a new custom event called Pickup SFX.

3. Configure the new **Pickup SFX** event as shown in the following screenshot:

4. Open the **Manage Player Collisions** actor behavior, and ensure that the **Collides with Collectibles** event is selected.

5. Add a trigger for the **PickupSFX** event as highlighted in the following screenshot, which shows an extract from the `Collides with Collectibles` event:

6. Test the game and collect some fruit!

What just happened?

We now have a second sound effect in our game: a pickup sound effect is played as each piece of fruit is collected.

After downloading the sound effect from StencylForge, the process to make the sound play took only a few changes.

We have created a `Pickup SFX` event in the `Sound Management` behavior, which plays the appropriate sound effect when the custom event `PickupSFX` is triggered. Now, whenever we need to play the pickup sound effect in our game, we can simply trigger the `PickupSFX` event in the `Sound Management` behavior! In our game, this sound effect is going to be played whenever the monkey collects a piece of fruit.

We already have a `Fruit Collected` event in the `Manage Player Collisions` behavior, so our final step was to insert a trigger for the `PickupSFX` event.

Have a go hero

The game file to import and load for this session is `5961_08_04.stencyl`.

We've created a behavior for managing sounds within our game, and we have worked step-by-step through the process of adding sound effects to different actions: jumping and collecting fruit.

Using the resources in StencylForge, try implementing sound effects for the following actions that occur within the game:

- ◆ Monkey collides with an enemy
- ◆ Player runs out of lives
- ◆ Level completed successfully
- ◆ Timer is running low

Also consider which other actions within the game would benefit from accompanying sound effects.

 Appendix, Planning, Resources and Legal Issues, contains information about locating and creating new sound effects for use within our games.

Be aware that too many sound effects can be very distracting for the player!

Adding a soundtrack

Now that we have implemented some interesting sound effects, let's introduce a soundtrack that will be played throughout our game.

 The soundtrack used in this section, is a short extract from *Pinball Spring* by Kevin McLeod, which has been made available under a Creative Commons license.

In order to keep the download file sizes small enough to be practical for the purposes of this book, the soundtrack we are using is a 15 seconds extract of the music previously described. For the full soundtrack, and for additional information about the licensing agreement for this soundtrack, please visit the web page: `incompetech.com/music/royalty-free/index.html?isrc=USUAN1100741`

Time for action – adding a soundtrack

The game file to import and load for this session is `5961_08_04.stencyl`.

1. Download **Stencyl Book Sound Track** from StencylForge, then close the tabs for the soundtrack and StencylForge.

2. Open the **Sound Management** scene behavior and create a new hidden Boolean attribute (not a game attribute) called `Sound Track Playing`.

3. Add a new custom event to the **Sound Management** behavior, called `Play Sound Track`, and configure it as shown in the following screenshot:

4. Open the **Main Menu** scene and add a new **when created** event (click on the gray **Events** button at the top of the main panel, then click on **+Add Event | Basics | When Creating**).

5. Rename the event to `Trigger Sound Track` and configure it as shown in the following screenshot:

6. Test the game play the game and enjoy the soundtrack!

What just happened?

We've added a soundtrack, which plays automatically when the game first loads!

After downloading the soundtrack from StencylForge, we created a new Boolean attribute in the `Sound Management` behavior. This attribute will be used to determine whether or not the soundtrack has already been started. Although we don't need it at the moment, it's a good idea to monitor the playing status of the soundtrack, so it will be easier to manage if more advanced sound features are added into the game in the future.

With the `Sound Track Playing` attribute in place, we then created a custom event called `Play Sound Track`, which listens for the `PlaySoundTrack` trigger. When the trigger occurs, this event checks that we haven't already started the soundtrack, and if we haven't, it starts playing the music in a **loop**, which means that it will start again as soon as it ends.

Our final step was to trigger the `PlaySoundTrack` event, and we did this by adding a `when created` event to the **Main Menu** scene. Now, as soon as the game loads, the soundtrack will be triggered after a one-second delay. A delay has been implemented to ensure that all the scene's attached behaviors have been activated and have completed their initialization tasks before attempting to trigger the soundtrack event. If the **Main Menu** scene attempts to trigger the `PlaySoundTrack` event before the `Sound Management` behavior has initialized, then the soundtrack will never play!

The issue of delaying the starting of events in Stencyl is one to look out for! If, during development, a behavior just doesn't seem to be doing its job when a scene is first loaded, then consider if a delay or some other logic may be required to ensure that associated events have enough time to be processed first.

Have a go hero

The game file to import and load for this session is `5961_08_05.stencyl`.

We've now implemented some sound effects and a soundtrack, but there are many other sound-management features that we could add to our game.

Have a go at implementing the following:

- Muting all sounds when a specific key is pressed on the keyboard
- Allowing the player to choose whether to mute the sound effects, the soundtrack, or both
- When a level is successfully completed, fade out the main soundtrack and play a jingle
- Fade out the soundtrack and play an appropriate sound effect when the monkey runs out of lives
- When all levels have been completed successfully, fade out the main soundtrack and play a different soundtrack

Research popular games and review how they manage sounds from the point of view of the player

Finally, take time to review the available instruction blocks that relate to sound management in Stencyl, and be aware that there are also two very useful sound-related events available (**+Add Event | Sounds**).

Understanding sound types in Stencyl

Although the available sound-control instruction blocks will play any sound that we have imported, it's important to understand that as far as Stencyl is concerned, there are two distinct types of audio that we can use in our game:

◆ Sound effects

◆ Music (soundtracks)

Although both of these types of audio start off life as files on our hard drive, once they are imported into Stencyl, they are treated differently for technical reasons. The sound effect type of audio is designed to be used for short, snappy sounds, such as the jumping and fruit-pickup sound effects that we have already implemented, whereas the music (soundtrack) type of audio is intended for playing back longer sound files. Sound effects are loaded into and stored in the computer's memory in order to reduce **latency** — delays that can occur when playing the effect. It would not be a good experience for players of our game if a sound effect was played shortly after it was required; we need it to be played instantly! In contrast, music audio is **streamed**, that is, the audio is loaded into memory in smaller parts as required.

Audio file requirements

Stencyl currently supports two different types of audio files:

◆ MP3

◆ OGG

The **MP3** file format is required when creating games for Flash, HTML5, Android, and iOS. Stencyl manages any format conversions that are required for these target platforms, but we do need to ensure that the MP3 file is encoded, or configured correctly, before we import it into Stencyl. While most MP3 files will work in Stencyl without us having to modify them, not all MP3 files are encoded in the same way, which can cause problems when compiling our game. If unexpected errors are displayed when a game is being compiled by Stencyl, or if sounds simply fail to play as expected in a game, ensure that the MP3 files used in the game conform to the following requirements:

◆ Frequency of 44.1 kHz

◆ 16-bit constant bitrate (as opposed to VBR, which is a variable bitrate)

◆ No metadata

OGG is an alternative audio file format that Stencyl requires when targeting desktop platforms (MS Windows, Mac OS X, and Linux). There are many utilities available for converting MP3 and other audio formats to OGG files, including free ones.

While this is a lot of technical information to consider, the good news is that many MP3 files work just fine in Stencyl! For further information about audio requirements, refer to the Stencyl help pages relating to sounds at `www.stencyl.com/help`.

 Refer to the section entitled, *Third-party tools*, in *Appendix, Planning, Resources & Legal Issues*, for additional resources relating to working with audio in Stencyl.

Looping music

It's useful to note that looping music, such as the soundtrack in our game, will continue to loop and play even when a different scene is loaded. This means that we do not have to tell each scene to play our soundtrack; it will continuously loop and play automatically. If we want to stop the music when a scene is over, we must implement those instructions ourselves; perhaps we would fade the soundtrack out in that scenario.

Importing sounds into Stencyl

For the purposes of this chapter, we have been using sound effects and a soundtrack that we have downloaded from StencylForge. However, it's almost a certainty that we'll want to create our own sounds, or download sounds from other sources, in order to improve our games.

Now that we have a better understanding of the requirements for our audio files, let's have a go at importing an MP3 sound effect into Stencyl.

Time for action – importing a sound effect

The game file to import and load for this session is `5961_08_05.stencyl`.

1. Select **Dashboard | Sounds**.
2. In the main panel, click on the **Click here to create new Sound** option.
3. Name the sound `Monkey Dies` and click on **Create**.
4. In the **Properties** panel, ensure that **Sound Type** is configured as **Sound Effect**.

5. In the **Import a Sound** panel, click on the **Import MP3 option to display the file-locator** dialog box.

6. Locate and open the file `5961_08_Monkey_Dies.mp3` from the book's download files.

7. Note that, in the **Import a Sound** panel, the **MP3 is imported?** status is now checked, as shown in the following screenshot:

8. Also note that, in the **Properties** panel, the **Type** is set to: **Mono / 44100 Hz / No VBR**.

9. Click on the play button in the **Sound Player** panel at the lower-left corner of the screen to hear the newly imported sound effect.

What just happened?

We have imported an MP3 audio file as a sound effect, and it can now be used in our game as required.

As we have discovered, as long as our audio files are in the correct format, importing our own sounds into a game is a straightforward process.

We created the new sound in the **Sounds** section of the **Dashboard** tab, and specified that the sound was a **Sound Effect**. We then selected the required MP3 file using the file locator and tested the sound to ensure that it had been imported correctly.

 If we want to publish our game to a desktop platform, such as MS Windows, we must create an OGG version of the audio file, and import it using the same process by selecting the **Import OGG** option.

Have a go hero

The game file to import and load for this session is `5961_08_06.stencyl`.

We've now imported our own sound effect for use in our game and we also have the skills to import other sounds that we may require, so let's put these skills to good use.

- Implement the required instructions to play the `Monkey Dies` sound effect on channel 1, each time the player loses a life.

- If the monkey jumps immediately after collecting a piece of fruit, the pickup sound effect is interrupted by the jump sound effect. A very simple modification to the `Jump SFX` event can resolve this problem. (Hint: channel!)

- Consider where it may be appropriate to play additional sound effects within the game, and implement those sounds.

Take care not to overwhelm the player with sounds, and remember to specify whether the sound is a sound effect or music soundtrack, when importing audio files.

A suggested solution for implementing the `Monkey Dies` sound effect, together with comments can be found in the download file `5961_08_07.stencyl`. The modifications are in the `Show Angel` event in the `Health` actor behavior, and the `Play Monkey Dies SFX` event in the `Sound Management` scene behavior. The solution to the sound effect interruption can be found in the `Jump SFX` event.

Summary

The very last features that we implemented relate to the use of sound; we added some sound effects to further immerse the player into our game, and we also added a soundtrack.

We also considered how to organize the management of audio within a single behavior, in order to make it easier to maintain the use of sounds within our game.

Finally, we learned how easy it is to import sound files into Stencyl, and we took a quick look at some of the considerations that those developers with a more advanced knowledge of audio files should take into account.

The gameplay elements of our game have now been completed, and with only a little more tweaking and polishing, it will be ready to publish. However, before we publish our game, we might like to consider that creating games with Stencyl can offer financial rewards, and that's what we'll be discussing in *Chapter 9, Publishing and Making Money from Your Games*

9
Publishing and Making Money from Your Games

Now that we have completed our game, it would be a great idea to share it with the rest of the world, otherwise it is going to languish unloved on our computer's hard drive!

Publishing any game that we have made with Stencyl is a very straightforward process but, as is so often true when it comes to game development, we have many alternatives available to us. In this chapter, we'll examine some of the options available to us when publishing games that we have created for the Flash platform, which will enable us to upload our game to the Internet and share it with our friends, family, and anyone else who chooses to play it.

In addition to making our game available on the Internet, we'll also be taking a look at some of the different choices that are available to us if we would like to make some money from our game—many developers earn a reasonable living from publishing their games, so it's certainly something that we should consider. However, the great news is that even if we just want to develop games for fun, it is incredibly easy to earn some money using the tools that Stencyl makes available to us free of charge.

Completing the development of a game immediately leads us onto some additional, very important steps! In this chapter we'll be learning about:

- ◆ Publishing to the Stencyl Arcade
- ◆ Making money with in-game advertising
- ◆ Obtaining sponsorship
- ◆ Improving our opportunities for sponsorship

Before we start, let's discuss how this chapter relates to the Monkey Run game that we have created.

Because we have been learning how to create our game from a book, there are going to be many other developers who have also created a game that is identical, or similar, to our Monkey Run game. For this reason it is inadvisable to attempt to sell or otherwise commercialize Monkey Run in its current form—it will just be one of many similar versions of the same game, with the same graphics, and the same audio. Game publishers will most likely be very unhappy about having their time wasted in considering sponsorship of a game that is already freely and widely available on the Internet!

Although we will be using our Monkey Run game to learn the required skills in this chapter, the author recommends that the information learned here should be put into practice in an original game that you create using the skills that have been learned from this book.

Feel free to substantially modify the Monkey Run game, perhaps improve the gameplay and change the graphics and music, and then publish it or sell it as your own work. If you make substantial modifications to the Monkey Run game, and give it a different name, the author will be happy for you to call the game your own, and he will be very pleased if you are able to earn some income from your new found skills.

 It is the game developer's sole responsibility to ensure that they fully understand and adhere to the licensing terms related to any of the assets used in a published game (for example, providing correct attributions for audio and graphics). The game developer must also accept full liability for the incorrect use of such assets. For further information about some of the legal aspects of game development and publication, please see *Appendix, Planning, Resources, and Legal Issues.*

If you are planning to sell your game, or you are planning to obtain sponsorship for it, you should not upload your game to any location where it can be played by the general public, as this can severely reduce or possibly entirely eliminate the commercial value of your game. This issue is discussed later in this chapter in the section entitled, *Obtaining sponsorship*.

Now that we have discussed the formalities, let's go ahead and publish our game.

Publishing to the Stencyl Arcade

The Stencyl Arcade is an ideal place to publish our first game and, as we might guess from its title, the Stencyl Arcade is part of the `stencyl.com` website! It has been created for users of Stencyl to upload their creations and can be found at `www.stencyl.com/game`.

In the following screenshot we can see that the Stencyl Arcade is a curated environment with the most interesting games being marked as **Staff Picks**:

It's certainly worth taking the time to examine some of the games in the Stencyl Arcade, if only to see the high quality of the productions that can be created with Stencyl. However, don't allow the high standard of many of the games to discourage you—we all have to start somewhere!

While we're looking at these games, it should also be noted that popular and successful games do not necessarily need to have amazing graphics. For example, we can see in the previous screenshot that the excellent game **Hex Rotate** (created by Robert Alverez) is a puzzle game based on basic hexagonal shapes.

Uploading a game into the Stencyl Arcade is a very straightforward process, so let's get our first game online.

Time for action – publishing to the Stencyl Arcade

Before proceeding, ensure that the final, ready-to-play version of your game is open in Stencyl.

1. On the main Stencyl menu, at the top of the screen, select **Publish | Stencyl | Stencyl Arcade**.

2. Wait for the game to compile, after which the following dialog box will be displayed:

3. Click on **Yes** to confirm that this game is a work in progress.

4. A progress box will be displayed as the game is uploaded to the Stencyl Arcade (this may take a few minutes).

5. When the **Congratulations!** dialog box is displayed, click on the **Play it Now** button.

6. A new web browser page will open and after the game has loaded, test the game.

7. After testing the game, sign in to `stencyl.com` using the link in the upper-right corner of the web page, then click on your Stencyl username (upper-right corner of the screen) to display your user page which contains information about you, including your uploaded games, as shown in the following screenshot:

8. Click on the title of the game, below the joystick icon, to display your game's information page.

9. Note the banner advising that the game is unpublished, and also the **Actions** and **Edits** options towards the top of the web page.

What just happened?

We have published our game to the Stencyl Arcade, so anyone can now play it!

During the publishing process, we specified that the game is a work in progress, but the game is still available for public access in the Stencyl Arcade—it just means that players will have to choose to see games labeled as work in progress in order to see our game.

When the upload completed, we chose to open the game in a web browser so that we could play the game, and we tested it to ensure that it worked as expected. It's a good idea to immediately test any game that we upload, to ensure that everything has gone according to plan, so do take the time to test your uploaded game thoroughly.

Finally, we ensured that we were logged into `stencyl.com`, and we selected our game from our user page, so we could see its information page, along with the **Actions** and **Edits** options that will enable us to configure our game in the Stencyl Arcade.

Although we could have uploaded our game into the Stencyl Arcade as a fully published game, it's a good idea to initially upload it as a work in progress, so anyone can still play our game, but it is labeled as an incomplete work. Once we have tested our game online, it's a simple matter of changing the status of the game to **Published**, so that it appears in the main section of the Stencyl Arcade.

Have a go hero – changing our game's configuration

Our game is currently configured as a work in progress in the Stencyl Arcade. Once we have tested our game, and we are confident that it is ready to join all the other completed Stencyl games online, we need to change its status to **Published**, by accessing the appropriate **Actions** option above the game in the Stencyl Arcade. To change the game's configuration perform the following tasks:

- Ensuring that you are logged into the Stencyl website, locate your game in the Stencyl Arcade, and modify its settings using the appropriate **Actions** option, so that it becomes a fully published game

- Using the **Edits** option, update the **Game Details** to include some useful information about the game

- Also consider creating a logo for your game, a 120 x 90 pixel image that will be used in the Stencyl Arcade index, and uploading it using the **Logo** option in the **Edits** section

A game logo can also be added within Stencyl. In the main **Game Settings** dialog box, select **Settings | Main**, then click the **Select Image** button in the main panel of the dialog box. This image will be used as the game's logo when the game is next uploaded to the Stencyl Arcade.

Making money with in-game advertising

Anyone who has played more than a handful of online games will be familiar with the experience of seeing an advertisement within a game. These advertisements are included in the game by the developer, to earn some money!

It is the game developers' responsibility to ensure that they declare their income to the relevant authorities, and to pay any taxes as required by law.

All versions of Stencyl include instruction blocks relating to the display of advertisements, which provide a very easy way for us to earn some money from our games. However, before we examine these instruction blocks in detail, we need to consider how much money can be made from advertisements in online games.

We need to lay our cards on the table right now, and advise that most game developers do not earn much money from in-game advertising alone! However, this does not mean that implementing in-game advertisements should be overlooked, because many game developers receive a useful **residual income** from in-game advertisements. Furthermore, many amateur game developers are very happy to regularly receive small amounts of money to fund their hobby!

Residual income—or **passive income**—is the money that is earned automatically once the initial work has been completed—in our case, that work is the development of a game. To earn this residual income, we need to create a game with the ability to display advertisements and then each time an advertisement is displayed to a player of our game, we make some money! Before we get too excited about the prospect of earning money for nothing, now that our game has been completed, we need to be realistic about the financial returns from in-game advertising.

Payment for in-game advertisements is based on **Cost Per Mille (CPM)**. The CPM is the amount paid to the game developer for each one-thousand times that an advertisement is displayed. Although it's quite difficult to determine average CPM payments, because of confidentiality clauses in advertising contracts (developers are generally unable to publicize their income for contractual reasons), research shows that typical rates for CPM are between $0.10 and $1.00, with a common amount being around $0.25 to $0.30 CPM.

Let's examine that information more closely: it appears that, using one of the most popular in-game advertising systems, many developers are being paid about 25 cents for each thousand times that an advertisement is shown in their game! Although that sounds like a very small amount of money, the amount paid to the developer will depend upon how many times a game is played, and how many times an advertisement is shown within the game. If we consider that we might have 10,000 players, who each play the game one day each week for one year, we have the potential to display 520,000 advertisements, which at the rate of $0.25 CPM, will give us an annual residual income of $130. Research in various game developers' forums has indicated that this is a fairly realistic estimate of the income that might be earned from each game created by an amateur or hobbyist game developer but, of course, the income will depend very much upon the quality and popularity of the game. If we have five games, each earning $130 per annum, then we'll have a residual income of $650 every year. The more popular our game is, the greater the advertising income will be!

Some of the most popular online games have gained tens of millions of plays each year, which has the potential to earn the developers thousands of dollars in advertising revenue. Ninja Kiwi, the developer of Bloons—one of the most successful online games of all time— has stated that the game received over one billion plays in just over three years. If Bloons had an average CPM of $0.25 that would have brought in revenue of over $250,000 if an advertisement was shown just once each time the game was played!

Although we might dream of such success, we can see from the following screenshot that the graphics in Bloons are very basic (the developer has said that the monkey character was created in about five minutes).

Playing the game in which the monkey must pop a certain number of balloons with a limited number of darts, demonstrates that the gameplay mechanics are also somewhat rudimentary.

Simplicity is the hallmark of many popular and addictive games, and a game such as Bloons could easily be developed with Stencyl. In fact, one of the sample games currently provided with Stencyl is called Balloons, and is based on similar gameplay principles. In the following screenshot, we can see the similarities, and it might even be argued that the graphics in the Stencyl sample game are an improvement on those that can be found in the Bloons game on which it is based:

Although we can now see the potential for making money from in-game advertising, we should be realistic and understand that only the most successful games have such great earning potential!

Third-party advertisement providers

Stencyl provides instruction blocks that enable us to place advertisements, which are provided by the following third-party organizations:

- ◆ Mochi Media
- ◆ Kongregate
- ◆ Newgrounds

Instead of the developer having to spend his or her time finding advertisers who are prepared to pay for in-game placement of advertisements, the above organizations, effectively, act as brokers between the developer and the advertisers. The developer simply adds some instructions into his or her game and the advertisements magically appear at the required time!

Implementing in-game advertising

Now that we have discussed potential earnings from in-game advertising, let's look at the practical requirements for placing an advertisement in our own game.

Displaying advertisements from any of the above third-party organizations is a straightforward process, but we'll be implementing advertisements using the MochiAds service by Mochi Media, in our game.

Before we can start displaying advertisements with MochiAds, we must register as a developer with Mochi Media at `www.mochimedia.com/register/`. Registration is a straightforward process, requiring the following information:

- Username
- Email address
- Real name
- Password
- Language

 Always carefully read the terms of service when subscribing to an online service; it's important to understand what you are signing up for!

Once we have completed the signup process, we can create an entry for the new game in the MochiAds Dashboard. The game does not have to be ready for uploading at this point—in fact, it doesn't even need to exist, so we can prepare the game's entry in the dashboard in advance! The main section of the MochiAds **Add A New Game** screen is shown in the following screenshot:

Add A New Game

Setup Game → Insert Ad Code → Fill out Profile

Title:

Dimensions: Why is this importa[nt]
(width by height in pixels, example: 550x400) Which res[...]

Live Updates: ○ Yes ● No What is this?
Push live updates and encrypt your game! If you're not s[...]
always enable it at a later time.

Terms and Conditions ☐ By checking this box you agree to the MochiAd[s] work consists entirely of content you created yours[elf]

IMPORTANT NOTE: Do not upload any games without p[...] created yourself. Games should not include copyrighted [...] Nintendo's Mario, unless you are the owner or have per[m...] obscene games will not be accepted.

Create Game or cancel

As we can see in the above screenshot, we only need to provide a **Title** for the game and the **Dimensions**. The **Dimensions** field refers to the actual size of the game onscreen—not the size of the scene in Stencyl—and in our case, the dimensions are 640 x 480 pixels, but this may vary for other games that we create.

There is also an option to enable a feature called **Mochi Live Updates**, which enables developers to easily update their games with improvements and bug fixes, along with several other useful features. For the moment, we'll leave this option set to **No**—we can always change our minds if we decide that we need this feature at a later date.

 More information about the Mochi Live Updates feature can be found in the Mochi Media developer pages at www.mochimedia.com/developers/liveupdates.html.

Finally, we must agree to the terms and conditions of the MochiAds service, after reading the information carefully!

The next stage is to create the game's profile information, which includes a description, instructions, thumbnail images, and screenshots. We also need to provide information about the genre of the game, the language, and the keywords associated with the game.

On the profile page, we need to provide a link to a web page at which the reviewer (an employee of Mochi Media) can test the game to ensure that it meets the required standards. However, we haven't implemented advertising in the game yet, so this can be left for later.

Before we can implement advertisements, we need the unique Game ID for our game. When an advertisement is displayed, the Game ID is sent to the MochiAds servers, so they can track which advertisements have been displayed in which games. This process is vital so that the developers can be credited for the advertisements that are shown to players of their game.

To locate the unique Game ID, log in to the Mochi Media website and display the **Overview** screen for your game. In the left-hand side panel, towards the bottom of the web page, we should find a section entitled **Game ID** as shown in the following screenshot:

In the screenshot of the **Game ID** shown above, the information has been deliberately partially obscured. The Game ID must be kept private, and should only be used by the game's developer. Sharing a Game ID may be considered a breach of the Mochi Media Terms of Use and may lead to the user's account being terminated.

We need to make a note of the unique Game ID, as we will need it in the following *Time for action – inserting an advertisement into our game*, section.

Now that we have created a profile for the game in our Mochi Media account, and we have the unique Game ID, we are ready to place the advertisement in our game.

Time for action – inserting an advertisement into our game

Before proceeding, ensure that the final, ready-to-publish version of the game is open in Stencyl.

1. Open the **Main Menu** scene.

2. Click the **Events** button at the top of the Scene Designer screen.

3. Click **+Add Event | Basics |When Creating**.

4. Rename the event to `Display Mochi Ad`.

5. In the instruction block palette, select **Game | Flash**.

6. In the **Mochi** section of the palette, locate the **show ad with size (w: 0, h: 0)** block and drag it into the new **when created** event.

7. In the new **show ad with size (w: 0, h: 0)** block, change the **w:** entry to `640` and the **h:** entry to `480`.

8. Ensure that the new event appears as shown in the following screenshot:

9. Click on the **Settings** icon in the main Stencyl toolbar.

10. Select **Web** in the list of options in the left-hand side panel and ensure that the **Services** option is selected at the top of the main dialog box panel.

11. Accurately enter the unique Game ID into the **Mochi Game ID** text box and click **OK**.

12. Test the game. When the game loads the following message (or similar) will be displayed:

13. Click on the **Play** button, in the lower-right corner of the game's screen, to play the game.

What just happened?

We have successfully implemented the MochiAds advertising instructions in our game, and the message has let us know that our game has correctly communicated with the MochiAds servers.

The first step was to create a new **when created** event in the **Main Menu** scene. We then added the instruction block that displays the advertisement, but we needed to specify the size of the advertisement, so we provided the correct dimensions of our game—640 pixels wide and 480 pixels high. Providing the correct dimensions ensures that the advertisement will completely fill the screen, and failure to provide the correct information may lead to inappropriately sized advertisements being placed.

Once we had the Mochi Ad instruction block in place, we needed to let Stencyl know the unique Game ID, so that it can be passed to the MochiAds servers each time an advertisement is displayed. The Game ID was placed into the **Mochi Game ID** text box, in the **Web** section of the Stencyl **Settings** dialog box.

We're nearly at the stage where we can start being credited for each advertisement that is displayed in our game, but there's a little more work required to configure our game in the Mochi Media Dashboard.

Have a go hero – finalizing the MochiAds configuration

We haven't provided enough information for Mochi Media to start displaying real advertisements in our game and to start being paid, so sign in to the Mochi Media website, display the overview page for your game, and click on the **Activate NOW!** button under the **Ads** heading.

The page that will be displayed will take you step by step through completing your game profile, uploading your game, and having it reviewed by a member of the MochiAds team to ensure that it meets the required standards.

Before Mochi Media can transfer any money to you, you will also need to provide some payment details. Note that payment information does not need to be provided immediately—Mochi Media will continue to credit your account and will hold payment until the required information has been provided.

The Mochi Media review process

Mochi Media needs to ensure that advertisements are only displayed in appropriate games, so a Mochi Media employee will check your game to make sure that it works, and that the content of the game is appropriate for the target audience. As long as your game is playable, is of a reasonable standard, and does not contain obvious bugs, your game should be accepted within approximately 24 hours of correctly completing the game profile.

 The Monkey Run game, exactly as developed throughout this book, was submitted for review and was accepted into the MochiAds program within 24 hours.

Preloaders and advertising

While this book has primarily been designed to be used with the free version of Stencyl, it should be noted that the subscription versions of Stencyl that output Flash games include the ability to create a custom **preloader**—the graphics and progress bar that are displayed as the game is loading on a web page. One of the custom preloader options provides the facility to display advertisements while the game is loading. This provides a more professional impression of the game and is accepted within the gaming community as an acceptable method of displaying advertisements without interfering with, or slowing down, the player's entry into the game.

Obtaining sponsorship

Earning money via advertisements is just one, very easy, way to bring in revenue from a game but, as already discussed, it is not likely to earn the game developer very much money unless the game is extremely popular.

An alternative way of making money from a game is to obtain sponsorship from a publisher. There are several different types of sponsorships, and it's a good idea to carry out full research before committing to a contract, but the most common types of sponsorship are explained in this section.

 Sponsors may offer varying terms and will often have their own customized sponsorship deals. Please ensure that you fully understand the terms of any contract that you enter into, taking professional legal advice as appropriate. The following explanations are offered only as a guide to some of the types of sponsorship that are available.

Understanding sponsorships

Sponsors will pay you to put their logos and web links into your games so that each time your game is played on the Internet, the player will see the sponsor's logo and will have the opportunity to click through to the sponsor's website. The benefit to the sponsors is that displaying their logo raises the profile of their brand name, which leads to more game players visiting their website. The sponsors may then earn revenue from advertising on their website, or they may encourage their website visitors to spend money—for example, they may sell premium mobile games.

Typically, a sponsor will be a game publisher—they will specialize in branding games with their logo, and will encourage as many players as possible to visit their website and play games branded with their logo. However, other organizations not related to the computer games industry do sponsor games in order to promote their products, although this is less common.

Each sponsor's terms and conditions will vary but, in broad terms, there are three main types of game sponsorship.

Primary sponsorship

With a **primary sponsorship**, also known as a **non-exclusive sponsorship**, a sponsor will pay the game developer to brand a game with the sponsor's logos and with links to the sponsor's website. The game will then be released publicly for display on as many websites as possible. The sponsor derives maximum benefit when the game is very widely distributed—it's not untypical for such a sponsored game to feature on many thousands of Flash game websites and to receive millions of gameplays! It is in the sponsors' best interests to ensure that the game is seen by as many players as possible, so they will make their best efforts to have the game promoted extensively.

The benefit to game developers is that they receive an up front payment, and their game can achieve a very high profile within the gaming community—that's free advertising for the game developer's skills, which may then lead to further paid game development work!

An additional financial benefit to the game developer is that primary sponsors will often allow the developer to include advertisements in the game, so the developer will receive revenue from the advertisements in addition to the initial up front sponsorship fee.

Primary sponsorship will usually provide the game developer with the benefit of exploring revenue opportunities from **secondary sponsorships**.

Secondary sponsorship

Secondary sponsorships can provide additional income from a game that has already received primary sponsorship! The game developer can receive sponsorship payments from secondary sponsors who wish to pay for the game to be published on their own websites with their own branding. With this type of sponsorship, the developer will remove the primary sponsor's branding and will site lock the game to the secondary sponsor's website.

 Site locking ensures that a game can only run on a specified website—this is a built-in feature of Stencyl, and is easily implemented by selecting **Settings | Loader | General**.

Because secondary sponsorships target a much smaller audience of game players, fees are much lower than they are for primary sponsorships.

Exclusive sponsorship

As we might guess from its title, an **exclusive sponsorship** is exclusive! With this type of sponsorship, the game developer sells the sponsor the exclusive right to publish the game, which means that, in effect, the game developer is paid an up front fee for implementing the sponsor's branding in the game. The game developer then hands the completed game over to the sponsor so, effectively, the game becomes the sponsor's property.

While this type of sponsorship can be far more lucrative than a primary sponsorship, the game developer has no further opportunity to earn any money from the game.

With an exclusive sponsorship, the developer may be able to retain intellectual property rights to the game, which means that, if the original game is very popular, the developer could create a sequel using the same game characters and graphics.

Sponsorship payments

The details of most sponsorship deals remain private for contractual reasons, but some information about sponsorship fees are freely available on the Internet. For example, at the time of publishing, Armor Games—a major player in the Flash game publishing industry—states on its website, that typical sponsorship payments range from $1,500 to $7,000. They also advise that they are prepared to pay more for higher quality games! More information about sponsorship by Armor Games can be found at `armorgames.com/page/sponsorship`.

Investigation within various industry-related Internet discussion forums indicates that typical fees for secondary sponsorships range from a few tens of dollars to the low hundreds of dollars, although higher amounts have been paid for top-quality games.

We can see that, for well designed games, the earning potential is quite great—there are certainly many developers who make a full-time living from game development. However, we must temper our enthusiasm, and understand that although the market for games is vast, there are many people attempting to earn money from game development. Nevertheless, we shouldn't let the possibility of competition put us off. If we develop games for fun, then any money we earn is a bonus and, if we are planning to make a living from game development, it's better to know the facts before starting a project!

Where to find sponsorship

Understanding the different models for sponsorship of games is vital but, equally important, is knowing where to find sponsorship!

Flash Game License (FGL)

`FGL.com`, formally known as **Flash Game License**, is a popular market place dedicated to bringing together game developers and sponsors. In essence, FGL allows developers to auction their games to an audience of sponsors. However, the developer is not obliged to accept the highest bid (or any bid)—the developer can choose which, if any, bid they consider to be the best overall deal. When a deal is agreed, the developer pays a commission of 10% to FGL.

While FGL was originally dedicated to marketing Flash games, it later rebranded in order to widen its scope to include other gameplaying platforms such as iOS, Android, and HTML.

`FGL.com` is a valuable resource for game developers, and it's certainly worth visiting the FGLopedia (`www.fgl.com/view_library.php`), which contains information about sponsorship and licensing models, a guide for new game developers, and other useful useful resources, including information about how to maximize sponsorship revenue.

Before openly marketing a game on FGL, developers must firstly have the game approved by an FGL employee to ensure that it meets the required standards. Once a game has been approved (usually within 72 hours according to FGL), the developer can choose to provide access to other developers in order to receive feedback about the game. This is an excellent opportunity to receive constructive criticism and advice from professional game developers—the FGL community has an overwhelmingly positive attitude with helpful advice being offered by game developers, many of whom have already successfully received sponsorship for their own games.

If appropriate, and it usually is appropriate, the game developers can then make the suggested improvements to their game and upload it again in order to elicit further feedback. This process can be repeated as often as desired until the developer is confident that his game is ready for marketing, at which time it can be made visible to sponsors, who can then start to place bids.

Do take the time to become part of the FGL community—review other developers' games and offer your own feedback!

Industry networking

Another way to obtain sponsorship is by directly contacting sponsors and cultivating relationships with in the industry. Many sponsors are happy for developers to contact them directly, and provide information about how to approach them with regards to receiving sponsorship.

Some examples of industry-leading sponsors, together with their contact details are given in the following list:

◆ **Miniclip**—`corporate.miniclip.com/page/view/developers`

◆ **Addicting Games**—`www.addictinggames.com/game/upload.jsp`

◆ **King**—`www.king.com/support/partner_program.jsp`

◆ **Armor Games**—`armorgames.com/page/sponsorship`

Always communicate with sponsors in a professional manner, and understand that some sponsors will receive communications from hundreds of developers each week, so they may take some time to respond—patience is the key!

Improving our opportunities for sponsorship

Clearly, sponsors are only going to be interested in paying for games that they consider to have great potential for popularity among game players. After all, the sponsor is paying for as many people as possible to see his branding in the game!

It is important, therefore, to ensure that any game we intend to put up for sponsorship is of the highest quality that we can achieve. When your game is complete, ensure that, at minimum, you check the following points prior to pursuing sponsorship:

- Ensure that the game has been tested thoroughly and that all known bugs have been eliminated
- Check that you have adhered to any licensing requirements for third-party assets used in your game (for example, artwork, music, sound effects)
- Keep a record of any license agreements relevant to your in-game assets
- Have a *written* agreement with anyone else who has contributed to the development of the game (for example, artists, musicians, designers)
- Do not release the game publicly—this will devalue your game and is highly likely to eliminate any possibility of a sponsorship deal
- Adhere to any legal requirements relevant in your region

Finally, do your own research—the information in this book is offered as a guide, but the game developer must take responsibility for his or her own actions! Time passes very quickly on the Internet, and industry standards change frequently, so be sure to research and participate in appropriate discussion forums to determine the latest industry standards. And, where appropriate, take professional advice prior to entering into any legal contracts.

Mobile game monetization opportunities

In-game advertising and obtaining sponsorship are popular methods of monetizing both desktop and mobile games, but Stencyl does offer additional methods of earning revenue from mobile games.

In-app purchases

A popular model for generating revenue from mobile games is to initially provide the game free of charge, but then to encourage players to purchase items throughout the game. **In-app purchases (IAPs)**, on mobile devices provide a facility whereby game players can purchase virtual items to aid their progress throughout a game. For example, in a motor-racing game, the player may be able to purchase a larger engine for his car or maybe they could purchase special tires to gain a speed advantage on a particular type of race track.

Stencyl makes the implementation of IAPs within our mobile games quite straightforward—the instruction blocks for working with IAPs are shown in the following screenshot:

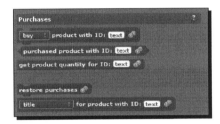

In addition to implementing IAPs within the game itself, the developer must enter into a contract with the relevant app store (that is Google Play or Apple App Store on iTunes), and it is also necessary to configure the items to be purchased in the relevant app store developer portal.

 The configuration and implementation of IAPs is beyond the scope of this book. However, step-by-step instructions for implementing, testing, and trouble shooting IAPs are available on the Stencyl help pages at `www.stencyl.com/help`.

App store sales

Many game players are happy to pay a one-off fee for good-quality games, and making our mobile games available for purchase in the Google Play and Apple App Store on iTunes is a topic that we'll be discussing in *Chapter 10, Targeting Mobile Platforms*.

Summary

In this chapter we took our first step into the world of publishing Flash games—we uploaded our game to the Stencyl Arcade so anyone with Internet access can play it. We then learned about the possibilities of earning some money through in-game advertising, which led us to implement MochiAds into our game. And we discovered that implementing advertising is a very straightforward process requiring just a single instruction block from the Stencyl palette.

We then examined some of the different sponsorship models that enable us to license our work, and how revenue can be maximized by choosing the correct type of sponsorship.

Finally, we took a quick look at the additional monetization opportunities available to developers of mobile games.

We have completed our game, published it, and perhaps earned some money from advertising or sponsorship! It is now a great time to widen our horizons from the development of web games, and consider how we can get a game up and running on some mobile devices such as smartphones and tablets, so let's head off to *Chapter 10, Targeting Mobile Platforms*.

10
Targeting Mobile Platforms

The mobile game market is growing dramatically. Although data does vary depending on the sources of information, the general consensus from analysts is that the mobile game market generated in the region of US $10 billion in revenue in 2012, and it is expected to be around double that amount by the end of 2016.

In the past, developing for mobile platforms, such as smartphones and tablet devices, required very specialist skills (each mobile platform has its own SDK (software development kit)), and special tools were required to create applications for each target platform. For example, developing for Apple's iOS operating system for iPad and iPhone required the developer to learn Objective-C (a unique variant of the popular C programming language), and Google's Android platform required different tools and another programming language called Java.

As a result of this mobile-platform diversification, developing games for mobile devices was more expensive and time-consuming than it should have been. Larger software houses were required to have teams developing for each platform, and the only option for independent developers was either to learn multiple programming languages or to find someone who could convert their game for them!

Stencyl alleviates this multiplatform problem by allowing us to develop games on a single platform, and to output those games to many different target platforms including mobile devices. We're going to learn how we can easily utilize some of the unique features of mobile devices to control games and provide feedback for our players.

In this chapter we will be:

- Understanding testing versus publishing
- Considering certification requirements
- Examining platform differences
- Testing on a mobile device
- Utilizing the accelerometer
- Implementing touch controls
- Exploring additional mobile device features

Before proceeding, be aware that mobile device technologies and development techniques can change very rapidly. The information in this book was accurate at the time of publishing, but the Stencyl toolkit and its features may have been updated since publication, and the third-party organizations that have been referred to may have updated their tools and licensing requirements.

While Stencyl makes developing games for mobile devices very easy when compared to traditional coding requirements, the configuration processes required outside of Stencyl in order to provision mobile development on iOS devices are notoriously complex (testing on Android devices is much more straightforward). The purpose of this chapter is to provide guidance for creating mobile games with Stencyl, along with hands-on tutorials that will enable us to quickly implement the unique features of mobile devices, such as the accelerometer and touchscreen controls. Where appropriate, links to external resources, which will aid the developer in configuring their computer ready for mobile development, have been provided.

 For the latest information relating to mobile game development with Stencyl, and for the latest news relating to the features of the Stencyl development toolkit, please read the online help and also visit the official Stencyl forums at www.stencyl.com.

Let's start by looking at what we need, in order to start creating games for platforms other than Flash and HTML.

Understanding testing versus publishing

One of the most amazing features of the free version of Stencyl is that it enables developers to develop games for and to test games on all the supported platforms listed as follows:

- Flash (desktop Player and web browser)
- HTML5 (web browser)

- Microsoft Windows (desktop)
- Mac OS X (desktop)
- Linux (desktop)
- iOS (iPhone / iPad / iPod touch)
- Android (tablets / smartphones)

For more details about the supported versions of each of the above platforms, please refer to *Chapter 1, Introduction*, and for the very latest information, visit `www.stencyl.com`.

Before we learn how to use the mobile development tools available to us in Stencyl, it's important to understand the difference between testing and publishing games.

Testing games with the free version of Stencyl

When we develop a game in Stencyl, we not only design and create the game, but we also test it. During the development of our Monkey Run game, we were testing it using the desktop Flash Player application. When we first installed Stencyl, the Flash Player was installed automatically, so that when we click on the **Test Game** button in Stencyl, the game is automatically compiled and then run in the Flash Player on the desktop. However, if we had access to the appropriate hardware, we could have tested our game on any of the available target platforms listed previously.

 Although unrelated to mobile development, it's also worth noting that when creating desktop applications, the target desktop platform is limited to that of the development platform. That is, Microsoft Windows desktop games can only be created on a Windows PC, Linux desktop games can only be created on a Linux PC, and Mac OS X games can only be created on a Mac.

When developing for mobile devices, the most practical way in which to test our games is to connect the mobile device to the desktop computer with the appropriate cable, so Stencyl can send the game directly to the device. The following table shows the mobile devices that we can test on with the free version of Stencyl:

		Target test-device	
		iOS	Android
Development platform	Windows	experimental feature	✓
	Mac OS X	✓	✓
	Linux	✗	✓

As shown in the previous table, the free version of Stencyl includes the ability to test games on iOS devices when developing on the MS Windows platform. However, this is, at the time of writing, an experimental feature with technical limitations.

 More information about this experimental feature can be found in Stencyl's online help at www.stencyl.com/help/view/testing-ios-windows.

Developers with an appropriate paid subscription version of Stencyl, running on Microsoft Windows, can create games for iOS devices using an online service called StencylBuilder. The Stencyl game file is automatically uploaded to Stencyl LLC's servers, and is compiled on a Mac. The developer can then download the target file for testing on an iOS device, or for publishing to the Apple App Store (both subject to membership of Apple's iOS Developer Program).

It's important to understand that in terms of mobile target platforms, there is a difference between testing Stencyl games and publishing them. When we test a mobile game using Stencyl, we compile the game and then run it on the target device, such as a smartphone or tablet, but we cannot publish the game for others to download and install on their mobile devices. However, the ability to run the game on the device enables us to ensure that the game works correctly — we'll see exactly what the players of our game can see, and we can modify or improve the game as required. This means that we can fully develop and test our game without paying for a subscription to Stencyl. We only need to part with our money when we are confident that our game works on the target platform, and we are then ready for publishing.

Publishing Stencyl games

When we publish to a mobile platform, we mean that the game is ready to be uploaded to the relevant app store; for Android, it is the Google Play Store, and for Apple, it is the App Store on iTunes.

Each of the above app stores has its own requirements for licensing, so be sure to read the relevant terms and conditions carefully before making a commitment to either organization. However, the most important consideration for many developers is cost.

In order to publish a Stencyl game for a mobile device, a premium Stencyl subscription is required. Stencyl's Mobile and Studio subscriptions include the facility to publish to the Google and Apple app stores, so one of these Stencyl subscriptions will be required. In addition, both Apple and Google charge a fee to join their developer programs.

Developer licensing for Google Android devices

Google's fee (currently a one-time US $25 payment) is only required for developers who wish to publish to the Google Play Store; neither a fee nor any kind of registration is required in order to develop, test, or distribute apps for Android devices. This means that we only need to pay Google if we wish to upload our games to the Google Play Store!

In practice, the vast majority of developers pay the one-off registration fee to Google, so that they can upload their apps and games to the Google Play Store and gain the widest possible exposure for their work. However, some developers do choose to distribute their apps and games from their own websites, and to manage customer payments using their own or a third-party system, or they simply give away their games and apps for free!

Developer licensing for Apple iOS devices

Apple's fee for developers wishing to join the iOS Developer Program is currently US $99 per year. Membership of the iOS Developer program is required for both testing games on an iOS device and for publishing to the Apple App Store on iTunes. Currently, there is no Apple-authorized method to bypass Apple's registration and licensing requirements.

 Be aware that membership of the iOS Developer Program is required to maintain apps in the Apple App Store. If a developer's annual membership lapses, any existing apps will no longer be available in the App Store for customers to download.

As discussed previously, the free version of Stencyl can be used to develop games and to test them on an iOS device. However, paid membership of the Apple Developer Program is a mandatory requirement.

Mobile game distribution costs

When using the Apple App Store or the Google Play Store to distribute games, the respective organization will charge an item fee for processing each sale. Currently, both Apple and Google charge a fee of 30 percent of the sale price of the game. They will take care of receiving payments from customers and will make the relevant payments to the developer, subject to the terms and conditions of the relevant developer agreement.

The Apple and Google app stores can also be used to distribute free games, in which case, there is no item processing fee.

Considering certification requirements

Before an application can be tested or published on a mobile device, a **certificate** is required. A certificate is an electronic document in the form of a file that is stored on the developer's hard drive, and it is accessed by Stencyl when creating the game for testing or publishing on the mobile device.

Certificates for publishing games to the Google Play Store and to the Apple App Store can be obtained by signing in to the developer's account on the respective organization's website. For the specific steps, please follow the instructions provided by Apple or Google as required.

It is very common for developers to experience difficulties with creating, obtaining, and implementing the required development certificates (especially for iOS devices, for which provisioning profiles are also required), as the process is widely acknowledged to be somewhat convoluted!

One of the most important things to understand about certificates is that the certificates used for testing are different to the certificates used for publishing. So do bear this in mind when working through the certificate-creation process.

If difficulties arise while working with mobile device certificates and provisioning profiles, read the relevant topics in the official Stencyl online help, where step-by-step guides have been provided, and visit the official forums at `www.stencyl.com`.

A comprehensive two-part guide to the process of understanding, creating, and configuring certificates for iOS can be found on the Stencyl help pages at `www.stencyl.com/help/view/ios-certificates-guide`. It is highly recommended that iOS developers follow the guide carefully prior to proceeding with the tutorials in this chapter.

Testing Stencyl games on Android devices is very straightforward; just connect the device to the computer, change the target device in Stencyl to **Android**, and click on **Test Game**. Stencyl automatically creates a certificate for testing!

Examining platform differences

When designing a game for use on a mobile device, we need to take into account a number of considerations relating to the form of the device, the way that the user holds it and interacts with it. We may also need to take other issues into consideration — mobile devices are usually far less powerful than desktop computers and laptops, so we need to be careful to ensure that our game will not slow down due to intensive processing of graphics. Following is a list of some of the issues that we need to consider when developing for mobile devices:

- Large or numerous graphics can quickly deplete a mobile device's memory capacity

- Too many onscreen actors can slow a game down so that it is no longer playable

- The player is unlikely to have a keyboard or mouse with which to control the game

- The mobile device may have a small screen, making it difficult for the player to see important gameplay elements and controls

- Mobile games can be stopped and restarted at any time, such as when an incoming call occurs on a mobile phone

The above issues might be considered to be a list of disadvantages; the points listed are overwhelmingly negative! However, we should also consider that mobile platforms also offer several advantages over traditional PCs:

- Touchscreens offer opportunities for increased and more natural and entertaining interactivity

- Many mobile devices include features, such as vibration feedback, that are not found on desktop computers and laptops

- Accelerometers are now common in many mobile devices; this enables us to determine at what angle the mobile device is being held

- Most mobile device owners have an app store account, which is associated with some form of instant payment

We can see that, although there are some obvious limitations to games running on mobile devices, there are also some exciting features that can be introduced into a game; both from the player's point of view (more fun) and the developer's point of view (more money)!

The previous lists are not exhaustive. There are many issues and benefits related to mobile device development, so do plenty of research and think carefully when planning games for specific or multiplatform use, and try to be creative and original.

The great news for us (as game developers) is that Stencyl doesn't care which type of mobile device we are developing the game for! In the vast majority of cases, we can simply use the instruction blocks that access mobile-device features such as touchscreen, vibration, and accelerometer, and Stencyl will correctly create the appropriate code at compilation time, regardless of whether the device is a tablet or smartphone or whether it is running iOS or Android. If the hardware isn't available on the device (for example, not all tablets have a vibration feature), the game will run on that device, and simply ignore the missing feature.

Testing on a mobile device

In the following two practical sessions, we will be separately testing a basic game on an Android device and then on an iOS device. For those users who only have an Android device, the section entitled *Time for action – testing on an iOS device*, can be skipped, and for those users with only an iOS device, the section, *Time for action – testing on an Android device*, can be skipped!

We're going to create a very basic game, so that we can speed up the process of testing the mobile development platform, and to ensure that it is working correctly. Compiling complex games for transferring to a mobile device generally takes much longer than it does for Flash games, and it can be frustrating to wait for a large game to compile, only to find that it will not transfer to the mobile device because of an incorrect configuration.

The first time Stencyl compiles for a mobile device, the process can take several minutes — perhaps 10 minutes or more on a slow desktop computer. So do be patient during the compilation process. Once a game has been compiled for the first time, it will generally be much faster for future compilations — perhaps just a few minutes. But this does depend on any changes made to the game, the speed of the development computer, and the complexity of the game. Patience is the keyword when testing on mobile devices!

Testing on an Android device

Stencyl can output a game for testing on an Android device using any of the three supported development platforms: Microsoft Windows, Mac OS X, and Linux.

It's important to ensure that any drivers required for communicating with the Android device are installed on the development computer. Typically, most users will already have these installed, but it's easy to test the drivers by connecting the Android device to the computer and seeing if it is a recognized device. If the device is not recognized, follow the device manufacturer's instructions for installing the required drivers on the computer.

USB debugging must be enabled on Android devices. This is usually achieved by viewing the settings screen on the phone or tablet, and selecting either **Development**, or **Applications | Development**, to find the **USB debugging** option. The exact steps required to enable USB debugging may differ depending on the model of the device, so check the reference manual, or search the Internet for instructions.

Note that if USB debugging is not enabled, the development computer may still recognize that the Android device is connected, and Stencyl will probably complete the whole compilation process, but it will fail to send the test game to the device!

For further information and troubleshooting tips for working with Android devices, see the following Stencyl help page: www.stencyl.com/help/view/setup-android.

During the following practical session, there may be several on-screen prompts requiring the downloading and installation of various development tools. So take care to read the instructions carefully, and be patient while any required software is downloaded and installed — some of the toolkits are very large downloads.

Also be aware that the instructions for downloading the third-party toolkits may vary slightly from the instructions provided by Stencyl. Unfortunately, the developers of these toolkits do change the download locations and instructions from time to time, and this is beyond the control of the developers of Stencyl. If in doubt, take some time out and ask for assistance on the official Stencyl forums at www.stencyl.com. The development computer will patiently wait as long as required for the relevant buttons to be pressed, so there's no hurry. Getting it wrong and having to start from the beginning will take much longer and be more frustrating than working at a steady pace and getting it right the first time!

Time for action – testing on an Android device

A game file is not required for this session. We're going to create a blank game for our initial mobile test.

1. Attach the Android device to the development PC using the appropriate USB cable.

2. Open Stencyl and create a new game called Mobile Testing Android.

3. Create a new scene called Test Scene, and set the **Background color** to **Light Turquoise**.

4. In the main Stencyl toolbar, select **Android** in the target device drop-down box next to the **Test Game** button, as shown in the following screenshot:

5. Ensure that Stencyl's **Log Viewer** window is open: **View | Log Viewer** in the main Stencyl menu.

6. Click on **Test Game**.

7. Follow any prompts to download and install the relevant **software development kits** (**SDKs**), which may be required if not already installed on the computer.

8. After the installation of any required SDKs, there may be a prompt to restart Stencyl. So quit and restart Stencyl, load the **Mobile Testing Android** game, ensure the **Log Viewer** window is open, and test the game again.

9. The compilation process can take several minutes, depending on the speed of the development computer. Be patient!

10. When the compilation process has completed, Stencyl will display a **Sending to Device...** message, and shortly after this, the game (a blank blue screen) will appear on the mobile device!

What just happened?

We have created an empty test game with a colored background, and tested it on our Android device. We selected a colored background to help us determine if the game is being displayed correctly on the mobile device's screen; if we had selected a white or black background, it might not be very clear whether or not the game is running correctly. However, with the colored background, it is clear that our game is being displayed as expected.

The first time we attempt to test a game on a mobile device, Stencyl checks if the relevant SDKs have been installed. The two required SDKs are the Java Development Kit and the Android Development Kit, and Stencyl provides the relevant prompts and instructions where these are required. Some users may already have one or both of these kits installed on their development computer, so Stencyl will only prompt for installation if needed.

During the compilation process, a detailed log of events is displayed in the **Log Viewer** window, which can provide useful information in the event when something goes wrong.

Testing on an iOS device

As discussed earlier in this chapter, it is important to understand that creating games for iOS devices (even test games that will not appear in the Apple App Store) requires paid membership to Apple's iOS development program.

Also, prior to testing on an iOS device, it is important to ensure that the relevant certificates and provisioning profiles have been created, downloaded, and configured in advance; otherwise the compilation process will fail at the final stages. See the earlier section, *Considering certification requirements*, for further information.

Time for action – testing on an iOS device

A game file is not required for this session. We're going to create a blank game for our initial mobile tests.

1. Attach your iOS device to your Mac using the supplied USB cable.
2. Open Stencyl and create a new game called `Mobile Testing iOS`.
3. Create a new scene called `Test Scene`, and set the **Background color** to **Light Turquoise**.
4. In the main Stencyl toolbar, select **iOS Device** in the target device drop-down list next to the **Test Game** button, as shown in the following screenshot:

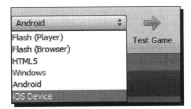

5. Ensure that Stencyl's **Log Viewer** window is open: **View | Log Viewer** in the main Stencyl menu.
6. Click on **Test Game** to start the compilation process.
7. The compilation process can take several minutes, depending on the speed of the development computer. Be patient!
8. When the compilation process has completed, Stencyl will display a **Sending to Device...** message, and shortly after this, the game (a blank, blue screen) will appear on the iOS device!

What just happened?

We created an empty test game with a colored background and tested it on our iOS device.

A colored background was selected to help us determine if the game is being displayed correctly on the mobile device's screen; if we had selected a white or black background, it might not be very clear that the game is running correctly. However, with the colored background, it is clear that our game is being displayed as expected.

With a correctly configured development system, getting a test game up and running on an iOS device is as straightforward as selecting the appropriate target device from the drop-down box, clicking on **Test Game**, and then waiting patiently!

During the compilation process, a detailed log of events is displayed in the **Log Viewer** window and this information can be useful if something goes wrong.

Utilizing the accelerometer

Most mobile devices now have an **accelerometer** embedded in them. This is the electronic component in a tablet or smartphone that enables applications and games to determine at what angle the device is being held. Typically, the mobile device's operating system will use the accelerometer to rotate the screen to display content in either portrait or landscape mode. However, game developers can access this positioning information and use it to allow players to control the action within their games!

Note that the rest of *Time for action* sections in this chapter apply to both iOS and Android devices, and will work on all the supported development platforms. However, if the mobile device being used for testing does not support the feature being tested, it will not work on that device!

> iOS developers should ensure that, if using the download file provided on the Packt Publishing website, a valid provisioning profile and certificate should be specified in Stencyl's **Settings** dialog box.

Time for action – experimenting with the accelerometer

The game file to import and load for this session is `5961_10_01.stencyl`.

Before we attempt to use the accelerometer in a practical test game, let's carry out an experiment to learn how Stencyl accesses the accelerometer information on a mobile device.

> The mobile device must have a built-in accelerometer in order for the following instructions to work.

1. Attach the mobile device to the development computer using the supplied USB cable.

2. Continue to use the blank game created in either of the sections, *Time for action – testing on an Android device*, or *Time for action – testing on an iOS device*. Alternatively, import the specified download file for this session.

3. Open **Test Scene** and select the **Events** button at the upper-center of the screen.

4. Select **+ Add Event | Basics | When Drawing**.

5. In the new **when drawing** event, add the instruction blocks shown as follows, noting that the **... of accelerometer** block can be found in the instruction block palette under **User Input | Mobile-Only**:

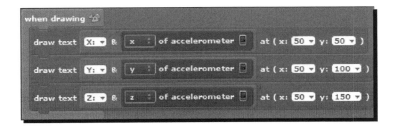

6. Ensure that the target device drop-down box next to the **Test Game** button, on the Stencyl toolbar, is set to **Flash (Player)**; we're going to test the game in Flash first!

7. Click on the **Test Game** button and view the game on the development computer's screen. It should appear as shown in the following screenshot:

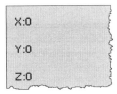

8. Close the **Flash Player** window.

9. Change the target device drop-down box to either **Android** or **iOS Device**, as appropriate for the attached mobile device, and click on **Test Game**.

10. Wait for the game to be compiled and sent to the device.

11. The game should appear on the mobile device's screen, shown as follows (note that the numbers will be constantly changing, and the numbers in the following screenshot are for illustration only):

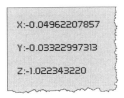

12. Hold the mobile device and tilt it at various angles, noting that, the greater the angle, the greater the change in the numbers being displayed.

What just happened?

We have created a test environment to discover how feedback from the mobile device's accelerometer is sent to a game in Stencyl. Our test environment is very basic; it simply consists of a `when drawing` event that draws the **X**, **Y**, and **Z** values of the mobile device's accelerometer on the screen.

Prior to testing the game on the mobile device, we first tested it in the Flash Player. But, why did we do this when we know that our development computer doesn't have an accelerometer? Compiling and testing on mobile devices can be a time-consuming process, and when errors occur within our code (errors will sometimes occur within our code because we're human), a lot of time can be wasted because of the relatively long compilation and testing process. However, testing in the Flash Player is much faster (typically a few seconds, rather than several minutes for a mobile device), and it is a great way to find basic errors before committing to testing on a tablet or smartphone. For example, if we miscalculated or mistyped the x and y screen-location values for any of the three `draw text` blocks in our test game, the game would successfully compile and run on the mobile device, but we might not be able to see the required information. Testing using the Flash Player in the first instance can help to avoid this kind of time-consuming error.

Once we knew that the game compiled and displayed the information in the correct location in the Flash Player, we then tested the game directly on the mobile device, and we learnt that information from the accelerometer is provided as constantly changing numbers. We also learnt that holding and tilting the device at various angles caused changes in the numbers provided by the accelerometer.

Understanding accelerometer feedback

Initially, the x, y, and z information provided by the accelerometer may appear difficult to understand. So let's have a look at the following diagram, which shows the position of each axis as it relates to a typical mobile device held in the portrait position:

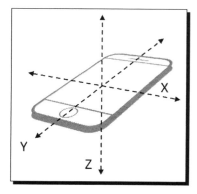

Many readers will have had a quick look at the previous diagram, and will now have a full understanding of the workings of the accelerometer, and how the onscreen numbers relate to the mobile device's position. The rest of us need to experience something a little more practical!

Let's take a few moments to examine how our test game's onscreen numbers change in relation to the physical position of the device, so we can start to make sense of them. This requires some methodical experimentation, and in each case, we will start the experiment by holding the mobile device in the same position — in front of us in the portrait position with the screen facing directly upwards (towards the ceiling), and with the accelerometer information being displayed onscreen, the correct way up:

Disconnect the device from the development computer and hold it so that both the x and y axes numbers are fairly close to zero. It should be possible to maintain the device in a flat position, where both the x and y feedback numbers are somewhere between *-0.09* and *0.09*. Don't worry about the z feedback for the time being!

We can now start to move the mobile device, in order to more clearly demonstrate the feedback from the accelerometer.

Understanding the x axis feedback

With the test game running, hold the mobile device in the starting position, and while watching the x feedback on the device's screen, tilt the device slowly to the right. We can see that the x feedback decreases from *0* towards *-1* (negative 1).

Slowly return the device back to the starting position, so x is approximately zero, and then start tilting the device slowly to the left, again watching the screen as the x feedback increases from approximately *0* towards *1*.

Understanding the y axis feedback

Repeat the experiment that we just carried out for the x feedback, but this time, tilt the device forwards, so the top of the device is lower than the bottom. We can see that the y feedback decreases from *0* towards *-1* (negative 1). If we tilt the top of the device towards us, so that the bottom of the device is lower than the top, the y feedback increases from approximately *0* towards *1*.

Understanding the x axis feedback

Changes in the z axis feedback from the accelerometer are rather difficult to demonstrate by gently moving the mobile device, because the accelerometer is actually measuring the acceleration of the device relative to free fall — it is measuring the magnitude and direction of the acceleration. This is quite easy to visualize and demonstrate for the x and y axes, but the z axis is somewhat different. We don't want to put our expensive mobile device into free fall, because this generally entails lowering it very quickly (that is, dropping it), while viewing the onscreen output, which is not a recommended experiment!

However, it is possible to see changes occurring on the z axis if we place the mobile device flat on a table (screen facing upwards), and then quickly raise the device while watching the information on the screen. We can also see the changes in the z axis information if we lower the device quickly, but these changes are even more difficult to see!

In practice, the z axis input is probably not as useful in games as the x and y axes, although it does have its uses; for example, to detect shaking of the mobile device.

Using the accelerometer in a game

Now that we have carried out some experiments with the accelerometer (perhaps along with some unexpected physical exercise), we can put our newfound knowledge into practice. So let's create a test game that enables the player to move an actor by tilting the mobile device.

Time for action – creating an accelerometer-controlled game

A game file is not required for this session!

1. Create a new blank game called `AccelloSoccer`.

2. Create a blank scene called `Soccer Pitch`, leaving all other scene settings at their default configurations.

3. Download the actor called `Stencyl Book Soccer Ball` from StencylForge.

4. Add the **Stencyl Book Soccer Ball** actor into the **Soccer Pitch** scene (so we don't forget to do it later).

5. Attach the built-in **Bounce off screen bounds** behavior to the **Stencyl Book Soccer Ball** actor.

6. Create a new actor behavior called `Ball Movement`, and attach it to the **Stencyl Book Soccer Ball** actor.

7. Return to the newly created **Ball Movement** behavior, select **+ Add Event | Basics | When Updating**, and rename the new **Updating** event to `Move Ball`.

8. Add the instructions, shown in the following screenshot, to the new **Move Ball** event, noting that the accelerator's **x** multiplier is **-100** (negative 100):

9. Ensure the target device drop-down list is set to the correct mobile device, and the device is connected to the development computer.

10. Click on the **Test Game** button, wait for the game to compile, and then play the game on the mobile device. Note how the ball acceleration increases when the device is tilted at a greater angle!

What just happened?

We have created the rudiments of an accelerometer-controlled game in only 10 steps!

 The completed `AccelloSoccer` sample game file, named `5961_10_03.stencyl`, can be located in the book's download files.

We should by now be familiar with creating blank games, scenes, and adding behaviors. So, we only need to look in detail at the `Ball Movement` behavior that we have attached to the soccer ball actor.

The `Move Ball` event always checks the values of the x and y feedback from the device's accelerometer and it sets the scene's x and y gravity based on those values. As we learned in our earlier experiments, the accelerometer returns values between *-1* and *+1*; however, these values are far too small to have any effect on the scene's gravity. To increase the feedback returned by the accelerometer to values that will be useful to our game, we have simply multiplied them by a factor of *-100* for the x axis, and *+100* for the y axis.

While these multipliers are a good starting point, experimentation is often required to achieve accelerometer controls to which the player can easily assimilate; so, do experiment with the multiplier numbers to attain a better understanding of how they will affect gameplay.

Autorotate

It's important to be aware that, typically, the accelerometer should not be used with the autorotate feature on iOS devices (at the time of writing, Stencyl does not support autorotate on Android). This is configured in the game settings, and can be found in the main Stencyl menu under **Settings | Mobile | User Input**.

By default, autorotate is disabled in Stencyl, because most games do not use this feature. However, it can sometimes be useful — imagine a game in which the normal gameplay display mode was portrait, but when turning the device to landscape, an in-game information screen was displayed. This could offer some interesting design possibilities if implemented appropriately, but if a game, such as our sample soccer game had autorotate enabled, this would cause havoc for the player, as the accelerometer feedback would appear to be reversed each time the device was rotated. iOS developers can try enabling autorotate in the soccer game's settings (select **Settings | Mobile | User Input**), and test the game on their mobile device to experience the problem firsthand.

Implementing touchscreen controls

When using mobile devices, we often take touchscreen control for granted. It's a feature that feels very natural, and for that reason we tend to forget about the feature and we just use it!

Detecting when a user taps the screen is incredibly easy in Stencyl; detection of mouse clicks is automatically converted to screen-touch detection in Stencyl games. However, there are also some very useful instruction blocks for detecting **gestures**, also known as swiping the display. Let's modify our `AccelloSoccer` test game to react to screen gestures instead of accelerometer feedback.

Time for action – implementing touchscreen controls

The game file to import and load for this session is `5961_10_03.stencyl`.

1. In the **Ball Movement** behavior, disable the **Move Ball** event by removing the check mark next to the behavior name as indicated in the following screenshot:

2. In the **Ball Movement** behavior, create a new `always` event: **+Add Event | Basics | When Updating** and rename it to `Swipe Control`.

3. Add the instructions as shown in the following screenshot, taking care to ensure that the **swiped ...** blocks' drop-down options are configured as shown, and that the number of degrees in each **push self sharply towards ... degrees at ... force** instruction block is entered correctly:

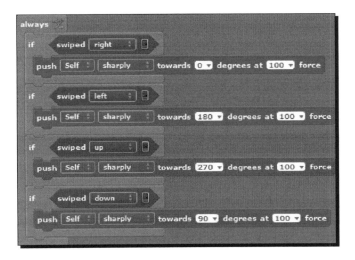

4. Mac users should skip steps 5 and 6, and move directly to step 7.

5. Add a new **when created** event and rename it to `Allow Gestures`.

6. Add the **Enable gestures** block as shown in the following screenshot:

7. Ensure that the mobile device is connected, and the correct device is selected in the target device drop-down list.

8. Test the game and use a finger to swipe the screen in the up, down, left, and right directions.

What just happened?

With just a few, minor modifications, we have converted our `AcceloSoccer` test game to a `SwipoSoccer` test game!

 The completed sample game file, named `5961_10_04.stencyl`, can be located in the book's download files.

Because we do not need the accelerometer event, we disabled it. We could have deleted it entirely, but we might want to use it again at a later date.

With the unrequired event disabled, we then created a new `Swipe Control` event which always reacts to the swipe gestures for each of the four detectable swipe directions. Windows developers also added a `when created` event called `Allow Gestures`, which contains the `Enable gestures` block.

 The `Enable gestures` block is not required according to the current Stencyl documentation. However, it was found that when developing on the Windows platform, the swipe events were not being detected on Android devices unless this block was implemented. This anomaly may be accounted for by the nature of the beta software that was being used during the production of this book, and may be resolved in upcoming updates to Stencyl.

Rather than controlling the soccer ball with gravity, which is controlled by the accelerometer feedback, we are now controlling the ball by swiping the screen in the required direction.

These are the only instruction blocks required to react and respond to touchscreen gestures!

Note that, in addition to the `swipe` ... instruction blocks that we have used in our test game, there is also a `when the device is swiped` ... event, which provides the same results but offers a different way to structure the events in our behaviors. The `when the device is swiped` ... event can be found by selecting **+ Add Event | Input | Swipe**.

Exploring additional mobile device features

In this *Beginner's Guide*, we have only been able to touch upon some of the available mobile device features that we can utilize within our games. There are many more mobile features to explore and experience, so do take the time to research Stencyl's instruction blocks and experiment with the available tools. Particularly be aware of and research the following features, using the instruction block palette's `search` feature, online help, and the Stencyl forums:

◆ Joystick

◆ Vibrate (usually only available on smartphones)

◆ Keyboard

Also, take time to view each of the mobile development settings in the main **Game Settings** dialog box: **Settings | Mobile**.

Of particular interest are the following configuration options:

◆ **App Name**

◆ **Orientation** (Portrait, Landscape)

◆ **Scale Mode** (affects how the game will display on devices with different screen ratios)

◆ **Multitouch**

◆ **Monetization** (paid, mobile subscriptions only)

There are numerous configurations offering almost endless opportunities for mobile game customization, so have fun experimenting with them!

Summary

In this chapter, we have taken a quick tour of mobile game development using Stencyl. Before we dived into testing a few of the features that are unique to mobile devices, we had a look at some of the configuration issues relating to the creation of mobile games: understanding the difference between testing and publishing mobile games, membership of the relevant app store programs, along with a quick look at certification requirements.

We then examined some of the practical differences between the platforms that Stencyl can target, and found that there are some interesting features available on many mobile devices that can be used to great effect when developing games.

The last step of our short journey into the world of mobile development with Stencyl was to carry out some practical experiments and exercises to learn how to use a mobile device's accelerometer and touchscreen for controlling gameplay. We discovered that, despite the technical complexities of the built-in hardware of mobile devices, implementing those features into our games can be a very straightforward process.

With the introductory knowledge that we have gained from this chapter, we can now start to experiment with the available tools and create some interesting games that can take advantage of the sophisticated hardware that many game players hold in their hands every day!

This is the final hands-on chapter of this book, but there is more to game development than sitting in front of a computer screen and tapping away at a keyboard! Before we even touch our development computer, it's a good idea to put some plans into place, consider the legal issues relating to game development, and be aware of some of the third-party tools that can help us to create our video game masterpieces. We'll be examining these topics in *Appendix, Planning, Resources, and Legal Issues*.

Planning, Resources, and Legal Issues

Our game is now complete! We've implemented all the features that our game requires, including sound and visual effects, and we've also considered the commercial aspects of our game and examined how to benefit financially from our hard work.

Because this is a practical guide book, we jumped straight into the development of our game in Chapter 2, Let's make a game!. Quite understandably, we just wanted to learn the required skills and get our game up and running. After all, rolling up our sleeves and getting our hands dirty is always good fun when it comes to game development!

Although it's fun to jump in and to start creating a game, when first learning the tools of the trade, in practice, it's not the most advisable way to develop a successful game—it's a good idea to put some plans into place first and also to ensure that we have all the right tools for the job.

In this final section of the book, we'll take a quick look at the basics of planning a game, and we'll also consider some of the third-party tools and resources that can help us in the development of our games. Finally, we'll reflect upon some of the legal issues that we, as developers, must take into account before presenting our completed game to the public.

The topics we'll be investigating are:

- The planning process
- Third-party tools
- Third-party assets
- Additional resources
- Legal issues
- Progressing with Stencyl game development

The planning process

Planning the development of a video game is a contentious topic—every developer has his or her own ideas about planning, and many books have been written on this topic! We're going to have a quick look at how professional game studios approach the planning of a video game, and then we'll examine some of the more practical aspects that will benefit an independent or hobbyist game developer.

Professional game studios follow a very formal planning process using a **game design document (GDD)** that specifies every aspect of a game's design in great detail. It will include all the information required to aid the smooth running of a game development project and although a GDD is usually considered to be a **living document**—it is expected to be updated as the project progresses—work will not start on the development of a game until the initial GDD has been completed and approved by the senior management.

A complex game design document is probably somewhat excessive for a lone, independent developer, and especially for a hobbyist, but it's certainly a good idea to do some planning before diving into a project. The contents of a game design document will vary within each organization, but it is typical for the following items to be included:

- Game concept
- Feature set
- Genre
- Target audience
- Game flow
- Gameplay
- Mechanics
- Objectives

The given list is certainly not exhaustive—a completed game design document will contain many additional headings, each with multiple subheadings. However, rather than re-inventing the wheel and creating our own GDD, we can take advantage of the many online resources related to the planning of games, and utilize some of the excellent game design document templates available for downloading from the Internet.

 A selection of planning resources and links for downloadable game design document templates can be found on the following web page: `thestencylblog.com/planning`.

Rather than investigating the finer details of a professional game design document, let's examine some of the aspects of planning that can help beginners to achieve their goals.

Where to start

Some developers prefer to start with a pencil and paper (or the electronic equivalent) and sketch out their ideas, so they can visualize the game before firing up their design and development tools. However, many developers prefer to start by creating a working prototype of the game, so they can very quickly get a feel of whether or not their idea is viable. Let's examine some of the advantages and disadvantages of these two approaches.

Starting with concept drawings

An individual, or team, with good graphics or drawing skills may have very firm ideas about the layout and appearance of the game. These visually presented ideas may be the driving force for the production of the game, and they will provide a good start, as the ideas will enable the developer to understand what to aim for as their final goal.

However, one of the risks for the small-scale developer of planning the graphics in great detail is that the mechanics required for the basic concept of the game may be too advanced for the skills of the developer. For example, if the plan is to have a character that travels at high speed on a roller coaster style landscape, the development of the game may fail in its very early stages if the developer has not already proven that this type of player movement can be achieved with the available development tools. Generally, it's not a good idea to spend too much time on creating detailed graphics until the gameplay mechanics have been demonstrated in a working prototype.

When initially planning our Monkey Run game, the initial concept drawing was created with graphics software, and the artwork is no more than outline drawings, as can be seen in the following screenshot:

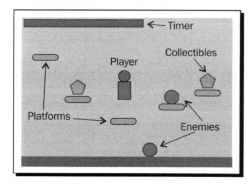

At this stage, there is no indication of a theme for the game—it's just a platform game in which the player will traverse a landscape while collecting objects and avoiding enemies.

There's also an idea that there will be some sort of time limit applied to the game but, so far, we cannot see any evidence of a jungle!

Starting with a prototype

A game may start its life as a prototype—a very basic, but workable version of the game that enables the developer to prove that the development of the concept into a working game is feasible. Very often, a prototype game will have basic graphics, and is simply used as a tool for the developer to create the type of player movement that is required. For example, if it's a game that is going to be set in space, the developer will want to be sure that the physics of the game will work as planned before spending excessive amounts of time designing the graphics.

Creating a working prototype enables the developer to ensure that their skills are a good match for the requirements of the game. If the developer can't create the mechanics for the game then the development will be abandoned at the very early stages!

Finding the fun

Developing games should be fun! Although it's a contentious topic, it has been suggested that following strict routines and plans is not necessarily the best way for a lone developer, or very small team, to make progress and, ultimately, create a completed product ready for publishing. Different people have different ideas about the best way to get the job done but the following tips are for beginners to help them on their way.

Starting small

Many new developers fall into the trap of trying to develop a blockbuster game on their first attempt, which often leads to disillusionment with the development tools.

Regular visitors to any online game development discussion forum will be familiar with reading comments from the excited beginner developer who has ideas for the most amazing game, only to read the follow-up comments of disappointment and frustration a few days or weeks later, when the same new developer realizes that game development requires a lot more hard work and planning than initially anticipated!

Before diving into a huge project, start with smaller manageable games that will enable you to build up a repertoire of skills that will, ultimately, lead you to being able to create the masterpiece that you have dreamed about.

 Using the game kits that are provided with Stencyl is a great way to jumpstart a new project. Several kits are installed along with Stencyl, and others can be downloaded from StencylForge.

For example, rather than trying to develop a huge, multilevel shoot-em-up game, start by creating a basic one-level game to prove that the gameplay mechanics are achievable, and that the game is fun to play. When the game concept is proven to work in practice, have a go at adding the onscreen scoring information, and then consider implementing the introduction screen. Having these skills in place helps to ensure that, when it comes to working on a larger project, there won't be delays and disappointments as numerous small problems arise.

Using placeholder graphics

During the initial stages of development, consider using **placeholder** graphics—temporary graphics that are used to get the development process up and running quickly. Of course, some developers are very artistically talented and may be able to create appropriate graphics quickly but, in many cases, the creation of the graphics for a game can cause frustration and delays in the development process.

Placeholder graphics might consist of simple shapes such as rectangles and circles, or they might be third-party graphics that have been legally obtained from the Internet—see the following section entitled *Third-party assets* for some suggestions as to where to find readily available resources that can be used for these purposes.

When initially planning the Monkey Run game, a mixture of placeholder and readymade third-party graphics were used. We can see in the following screenshot, which shows a very early working prototype of the game, that the tileset is the same one that we used in the final game, but the actors are basic placeholder shapes:

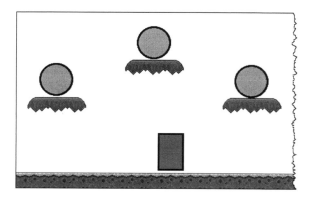

In this case, the player is a rectangle, and the collectible objects are circles. It was only at a later stage of development, after the platform mechanics were proven to work, that the basic actor shapes were replaced by the high-quality monkey and fruit graphics, and the animations were added.

The reason for immediately implementing the tileset was that it was very easily accessible from StencylForge, and was known to be available for use in commercial projects free of charge—an important criterion for this project! The style of the tileset led to further development of the jungle theme and, while the original concept for the game was a platform in which the player collects objects and avoids enemies, the style of the game was, in fact, influenced by the availability of the tileset! Don't forget that StencylForge is an excellent resource for actors and other resources, as well as tilesets.

Setting small goals

Rather than setting large, unspecific goals, such as completing the development of level one in a couple of weeks, consider specifying smaller milestones and recording them in a notepad or a spreadsheet. For example, some of the minor milestones specified for the development of Monkey Run are shown in the following table:

Task	Days required	Actual days	DONE
Prove platformer concept viable	1	1.5	✓
Research and finalize main actor graphics	1	1	✓
Import actor graphics as animations	1	0.5	✓
Create main collision behaviours	1	1	✓
Implement pause feature	0.5	0.5	✓
Implement level transitioning	0.5	1	✓

Each of the milestones stated in the previous table is small and realistic and, when each milestone was reached, a sense of achievement was experienced as the Done boxes were checked.

It's also a good idea, where possible, to set goals that have fun targets dispersed between the less-fun targets. If your idea of fun is to create graphics, then don't spend 10 consecutive days creating graphics, leaving the less-fun milestones to the end of the project! Try to work on smaller graphics-related tasks between some of the tasks that are, perhaps, less enjoyable. Working like this ensures that there is still some fun to be had regularly throughout the development process.

Avoiding burn-out

Don't become disheartened when difficulties arise! When an apparently insurmountable problem raises its ugly head, take a step back and consider your options, which include:

♦ Asking for help from other Stencyl developers—the official Stencyl forums are a great place to start, and the Stencyl developer community is very welcoming and generous: `community.stencyl.com`

♦ Working on a different part of the project, and coming back to the problem at a later time (perhaps when help has been provided on the Stencyl forums)

♦ Trying a completely different way of solving the problem—think out of the box

♦ Eliminating the problem from the game, and introducing an alternative feature

♦ Taking a break—play some video games and hope for inspiration

It's very rare that a problem cannot be resolved one way or another, so be patient, take a deep breath and relax—game development should be fun.

Third-party tools

Stencyl is an amazing game development tool, and it is even packaged with its own graphics editing application, Pencyl. However, most developers will want to progress to using some more advanced, third-party tools for the creation or modification of graphics, audio, and other assets that will be used throughout the game.

There are many commercially available software packages that can be used for the creation of video game assets. However, as we have created a completed game using the free version of Stencyl, in this section of the book, we'll have a look at some of the free tools that are available to assist in the creation of video games.

Please note that the author does not endorse the use of any specific software applications. Recommendations were solicited in the official Stencyl forums, and the most popular and long-lived applications have been included in this section!

Graphics tools

There are some amazingly high-quality graphics software packages, for creating **bitmap** and **vector** images, that are available for download and use free of charge.

 There is a detailed explanation of bitmap and vector images at the following website: graphicssoft.about.com/od/ aboutgraphics/a/bitmapvector.htm.

Following are some of the most popular packages as recommended by Stencyl users:

GIMP

GIMP is a bitmap graphics application that many users consider equal to the most popular commercially available graphics software. It can be used for creating and modifying many types of graphics images.

GIMP can be found at www.gimp.org. It runs on Windows, Mac OS X, and Linux.

Inkscape

Inkscape is a comprehensive vector graphics package. Although Stencyl can import both vector (SVG format) and bitmap graphics files, many graphics artists prefer to work with vector graphics, and then convert the final results to bitmaps for importing into Stencyl.

Inkscape can be found at www.inkscape.org. It runs on Windows, Mac OS X, and Linux.

GraphicsGale

GraphicsGale is an animation editor which is designed to ease the process of creating animations that can be used in video games. There is a freeware version of the software, and a more comprehensive version which must be paid for.

GraphicsGale can be found at www.humanbalance.net/gale/us. It runs on Windows.

Audio Tools

As we have learned during the development of Monkey Run, a soundtrack and sound effects can completely change the atmosphere of a game! Following are some useful audio utilities.

Audacity

This very popular audio editing and recording tool has an amazing range of sound editing features, including the ability to add special effects to existing recordings (for example, echo, reverb, and so on). Audacity also includes features which enable conversion among different audio formats, including the configuration of the sample rate and bit depth which, as we discovered in *Chapter 8*, *Implementing Sounds*, is essential for ensuring that audio files are compatible with Stencyl.

Audacity can be found at `audacity.sourceforge.net`. It runs on Windows, Mac OS X, and Linux.

SFXR

SFXR is a special effects generator that was created by Tomas Pettersson, originally for a computer programming competition in 2007. Since then, it has become an extremely popular tool for creating sound effects for video games. It's very easy to use and includes preset buttons for creating effects such as explosions, pickups, jumps, and blips.

The original application has now been ported to most development platforms, and there is even a handy web-based version that runs on most browsers.

SFXR can be found at `www.drpetter.se/project_sfxr.html`. For the web browser version visit `www.superflashbros.net/as3sfxr/`. SFXR is available for Windows, Mac OS X, Linux, and Flash-enabled web browsers.

inudge

This interesting browser-based application enables the user to paint sounds onto a grid using various musical instruments. It's very useful for creating short melodies and jingles.

inudge can be found at `www.inudge.net`. It runs on Flash-enabled web browsers.

Third-party assets

Assets are the objects that we use in our games and include graphics, audio, and fonts. **Third-party** assets are those assets which have been created by someone else!

Following are some resources for graphics and audio assets:

Graphics resources

There are many Internet resources for graphics, but finding good-quality images that can be used freely in commercial games can be a time consuming task! Following are several resources, some of which include very high-quality images for use in games:

- ◆ www.vickiwenderlich.com deserves to appear at the top of the list because this website is the source of most of the graphics used in the game we have created in this book! Vicki has created numerous collections of high-quality game art which can be used free of charge, even in commercial games, as long as Vicki is clearly attributed as the author of the graphics.

- ◆ Lostgarden.com is an excellent resource, not just for graphics, but for many other topics relating to game development. Daniel Cook, who maintains the website, is Chief Creative Officer at the game development studio Spry Fox, and he has made available a wonderful set of graphics at www.lostgarden.com/2009/03/dancs-miraculously-flexible-game.html.

- ◆ Opengameart.org is a huge resource of free-to-use graphics assets. The quality of the graphics varies from excellent to not so good but, if nothing else, it's a great source of graphics for prototyping. Note that the licensing is specified by the author of each of the graphics and, while many images can be used in commercial games, there are some exceptions, so be sure to check the licensing for each image.

- ◆ www.widgetworx.com/widgetworx/portfolio/spritelib.html—SpriteLib is a sprite library that has been available for many years, but it contains a wonderful collection of graphics that can be used in several genres of games. The author has released these sprites into the public domain, and they have been used in some commercially available games.

Sound resources

There are many high-quality sound effects and music tracks available for use in our games but, as always, be sure to check the licensing requirements of each asset:

- ◆ www.incompetech.com—Kevin MacLeod's website contains a large library of sound tracks that he has composed and made available free of charge, for use in any project, as long as Kevin is clearly attributed as the author of the music. The quality of the music is extremely high, and covers a wide range of genres.

- ◆ www.soundjay.com—A well organized and comprehensive collection of free music tracks and sound effects.

- ◆ www.partnersinrhyme.com—This commercial website also contains a large selection of free sound effects.

Additional resources

Graphics and audio are not the only assets that we use when developing games.

Fonts

Fonts are another important visual asset found in games, so don't forget to utilize fonts that are appropriate for the style of the game! Some popular web resources for fonts are:

◆ www.1001freefonts.com

◆ www.fontspace.com

◆ www.dafont.com

Be sure to check the licensing for each font before using it in a game—while some fonts are released into the public domain, many are licensed and may require payment or attribution.

StencylForge

Don't forget that StencylForge contains a large collection of all types of game resources including fonts, sprites, backgrounds, tilesets, and audio!

Books

The following books are not specific to Stencyl, but are references relating to the design of games:

◆ A *Theory of Fun for Game Design, Raph Koster*: An interesting, visual approach to understanding what makes games fun and entertaining

◆ *The Art of Game Design: A Book of Lenses, Jesse Schell*: This book breaks down each element of gameplay and examines the theory in great detail

Websites

The following links are for websites that contain further information, help, or tutorials about developing games with Stencyl:

◆ www.stencyl.com

◆ community.stencyl.com

◆ www.thestencylblog.com

Legal issues

Please note that the information in this section is only an overview of some of the important issues of which a game developer should be aware—it is the responsibility of the developer to ensure that they have the legal right to use assets in their game. Laws vary across states and countries, so be absolutely certain of your legal position prior to using any assets that you have not created yourself. In practice, it is always advisable to obtain written permission from a license holder, prior to using assets in a publicly released game.

Use of third-party assets

The Internet is awash with freely available graphics and sounds assets. However, when an asset is freely available, it does not necessarily mean that the asset can be used legally!

Other than using assets that you have created yourself (or that your development team has created), the other main source of assets is the Internet. Prior to using any assets obtained from the Internet, it is important to understand some of the issues relating to copyright and licensing.

Copyright

Although **copyright** is a very complex legal concept, the basics of copyright law are very easy to understand. Copyright gives the creator of a **work** the exclusive right to use that work. This means that only the creator of a work has the right to decide who can use that work and what they can use it for. When we refer to a work, in this context, we mean an original creation, examples of which include artwork, music, sounds, font designs, written text, and video games.

Although copyright laws vary between countries, most countries have very similar copyright laws. The main variations relate to the length of time for which copyright exists but, as a general rule, we can probably consider that for the purpose of game development, the types of asset that we will be using will almost always fall within those time limits and will, therefore, be subject to copyright laws.

Public domain

There are very specific legal definitions of the phrase **public domain**, with variations that may apply in different jurisdictions. However, the principle is that, once copyright has expired, a work enters into the public domain, which means that it can be used for any purpose. Additionally, the creator of a work may voluntarily pass the work into the public domain, therefore forfeiting the right to determine future uses for that work.

When using public domain works in video games, it is important to ensure that they are actually in the public domain and not simply categorized incorrectly! For example, some websites contain libraries of freely available works, but they will not necessarily guarantee that the works are public domain.

Licensed works

There are many different forms of licensing available when using other people's assets in your game.

If the work is in the public domain, then no license is required.

If an asset that is not in the public domain is being used in your game, it is important to ensure that the licensing agreement for that asset is adhered to. For example, some creators of a work will allow the use of their creative work in any other work (such as a video game) as long as they are clearly attributed as the creator of the specific assets.

An example of this kind of licensing has been used for many of the assets that have been used in our game, Monkey Run! Most of the jungle graphics and objects used in the game were created by Vicki Wenderlich (`www.vickiwenderlich.com`), who has released the graphics under a **Creative Commons Attribution** license. Although there are several variations of the Creative Commons license, Vicki has chosen to allow free use of the images as long as she is clearly attributed as the original author. The only exception as specified on the licensing page on Vicki's website is that the art may not be sold by itself—it must form part of another work. For legal reasons, it is important to understand that this is my interpretation of the license—if you wish to use the graphics that Vicki has created, please do visit her website and read the license carefully! You will note that on the opening screen of our game, we have clearly displayed credits for the assets we have used, including the graphics and sound track. For more information about Creative Commons licenses, visit the website at `www.creativecommons.org`.

Google's Advanced Image Search, which can be found at `www.google.com/advanced_image_search`, is a very useful resource for locating images based on a type of license. For example, the following screenshot shows the **Advanced Image Search** being used to find images that are **free to use, share, or modify, even commercially**:

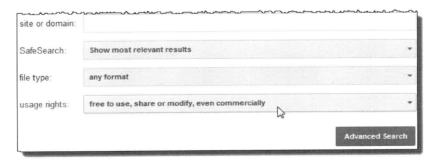

Another useful tool that provides searching by license type is `www.iconfinder.com`. Although, as its name suggests, this website is a resource for locating icons, many of the images can be used games as long as the license permits.

Royalty-free

Very often, when searching for free assets to use in our games, we will find that the term **royalty-free** is used in an asset's description. It's important to understand that if an asset is royalty-free it doesn't necessarily mean that the asset is free to use!

A **royalty** is a fee that is paid to the license holder for each use of an asset. For example, if a copyrighted sound-track is used in a game, the license holder may require a fee to be paid for each copy of the video game that is sold. Depending on the size of the royalty fee and the numbers of products sold, the final amount to pay to the license holder could be quite substantial!

If an asset is royalty-free, it means that no royalty is paid for each use—however, a one off payment may be required to use the asset. As always, be sure to read the license agreement carefully, and take legal advice when required.

A note about collaboration

When collaborating in the creation of a game with other developers, artists, and musicians, it is important to have a written agreement relating to the use of assets that are created for the project. While it is easy to ignore such issues in the excitement of creating a new game, failure to have a formal agreement in place can lead to disagreements and even legal problems at a later stage.

Some questions to consider are:

◆ Who legally owns each asset?

◆ Can the asset be used in other projects? If so, then who can use it?

◆ How will each contributor be rewarded for their work?

It's also important to ensure that ownership of the final product is determined before development work begins. Will each collaborator own an equal share of the work, or will some of the contributors receive a smaller or larger proportion of the rewards based upon their contribution to the project?

Ensure that these decisions are documented and agreed upon prior to starting development!

Clearing up some myths

There is a lot of misunderstanding regarding the subject of copyright and licensing, and it's important to understand which assets can and cannot be used in your game. Following is a discussion of some of the common myths related to the use of game assets.

Myth 1

> *If a commercial game isn't available for sale anymore, I can use the game's assets in my own games.*

If a game is no longer for sale, even if the publisher has gone out of business, copyright will probably still apply to those assets. Ownership of **intellectual property** (creative works) can be enormously complex, so never assume that game assets are available for use. The only sure way to know is to determine who has ownership of the assets, and then determine from the owner, in writing, whether or not the assets may be used in your games.

Myth 2

> *The graphics from an old, commercial game are freely-available on the Internet, which means that they are public domain.*

Just because game assets are freely available on the Internet, it does not mean that they are free to be used for any purpose. Very often people will copy and share game assets under the misapprehension that they are doing so legally, and they may even state that the assets are free or public domain. Do not believe everything that you read on the Internet! Ensure that you are certain as to the provenance of the information before utilizing any free graphics that you obtain from the Internet.

Myth 3

> *I'm not making a profit from my game, so the owner of the copyrighted assets that I have used won't/can't take any legal action against me.*

This is a very common myth! Although there are some intellectual property owners who are happy for others to use their assets for nonprofit purposes, it is very rare for such permission to be given. Most organizations take great care to protect their intellectual property, and are likely to employ lawyers to pursue legal action in the event that their intellectual property is used without permission.

Myth 4

I copied the assets from someone's game, but I've changed them a bit so no one can take legal action against me.

Changing someone's game assets prior to using them in your own games does not mean that copyright no longer applies. Some intellectual property owners will take legal action, even if there is the slightest resemblance to their copyrighted property. If a court decides that the modified works are too similar to the originals, or that some damage has been done to the public's perception of the owner of the original works, then financial damages are likely to be awarded.

Myth 5

There was no copyright information with the assets, so copyright laws don't apply to it.

In the vast majority of legal jurisdictions, copyright is implicit in all creative works. This means that copyright exists automatically when the work is created, and there is no legal requirement for the creator of a work to display a copyright notice. It is safest to assume that all works are copyrighted unless the legal owner of the intellectual property states otherwise!

Myth 6

I have some classical music on a CD, and it was composed hundreds of years ago, so it must be out of copyright and, therefore, I can use it in my game without permission.

Although there is a lot of classical music that is out of copyright, most of the recordings of that music are still under copyright! If you can perform out of copyright music yourself, and record it, then you can use it in your game!

When it is safe to use third-party game assets

It is safe to use game assets when you have written authorization from the owner of the copyright of those assets. Even then, there can be legal wrangles related to exactly who has the right to authorize such usage, so it is important to take legal advice when required.

Progressing with Stencyl game development

We've almost reached the end of this book! I hope that, at this point, you have learned and understood the basic skills needed, and have acquired the confidence to use Stencyl for developing your own video games.

But, don't stop here. Consider how our game can be improved—there are still a few rough edges!

Players of our game will be expecting a fully polished product that has received all the love and attention that it deserves, so do take the time to tidy up any loose ends that you find. Add your own finishing touches, introduce some additional challenges, and implement some different graphics then, if you wish, sell your game or use in-game advertising to make some money!

Remember that there are usually many ways to achieve the same results, and that the ideas and suggestions in this book are just that—ideas and suggestions. This is, after all, a guide book designed to help you on your way!

We've only scratched the surface of what can be achieved with Stencyl, so don't limit yourself to what we have learned in these pages. Research, ask questions to other Stencyl users, and experiment!

Summary

In this final section of the book, we have taken a look at some basic aspects related to the initial planning and ongoing development of a video game, including suggestions as to how of get started with a new project, and the importance of setting realistic milestones.

We've also been introduced to just a few of the many third-party creative tools that are available to assist us in developing a high-quality game—primarily, graphics editors and sound utilities for creating visual and audio assets.

For those who prefer to use third-party resources, we then considered where we can find freely available, readymade assets to use in our games, and found that there are some very generous, creative artists who are willing to share their work free of charge.

Finally, we took a look at some of the important legal aspects of game development—how to stay within the law, and ensure that we are using third-party game assets within the terms of their licensing requirements.

From this point on, the rest is up to you; you now have the tools and the skills, so enjoy making some amazing games with Stencyl and, most importantly, have fun!

Index

control key 196
copyright 296
Cost Per Mille. *See* CPM
Countdown expired event 148
countdown timer
  creating 118-122
  debug blocks, examining 122
countdown timer onscreen
  about 155
  displaying 155, 156
CPM 248
created games, Stencyl used
  Impossible Pixel 20
  Kreayshawn Goes to Japan 19
  Making Monkeys 18
Creative Commons Attribution license 297
custom behavior
  about 90
  action, attaching to an actor 92-95
  action, creating 92-95
  additional event, adding to 96
  behavior screen 95
  creating 90, 91
  event, adding 96-98
  future refinements 99
  gameplay review 99
  instruction block palette 98
  new challenge 100
  statue, configuring 100
  statue, downloading 100
custom events
  triggerring, in behaviors 127-129

D

decision making
  if ... block 125
  implementing 122-124
default animation 139
Delete key 86
downloaded game files
  using 34
Download Now button 23

E

Edit Frame (External) option 145
Enable Debug Drawing option 74

Enable gestures block 282
enemies
  adding 75
  downloading 75
Escape key 44
exclusive sponsorship 257

F

features, Stencyl 13-17
FGL 258
first special effect
  implementing 111
  status, disappearing 111, 112
  timings 113
flag 172
Flash Game License. *See* FGL
fonts
  configuring 157
  files, using, in Stencyl 158
  specifying, for game use 157, 158
foregrounds
  about 182
  viewing, in Scene Editor 181, 182
frames 136
free version, Stencyl
  limitation 16
Fruit Collected event 215

G

game
  actor count, optimizing 110
  fixing 174
  randomness, introducing 108, 109
  sounds, organizing 232
  testing 40, 52
  testing, for problem finding 52, 53
  timer, creating 110
game attribute
  creating 159
  debug instructions, removing 165
  lives count, decrementing 161, 162
  Lives game attribute, creating 159, 160
  using 160
  zero alert 162-164
game-completed scene
  implementing 223-225

Thank you for buying
Learning Stencyl 3.x Game Development
Beginner's Guide

About Packt Publishing

Packt, pronounced 'packed', published its first book "Mastering phpMyAdmin for Effective MySQL Management" in April 2004 and subsequently continued to specialize in publishing highly focused books on specific technologies and solutions.

Our books and publications share the experiences of your fellow IT professionals in adapting and customizing today's systems, applications, and frameworks. Our solution-based books give you the knowledge and power to customize the software and technologies you're using to get the job done. Packt books are more specific and less general than the IT books you have seen in the past. Our unique business model allows us to bring you more focused information, giving you more of what you need to know, and less of what you don't.

Packt is a modern, yet unique publishing company, which focuses on producing quality, cutting-edge books for communities of developers, administrators, and newbies alike. For more information, please visit our website: www.PacktPub.com.

Writing for Packt

We welcome all inquiries from people who are interested in authoring. Book proposals should be sent to author@packtpub.com. If your book idea is still at an early stage and you would like to discuss it first before writing a formal book proposal, contact us; one of our commissioning editors will get in touch with you.

We're not just looking for published authors; if you have strong technical skills but no writing experience, our experienced editors can help you develop a writing career, or simply get some additional reward for your expertise.

Sencha Touch Mobile JavaScript Framework

ISBN: 978-1-84951-510-8   Paperback:316 pages

Build web applications for Apple iOS and Google Android touchscreen devices with this first HTML5 mobile framework

1. Learn to develop web applications that look and feel native on Apple iOS and Google Android touchscreen devices using Sencha Touch through examples

2. Design resolution-independent and graphical representations like buttons, icons, and tabs of unparalleled flexibility

3. Add custom events like tap, double tap, swipe, tap and hold, pinch, and rotate

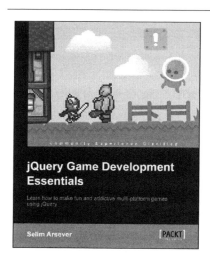

jQuery Game Development Essentials

ISBN: 978-1-84969-506-0   Paperback: 224 pages

Learn how to make fun and addictive multi-platform games using jQuery

1. Discover how you can create a fantastic RPG, arcade game, or platformer using jQuery!

2. Learn how you can integrate your game with various social networks, creating multiplayer experiences and also ensuring compatibility with mobile devices.

3. Create your very own framework, harnessing the very best design patterns and proven techniques along the way.

Please check **www.PacktPub.com** for information on our titles

Blender Game Engine Beginner's Guide

ISBN: 978-1-84951-702-7   Paperback: 206 pages

The non programmer's guide to creating 3D video games

1. Use Blender to create a complete 3D video game

2. Ideal entry level to game development without the need for coding

3. No programming or scripting required

Corona SDK Hotshot

ISBN: 978-1-84969-430-8   Paperback: 358 pages

A deep, solid guide with ten projects specifically designed to expand the fundamentals of exciting mobile development platform!

1. Ideal for Java developers new to Groovy and Grails—this book will teach you all you need to create web applications with Grails

2. Create, develop, test, and deploy a web application in Grails

3. Take a step further into Web 2.0 using AJAX and the RichUI plug-in in Grails

Please check **www.PacktPub.com** for information on our titles